Does the Bible Have Any Answers?

Practical Wisdom

Rick Thompson, Fran and Jill Sciacca

Too Tough?

Paul Borthwick and Jan Johnson

What Do You Think?

Paul Borthwick and Larry Keefauver

NEXGEN®

Building the New Generation of Believers

An Imprint of Cook Communications Ministries
Colorado Springs, Colorado

Does the Bible Have Any Answers?

© 2003 Cook Communications Ministries

Published by Cook Communications Ministries
4050 Lee Vance View
Colorado Springs, CO 80918
www.cookministries.com

Editorial Manager: Doug Schmidt
Product Developer: Karen Pickering
Series Creator: John Duckworth
Series Editor: Randy Southern
Cover Design: Granite Design
Interior Design: Becky Hawley Design, Inc.

Unit 1: Practical Wisdom
© 2003 Cook Communications Ministries
Editor: Randy Southern
Writers: Rick Thompson, Fran and Jill Sciacca
Option Writers: John Duckworth, Nelson E. Copeland, Jr.,
Michelle Geiman, and Lisa Anderson
Inside Illustrator: Eric Masi

Unit 2: Too Tough?
© 2003 Cook Communications Ministries
Editor: Anne Dinnan
Writers: Paul Borthwick and Jan Johnson
Option Writers: Stan Campbell, Nelson E. Copeland, Jr.,
and Ellen Larson
Designer: Bill Paetzold
Inside Illustrator: Al Hering

Unit 3: What Do You Think?
© 2003 Cook Communications Ministries
Editor: Randy Southern
Writers: Paul Borthwick and Larry Keefauver
Option Writers: John Duckworth, Nelson E. Copeland, Jr.,
and Sue Reck
Inside Illustrator: Eric Masi

Printed in the U.S.A.

Contents

How to Customize Your Curriculum   5

Unit One: Practical Wisdom

Getting the Most out of Proverbs and Ecclesiastes   9

Unit One Publicity Clip Art   12

SESSION 1
Words of Wisdom   14

SESSION 2
A Fool and His Happiness Are Soon Parted   30

SESSION 3
Hold Your Tongue!   46

SESSION 4
The Meaning of Life   62

SESSION 5
A Matter of Time   78

Unit Two: Too Tough?

Talking to Kids about the Tough Teachings of Jesus   93

Unit Two Publicity Clip Art   96

SESSION 1
Are Sexual Thoughts Always Sinful?   98

SESSION 2
Are Mountain-Moving Prayers Possible?   112

SESSION 3
What, Me Worry?   126

SESSION 4
Why Bother with Annoying People?   140

SESSION 5
Why Should I Give Money Away?   156

Unit Three: What Do You Think?

Tackling Controversial Issues   173

Unit 3 Publicity Clip Art   176

SESSION 1
Pro-Choice or Pro-Life? (Abortion)   178

SESSION 2
A Time to Die (Euthanasia/Medically Assisted Suicide)   196

SESSION 3
What God Has Joined Together...(Divorce)   212

SESSION 4
Just an Alternative Lifestyle?
(Homosexuality and Gay Rights)   226

SESSION 5
Hawks and Doves (War and Peace)   242

How to Customize Your Curriculum

We know your time is valuable. That's why we've made **Custom Curriculum** as easy as possible. Follow the three steps outlined below to create custom lessons that will meet the needs of *your* group. Let's get started!

 Read the basic lesson plan.

Every Custom Curriculum session in this book has four or five steps designed to meet five goals. It's important to understand these five goals as you choose the options for your group.

Getting Together

The goal for Getting Together is to break the ice. It may involve a fun way to introduce the lesson.

Getting Thirsty

The goal for Getting Thirsty is to earn students' interest before you dive into the Bible. Why should students care about your topic? Why should they care what the Bible has to say about it? This will motivate your students to dig deeper.

Getting the Word

The goal for Getting the Word is to find out what God has to say about the topic they care about. By exploring and discussing carefully-selected passages, you'll help students find out how God's Word applies to their lives.

Getting the Point

The goal for Getting the Point is to make the leap from ideals and principles to real-world situations students are likely to face. It may involve practicing biblical principles with case studies or roleplays.

Getting Personal

The goal for Getting Personal is to help each group member respond to the lesson with a specific action. What should group members do as a result of this session? This step will help each person find a specific "next step" response that works for him or her.

2 Consider your options.

Every **Custom Curriculum** session gives you 14 different types of options. How do you choose? First, take a look at the list of option categories below. Then spend some time thinking and praying about your group. How do your students learn best? What kind of goals have you set for your group? Put a check mark by the options that you're most interested in.

 Extra Action—for groups that like physical challenges and learn better when they're moving, interacting, and experiencing the lesson.

 Media—to spice up your meeting with video, music, or other popular media.

 Heard It All Before—for fresh approaches that get past the defenses of students who are jaded by years in church.

 Little Bible Background—to use when most of your students are strangers to the Bible or haven't yet made a Christian commitment.

 Extra Fun—for longer, more "festive" youth meetings where additional emphasis is put on having fun.

 Fellowship and Worship—for building deeper relationships or enabling students to praise God together.

 Mostly Girls—to address girls' concerns and to substitute activities girls might prefer.

Mostly Guys—to address guys' concerns and to substitute activities guys might prefer.

 **Small Group**—for adapting activities that might be tough with groups of fewer than eight students.

 Large Group—to alter steps for groups of more than 20 students.

 **Urban**—for fitting sessions to urban facilities and multiethnic (especially African-American) concerns.

 Short Meeting Time—tips for condensing the meeting. The standard meeting is designed to last 45 to 60 minutes. These include options to cut, replace, or trim time off the standard steps.

 Combined Junior High/High School—to use when you're mixing age levels but an activity or case study would be too "young" or "old" for part of the group.

 Sixth Grade—appearing only in junior high/middle school volumes, this option helps you change steps that sixth graders might find hard to understand or relate to.

 Extra Challenge—appearing only in high school volumes, this option lets you crank up the voltage for students who are ready for more Scripture or more demanding personal application.

3 Customize your curriculum!

Here's a simple, three-step plan to customize each session for your group:

1. Choose your options.

As you read the basic session plan, you'll see icons in the margin. Each icon represents a different type of option. When you see an icon, it means that type of option is offered for that step. The five pages of options are found after the Repro Resource student pages for each session. Turn to the option noted by the icon and you'll see that option explained.

Let's say you have a small group, mostly guys who get bored if they don't keep moving. You'll want to keep an eye out for three kinds of options: Small Group, Mostly Guys, and Extra Action. As you read the basic session, you might spot icons that tell you there are Small Group options for Step 1 and Step 3—maybe a different way to play a game so that you don't need big teams, and a way to cover several Bible passages when just a few kids are looking them up. Then you see icons telling you that there are Mostly Guys options for Step 2 and Step 4—perhaps a substitute activity that doesn't require too much self-disclosure, and a case study guys will relate to. Finally you see icons indicating Extra Action options for Step 2 and Step 3—maybe an active way to get kids' opinions instead of handing out a survey, and a way to act out some verses instead of just looking them up.

2. Use the checklist.

Once you've picked your options, keep track of them with the simple checklist at the end of the option section (just before the start of the next session plan). This little form gives you a place to write down the materials you'll need too—since they depend on the options you've chosen.

3. Get your stuff together.

Gather your materials; photocopy any Repro Resources (reproducible student sheets) you've decided to use. And…you're ready!

Unit One: Practical Wisdom

Getting the Most out of Proverbs and Ecclesiastes

by Fran and Jill Sciacca

The perfect paradigm of our present American culture is the corner convenience store. These shops thrive on our willingness to pay higher costs for goods and services in exchange for lower levels of inconvenience. Instead of encouraging prudent planning, selection, and control of our appetites, convenience stores stimulate impulse buying and careless spending. And we don't *think* about our wasteful decisions. As a culture, we also are increasingly willing to live with disposable relationships. Many partners choose to exchange long-term responsibility for immediate pleasure. One tragic result of this malady is that the children of today, even churched kids, are growing up with no understanding—much less appreciation—of how to live for the "long haul." Life is viewed more as a quick sprint rather than a marathon, an event more than a process. Paul's parting statement, "I have fought the good fight, I have finished the race, I have kept the faith" (2 Tim. 4:7), is a foreign concept and a crazy mentality to many of today's teens.

In *Streetwise* you'll have the opportunity to make significant advances in a very needed area. These sessions plunge headlong into Proverbs and Ecclesiastes, two books of the Bible that help us understand and deal with "convenience store" living, the notion that everything in life should come quickly. King Solomon, often called the wisest man who ever lived, played a role in writing both of these books. Even though God entrusted deep spiritual wisdom to Solomon, He also allowed the king to learn from the crushing consequences brought on by his own sin. Solomon, in short, was very qualified to speak and teach about both wisdom and foolishness.

Proverbs: If It's Important, It's Probably in Here!

The material in Proverbs is profound yet practical. Solomon paints a panoramic portrait of every human relationship we encounter (good *and* bad) with bold yet specific strokes. The first nine chapters address broad subjects using colorful, symbolic language.

Beginning with chapter 10, Proverbs virtually explodes with themes that are the brightest threads in any teen's personal tapestry. Solomon teaches about the differences between a wise man and a fool, and he warns the readers to choose carefully between the two. The tongue is a familiar topic in Proverbs. We are taught about its power to either build up or tear down our reputation and our relationships. Proverbs contains a special focus on the family, including topics like getting along with siblings, the relationship between parents and children, how husbands and wives should treat each other, and even growing old. Friends and friendship also get a lot of press in Proverbs, along with topics like emotions, decision making, true humility, money, and pride.

But Proverbs is more than a careful collection of pithy paradigms or marvelous metaphors about life on planet earth. One of the clearest notions running through the book is shouted in the introduction and echoes until the end: "The *fear of the Lord* is the beginning of knowledge" (1:7, emphasis mine). Help your kids recognize that Proverbs describes life *as it really should be lived,* because it was authored by the Lord of life itself. These are not "Solomon's Suggestions," an early version of Ann Landers! Eliminating God and then trying to figure out how to live a meaningful life is about as easy as pushing a chain. Proverbs begins and ends with the penetrating truth that God must be included in any equation that attempts to explain life and/or how to live it. Truth about living in the *real* world, not trendy suggestions for a "successful" life, is what Proverbs is all about. Its message is timeless because its author is the One who made both the players and the rules.

Ecclesiastes: Bad Choices and Meaninglessness

Ecclesiastes, like parts of Proverbs, probably was written by King Solomon. The primary difference between Ecclesiastes and Proverbs, however, is that Solomon probably wrote Ecclesiastes much later in life. In fact, some think that Ecclesiastes is a sort of "journal" about Solomon's pursuit of meaning in life without God—a search that he says is about as valuable as chasing after the wind! It's the diary of a man who made a career out of making bad choices.

Many people shy away from reading Ecclesiastes because they find it too depressing. After all, any book whose opening statement is "Meaningless! Meaningless!" is not destined for the *New York Times* Bestseller List! However, many readers of Ecclesiastes fail to unlock the beauty of this book because they do not understand the significance of one small phrase that appears and reappears. That phrase is "under the sun." It shows up at least twice in every chapter. "Under the sun" refers to a perspective about life on this planet that does not allow for God. Once you understand that Solomon is penning the memoirs of his own journey to find meaning "under the sun" (without God), the book begins to take on life. It becomes the clearest testimony in Scripture of the futility of living *as if there is no God.* Make sure your kids discover this key early on as you study Ecclesiastes. Ask them if they want to read the diary of someone who had access to every possible toy, tried every possible pleasure and every conceivable token of wealth and success. Most young people would be eager to savor such an opportunity.

Of Ballpoints and Backbones

Solomon indeed "did it all" and "had it all." He filled his mind with knowledge, his stomach with food and wine, his eyes with pleasure, his bedrooms with women, his stalls with horses, his calendar with travel, his vaults with riches, his time with thinking, and his nation with beautiful buildings. But each time he sat down and assessed his accomplishments and fulfillment, the answer was the same: "Meaningless, utterly meaningless!" Why? How do you explain the predictable outcome of his adventures? The answer can be found in a simple statement that summarizes a powerful principle: *Purpose is contingent upon design.*

Each year when we discuss the basis of meaning and purpose in my high school Bible classes, I introduce this notion. It is genuinely exciting to see the lights "come on" in the minds of students. The principle, simply stated, is that the purpose of anything (what it is intended to do and be) is totally dependent upon its design. In other words, the purpose of a ballpoint pen is to write on a limited variety of surfaces, normally paper. It is *not* intended to be used to pry open file cabinets, punch holes in sheetrock, or prop open windows. What's the point? The point is that something finds its purpose in doing what it was designed to do. The opposite is also true. Screwdrivers often break when used as chisels; plastic knives snap when used to exert great force; etc. Now if humans are really the product of random evolution, we are a product of chance, not design. Therefore, we have no purpose. In fact, in an evolutionary scheme, a ballpoint pen has more purpose than a person does because *it* has design and the person doesn't!

However, if humans were made in the image of God with a capacity to know Him intimately (Jer. 9:23-24), then trying to live as though that were not true is about as feasible as a fish enjoying a stroll down your street! When a human being seeks to find a purpose in life without God, he or she will eventually be forced to conclude, "Everything is meaningless." As you explore Ecclesiastes, emphasize the fact that Solomon was a man who fought to deny his design, and ended up with no lasting purpose. It wasn't because he failed to discover the right things. Happiness and purpose were not "just around the bend" for Solomon. He had no lasting purpose because he tried to be what he could not—someone who was *not* made in God's image.

Practical Wisdom is designed to do just what the title suggests: make your group members wise about life in the streets at home, school, work, and play. Someone has aptly said that adolescence is like a minefield. Our job is to teach kids how to make it to the other side without becoming another casualty. Two of the best books in the Bible for helping us with this task are Proverbs and Ecclesiastes.

As you prepare to lead these studies, open your own heart and mind to let God speak to you. Let your group members see your life growing to be more in tune with God's design for you, which is intimate fellowship with Him. Young people are yearning for "heroes" who have convictions about what really matters. *Your life* can be a lesson in itself.

Fran and Jill Sciacca have been involved in youth ministry for nearly two decades. Fran is a graduate of Denver Seminary. He has been teaching Christian high school Bible since 1980. Jill has a degree in journalism and sociology and is a full-time homemaker and freelance writer/editor.

The images on these two pages are designed to help you promote this course within your church and community. Feel free to photocopy anything here and adapt it to fit your publicity needs. The stuff on this page could be used as a flier that you send or hand out to kids—or as a bulletin insert. The stuff on the next page could be used to add visual interest to newsletters, calendars, bulletin boards, or other promotions. Be creative and have fun!

Don't Be a Fool

What's the difference between being wise and being a fool?
Find out as we begin a new course called *Streetwise*.
In Proverbs and Ecclesiastes, we'll explore some of the wisest
passages ever written. You'll discover practical advice on how to
find wisdom, when to take advice, and where to look for true happiness.
It would be foolish to miss this opportunity.

Who:

When:

Where:

Questions? Call:

Unit One: Practical Wisdom

Got something to say? We'd love to hear it.

I C I BUY

ALL WORK

Things aren't always as they seem.

Look before you leap.

I PARTY

Words of Wisdom

Choose one or more

☐ To help kids recognize that wisdom is more than "book knowledge."

☐ To help kids understand that the way to become wise is to get to know God better and follow His ways.

☐ To help kids identify one thing they can do this week to overcome a barrier that keeps them from knowing God better.

☐ Other:_____

Your Bible Base:

Proverbs 1:1-7
Various Proverbs that deal with wisdom and the fear of the Lord

Who's the Wisest of Them All?

(Needed: Copies of Repro Resource 1, pencils, small prize [optional])

To get kids thinking about what wisdom is and isn't, hand out copies of "Wisdom Test" (Repro Resource 1) and pencils. These Repro Resources could be given to individuals or to teams. As you're handing out the sheets, explain to your group members that this is a test to see how wise they are in certain areas that they probably won't be tested on at school. Give kids a few minutes to work, then go over the answers together.

You might want to mention that the correct answers are like a very naughty taxi—A BAD, BAD CAB (1—A, 2—B, 3—A, 4—D, 5—B, 6—A, 7—D, 8—C, 9—A, 10—B). If you wish, award a small prize to your winner(s)—perhaps a packet of Kleenex (brain tissue).

Then ask: **How accurately do you think this test reflects how wise you really are?** (Not very, because it only covers a few areas—and some of the areas aren't that important [although #1 could be important if your kids are into eating flowers].)

What would be a better test to measure how wise someone is? Kids might mention things like SAT or ACT tests, essay tests, or other tests. Some might say that it's difficult to measure wisdom through a test. If they do, ask them why it's difficult.

Who's the wisest person you know? What makes this person so wise? Let kids share for a few minutes before moving on. Try to get beyond the "correct, churchy" answers like Jesus or Solomon.

STEP 2

What Is Wisdom?

(Needed: Paper, pencils, chalkboard and chalk or newsprint and marker)

OPTIONS

Say: **For the next few weeks we'll be taking a look at some parts of the Bible known as the "wisdom literature." We'll be looking mostly at Proverbs and Ecclesiastes. I guess the logical place to begin, then, is to define "wisdom." How would you define "wisdom"?** Have kids write their definitions on the back of Repro Resource 1, on the board, or on sheets of newsprint. Encourage them to come up with short definitions, like "being smart," "knowing a lot and how to use it," etc.

After several volunteers have shared their responses, say: **The dictionary defines wisdom as "accumulated philosophic or scientific learning: knowledge; ability to discern inner qualities and relationships: insight; good sense: judgment."** You might want to write these definitions on the board, or at least the three key words: knowledge, insight, and judgment.

Suggest: **A definition that takes the Bible's meaning of the word into account might be "Gaining insight from a study of God's ways and applying what you learn in daily life."**

Ask: **What do you think of these definitions? How is the Bible's definition different from the dictionary's?** (The Bible's definition goes beyond mere head knowledge and refers to how we live our daily lives. The Bible recognizes that God is the true source of all wisdom.)

Why should you care about what wisdom is, anyway? What benefits are there to being wise? Group members may have difficulty answering these questions, but it's essential that you get kids thinking about them. If they don't see any reason or personal bene-fit from studying about wisdom, they probably won't really care about anything else that follows. Try listing some of the benefits of wisdom. Here are a few ideas to get you started: It helps us avoid mistakes; it helps us make better choices; it helps us get to know God better. (Further benefits are listed in Prov. 2 and 3. You'll get to those later.)

What might it cost you to become wiser? If you listed some of the benefits, you might also want to list some of the costs. For instance, becoming wiser might mean some changes in lifestyle. Once you gain wisdom in certain areas, you'll be challenged to act on what you've learned. Friends might think you're weird for pursuing wisdom.

Becoming wise takes time and effort. (Besides, many people think that ignorance is bliss!)

Summarize: **The bottom line seems to be that there's a real value in seeking after wisdom—but it will cost you something too. Your job as we continue in this study is to decide if the benefits of wisdom outweigh the costs. Only you can make that call.**

A Proverbs Primer

(Needed: Bibles, copies of Repro Resource 2, pencils)

Ask some questions to see how familiar your kids are with the Book of Proverbs. Can they recite any verses? Do they know who wrote it? Have they ever read it through from start to finish? What are their impressions of the book? Point out that a lot of people have trouble with the book because it seems like a hodge-podge of unrelated verses. Explain that in this session you'll try to sort some of it out.

Read Proverbs 1:1-7 together. Point out that these verses present the purpose and main theme of the book.

Ask: **Why was the book written?** (To help us gain wisdom, discipline, understanding, etc.)

Who was it written for? (The simple, the young [v. 4], wise people who want to add to their learning [v. 5].) Point out that you'll talk more about what it means to be "simple" in the next session.

Hand out copies of "A Proverbs Primer" (Repro Resource 2). Explain: **This sheet contains a few key words from the first seven verses of Proverbs. By understanding these key words, you'll have a better grasp of the whole book.**

Go over the first key word (Proverb) as a group. Point out that what we typically think of as the short-saying type of proverbs don't begin until chapter 10. The first nine chapters serve as an introduction to these sayings. It's as if the first nine chapters are there to show us why we should care about the sayings that follow.

Have group members form teams. Assign each team one or more of the three remaining words or phrases from the sheet. Give the teams a few minutes to look up their assigned passages and answer the questions for their word or phrase. After a few minutes, have the teams report back to the rest of the group what they learned about their word or phrase. Use the following information to supplement your discussion.

Solomon
• *Who was Solomon?* (He was the son of David and Bathsheba. He was a very wise and rich king. He was known for uttering three thousand proverbs during his lifetime [I Kings 4:32]. His many foreign wives and concubines eventually led him away from God.) Point out that when we consider Solomon's downward slide, we need to take a "do as I say, not as I do" approach to the Book of Proverbs.
• *Who wrote the Book of Proverbs?* (Prov. 1:1 attributes the entire book to Solomon, but other authors are mentioned in different places in the text. The bulk of the book [10:1–22:16; 25:1–29:27] is attributed directly to Solomon. It's possible that he compiled the book, sort of like an editor, or that most of it was compiled during his reign. Proverbs 25–31 were probably added to Solomon's collection at a later date during the reign of King Hezekiah of Judah. The other named authors, Agur and King Lemuel, were most likely Ishmaelites [Arabs]. Solomon was probably quite familiar with the wisdom of neighboring lands.)

Wisdom
• *What other words are used in the book that seem to mean something similar to wisdom?* (Discipline, understanding, insight, prudence, knowledge, discretion, instruction, teaching, commands.) Compare these words to the definitions of wisdom you developed earlier. Certainly, wisdom is the key concept contained in the book. Note that it is much more than head knowledge; it is very practical and active.
• *Where does wisdom come from?* (The source of all wisdom is God.) Point out that this same idea is found in the New Testament—in James 1:5.
• *What are some of the benefits of wisdom?* (Finding knowledge of God, victory, protection, understanding what is right and just, prolonged life, winning people's favor, riches, honor, etc.) Compare these benefits to those listed earlier.
Ask: **How can wisdom lead to prosperity and long life? How can wisdom protect us?** If no one mentions it, suggest that wisdom from God can keep us from making some foolish and life-threatening mistakes. Ask for some examples. (You may also want to point out that this isn't a guarantee that all wise people will live to be 100!)

Fear of the Lord
• *What does it mean to "fear" the Lord?* (Having a loving awe or reverence for God that involves getting to know Him and obeying His commands.) Point out that Proverbs 1:7 is sort of the motto of the whole book, so it's crucial to understand what the fear of the Lord is.

You might also want to call attention to the connection between knowing and obeying God, hating evil, and fearing (or respecting) God.

• *What's the connection between wisdom and fearing God?* (Only when we care enough to really get to know God better and choose to follow His ways do we discover what true wisdom is. In this sense, the smartest scientist or Nobel prize winner in the world isn't wise if he or she never respects God enough to establish a relationship with Him.)

Summarize: **Wisdom is much more about who you know than what you know. It's more about your attitude than your aptitude!**

Have group members share any additional insights or questions they uncovered during their group study time.

Wisdom Blocks

(Needed: Paper, pencils, bricks or yellow crepe paper)

Say: **We've established that wisdom is worth pursuing and that the key thing we need to do in order to gain wisdom is to fear God—that is, get to know Him better. Simple, right?**

In theory, maybe it is simple, but not in practice. Getting to know God is a life-long process. At times it'll be an adventure; at other times it'll be a real effort.

Have kids return to the teams they formed earlier. Give each team the task of developing a list of at least five barriers to intimacy with God—things that keep us from getting to know Him better. After a few minutes, reassemble the group and have each team share its list. Spend some time as a group discussing each barrier. To make the point more memorable, you might want to use some bricks to represent each barrier. Point out that like a brick wall, these barriers can keep us from having a more intimate relationship with God. If bricks aren't available, try taping up strips of yellow crepe paper to represent a police barrier at the scene of a crime.

For each barrier, ask the following questions: **What would be some signs or symptoms of this barrier in someone's life?**

What are some specific suggestions you'd give to someone who's trying to get around this barrier?

Use the following suggestions to supplement group members' responses:

OPTIONS

LITTLE BIBLE BACKGROUND

MOSTLY GIRLS

MEDIA

- Barrier #1—Lack of interest (apathy)

Symptoms—No priority given to prayer or Bible study, boredom with church, etc.

Suggestions—Spend some time with people who are excited about their faith, challenge God to be more real in your life, discipline yourself to pray and read the Bible for a few minutes at a time even if you don't feel like it, etc.

- Barrier #2—Lack of time

Symptoms—Involved in too many activities, high level of stress, etc.

Suggestions—Slow down, relax, spend some concentrated time alone, etc.

- Barrier #3—Unwillingness to give up a certain sin

Symptoms—Feelings of guilt or conviction, lies or deception to cover something up, etc.

Suggestions—Confession of the sin, talking with a trusted friend or counselor, etc.

- Barrier #4—Not knowing how to go about gaining wisdom

Symptoms—Feeling frustrated, not knowing where to begin, limited understanding of the Bible, etc.

Suggestions—Ask a more mature Christian to disciple you, go through a good devotional book for teens, etc.

- Barrier #5—Feelings of inadequacy or unworthiness

Symptoms—Low self-esteem, constantly putting yourself down, feeling like God doesn't really care about you, etc.

Suggestions—Spend time with God anyway, share your feelings with Him, keep a journal of your thoughts and feelings, etc.

- Barrier #6—Feeling that God is unapproachable or unknowable

Symptoms—Viewing God as far away and uninvolved in your daily life, never having committed to a personal relationship with Him, etc.

Suggestions—It's true that we can't fully understand God or know Him completely, but we can start by taking one small step at time. The first step might be submitting your fears and your doubts to God and starting a personal relationship with Him through acceptance of Jesus as Lord and Savior.

Barrier Breakers

(Needed: Bricks and hammer or yellow crepe paper and tape)

Have each group member choose one barrier that is most likely to interfere with his or her relationship with God. This could be something mentioned in the discussion, or something more private. Give each young person a brick (or a strip of crepe paper) to represent that barrier. In silence, have kids think of one specific step they can take this week to start overcoming that barrier.

If you're using bricks, give kids a very sturdy hammer (like a sledge hammer) and safety glasses, and let them pulverize their bricks. If you're using crepe paper, have kids tape their strips across a doorway and then break through to the other side. Either way, you'll be symbolizing the need to do something to get around (or through) the barriers that keep us from getting to know God better.

Before (or after) physically breaking through the barriers, let kids share as they are comfortable about their commitments.

Close the session by thanking God for the fact that He wants us to get to know Him better and has taken the initiative to do that. For in Jesus Christ, we see the essence of God's Wisdom. Ask God to help you get to know Him better in our own individual ways. You could end the prayer by reading Romans 11:33 together.

NOTES

1 2 3 4 5 6 7 8 9 10
| | | | | | | | | |
A BAD BAD CAB

A

Wisdom Test

Circle the correct answer to each scientifically formulated question to determine how wise you really are.

1. Which of the following plants is *not* poisonous?
   a. marigold   c. sweet pea
   b. daffodil   d. lily of the valley

2. Which household appliance has the highest yearly energy cost?
   a. light bulbs throughout the entire house
   b. water heater
   c. color TV
   d. refrigerator/freezer

3. Which of the following foods has the most cholesterol?
   a. chicken (three ounces, skinless, light meat)
   b. butter (one tablespoon)
   c. ice cream (one-half cup)
   d. bacon (two slices)

4. What's the best month to buy new curtains?
   a. November   c. May
   b. August   d. February

5. What do the letters M and M stand for in M&M candies?
   a. Mercury and Mars (two planets in the Milky Way)
   b. Mars and Murrie (two head honchos at the company)
   c. More and More (from the first advertising campaign)
   d. Malt and Milk (two ingredients)

6. When was *Xmas* first used to denote Christmas?
   a. 1511 (X represents a Greek symbol for Christ)
   b. 1827 (an English abbreviation to save typesetting space)
   c. 1959 (attempt by the U.S. press to secularize the holiday)
   d. 1978 (an advertising campaign that appeared in the *New York Times*)

7. What's the traditional anniversary gift for a thirteenth-year anniversary?
   a. ivory   c. silk
   b. pottery   d. lace

8. How many miles does the average person walk in a lifetime?
   a. 6,500   c. 65,000
   b. 26,500   d. 165,000

9. How many earthworms are in a typical square acre of soil?
   a. 50,000   c. 5,000
   b. 25,000   d. 500

10. Why do pigs take mud baths?
   a. The mud destroys bacteria that causes disease in pigs.
   b. To keep cool
   c. To keep warm
   d. Pigs really don't like mud at all.

How wise are you?

10—Wise guy, eh?
9-8—Solomon's got nothing on you.
7-6—Einstein's got nothing on you.
5-4—Bozo's got nothing on you.
3-2—You're at least as wise as the guy who made up these silly questions.
0-1—Get that daffodil out of your mouth!

A PROVERBS PRIMER

PROVERB
What is a proverb? (Proverbs 1:1, 6; 10:1; 22:17; 24:23)
• A parable, saying, or riddle spoken by a wise person
• A comparison, contrast, or simile
• An analogy
• Any short saying
• Wisdom passed on from teachers who know God's laws to their students

SOLOMON
Who was Solomon?
(Proverbs 1:1; I Samuel 12:24; I Kings 3–4; I Kings 11:1-6)

Who wrote the Book of Proverbs?
(Proverbs 1:1; 10:1; 22:17-21; 24:23; 25:1; 30:1; 31:1)

WISDOM
What other words are used in the book that seem to mean something similar to wisdom? (Proverbs 1:1-8, 20, 21; 2:1, 2)

Where does wisdom come from? (Proverbs 2:6)

What are some of the benefits of wisdom? (Proverbs 2–3)

FEAR OF THE LORD
What does it mean to "fear" the Lord?
(Proverbs 1:7, 29-31; 2:1-5; 3:7; 9:10;
10:27; 14:27; 15:33; 16:6; 19:23; 31:30)

What's the connection between wisdom and fearing God? (Proverbs 1:7, 29-31; 2:1-5; 3:7; 9:10; 10:27; 14:27; 15:33; 16:6; 19:23; 31:30)

STEP 1

Instead of using the quiz on Repro Resource 1, stage a "Streetwise Olympics." Have kids compete in the following events:

• *Sidewalk Sidestep*—Lay out a butcher-paper path on the floor. Dot it liberally with wads of freshly-chewed chewing gum. Each person must negotiate the path in 30 seconds or less without getting gum on his or her shoes. (Adjust the time to fit the length of your "sidewalk.") Give a prize to everyone who succeeds.

• *Street Search*—Give two teams identical maps of any city. Call out the name of a street; the first team to find it wins a prize.

• *Stickup Speeches*—Have kids line up. Pretend to rob each person, one at a time, saying, **This is a stickup!** See who can give the most creative verbal response to convince you not to rob him or her. Reward the best response with a prize.

Afterward, ask: **What does it mean to be "streetwise"? Who's the most "streetwise" person you know? What other kinds of wisdom do people need?**

STEP 3

Before the session, dress a group member or an adult helper as a "guru"—in a bathrobe, fake beard, etc. Hide this "wise man" somewhere in the building. Give him photocopies of the three answer sections ("Solomon," "Wisdom," and "Fear of the Lord") from the session plan. Have kids form three teams. Explain that the teams must find the wise man within two minutes (adjust according to the difficulty of the search) in order to get the photocopied answers. Those who don't find him must look up the answers.

STEP 1

Make two copies of Repro Resource 1 for each group member. Have kids complete the first version according to the instructions in the session. Emphasize that kids must work alone on the sheet. (But don't give the "very naughty taxi" clue.) Before you reveal the correct answers, distribute the second version of the sheet. Explain that this time kids may work together and ask each other for the quiz answers. For instance, if you have a "flower expert" among your group members, kids might consult him or her for Question #1. After kids get opinions from other group members, they must decide whose answer to use for each question. Use this activity to make the point that wisdom involves knowing whose advice to take.

STEP 3

Rather than having kids form teams to work on Repro Resource 2, give them a few minutes to look up the passages individually. However, they may *not* write down their answers. Instead, they must do their best to remember the information in the verses. After a few minutes, have kids close their Bibles. Then go through the questions on the sheet one at a time, pointing to the kids you want to answer each question. For instance, you might ask: **John, who was Solomon?** If John replies, "The son of David," ask the question to another group member—who must then give a different answer (perhaps "the king of Israel"). If a person cannot answer, he or she is out. Continue until you have all the answers you're looking for each question.

STEP 1

As group members arrive, seat them as though they're about to take their SAT exams. Space the kids apart as much as possible, give them each a #2 pencil, have them remain quiet, etc. When everyone is seated, explain that instead of taking the SAT in the traditional manner, kids will be working as teams on the exam. Have kids form three teams (the "S Team," the "A Team," and the "T Team"). You will ask a series of nearly impossible questions. After you ask a question, team members will consult together to answer it. When a team comes up with an answer, one of its members must run to the board and write it down. The first team to write the correct answer gets a point. The team with the most points at the end of the game is the winner. If possible, try to make your questions so hard that only one or two is likely to be answered. Then for your final question, ask: **What is wisdom?** Use this activity to lead into a discussion on the difference between knowledge and wisdom.

STEP 3

Before the session, write each of the questions on Repro Resource 2 on a separate sheet of poster board. Then post the signs in various places around the room. You'll also need to write each of the Scripture references listed on the sheet on a separate index card. Distribute the index cards to your group members (one card per person). Instruct kids to look up their assigned passage, decide which question it applies to, and stand under the appropriate sign. Then have the members of each newly formed group under each sign fully answer their question. After a few minutes, have each group share its findings.

STEP 2

Kids may think of biblical "wisdom" as something for old people. Like many people in our culture, they may value what current celebrities say over what an old Book says. Share the following examples of celebrity "wisdom": **"I will not change. When you are successful and you change, you are an idiot"— Arnold Schwarzenegger. "I watch [the movie Heaven Can Wait] constantly because it causes me to re-explore my values. I hope I can act half as cool as Warren Beatty in the years to come"—Dr. Dré, rap star. "My expression for the '90s is 'stash the cash.' I'm not willing to sell my very soul—but almost"— Daniel J. Travanti, actor. "Every time I perform, I have to have it [a "lucky" ring she's worn since tenth grade] on. If I can't wear it around my neck, I'll put it around my waist"—Mariah Carey, singer. "People who believe in voodoo are as serious as people who believe in any other religion. Making fun of zombies comes out of igno-rance"—Cicely Tyson, actress.** Ask: **How wise are these statements? Doesn't the wisdom of the Bible deserve at least equal time?**

STEP 3

Kids may think of Proverbs as irrelevant— a bunch of sayings that are either obvious or don't make any sense, about as useful as the messages in fortune cookies. Help them to see the book as the hard-won insights of a lifetime, shared out of con-cern for the reader. Say: **Pretend that you have only two minutes to live, and must pass along to your children two of the most important things you've learned in life.** Give group members two minutes to write; then share results. Ask: **If you really had to do this, how would you want people to treat what you'd written?**

STEP 3

If your kids aren't familiar with the Bible, they may have a hard time answering the questions on Repro Resource 2. So instead of having kids form teams to work on the sheet, work on it together as a group. You may even want to turn the activity into a game. Help your group members find the Book of Proverbs in their Bibles. Before you ask each question, write the accompanying passages on the board. Go through the questions one at a time, giving kids an opportunity to look up the passages and shout out the answers. The first person to shout out a correct answer gets a point. There's more than one correct answer for each ques-tion, so there are several points available. After you've gone through all of the ques-tions, you may want to award a prize to the person with the most points.

STEP 4

Kids with little Bible background may have difficulty brainstorming barriers to intimacy with God. So rather than having kids form teams to come up with barriers, try a different approach. Have kids form pairs. Assign each pair one of the barriers listed in the session. Also read some of the symptoms associated with each barrier, as well as suggestions for overcoming the barrier. Then have the pairs come up with some potential problems kids might face in applying the suggestions to the barrier problem. (For instance, one of the suggestions for "Barrier #1—Lack of interest [apathy]" is "Spend some time with people who are excited about their faith." One potential problem is that some kids don't know anyone who is excited about his or her faith.) After a few minutes, have each pair share what it came up with. You'll want to be prepared to offer some workable solutions to the problems the pairs name.

STEP 1

After completing Repro Resource 1, have each group member come up with one more trivia question that only he or she will know the answer to. One at a time, have each person ask his or her question. Then give the rest of the group 10 seconds to answer it. After all group members have asked their questions, say: **We're all knowledgeable in differ-ent areas. Likewise, we're probably all wise in different areas.** Point out that God imparts different kinds of wis-dom to people. So a good way to make maximum use of God's imparted wisdom is to seek advice from each other. Help your group members see that they're a team when it comes to gaining wisdom.

STEP 5

Distribute file folders and pencils to your group members. Explain that the folders are to be used as "faith files." Instruct kids to write in their folders any answered prayers or fulfilled needs they've experi-enced from God. Give kids a few minutes to begin their files. Afterward, ask volun-teers to share some of their faith-building memories. Then say: **Add to your fold-er every time God comes through for you or every time you over-come one of the barriers we just identified. Then, whenever you feel like you just can't get over the next hurdle in your way, you can pull out this file and be reminded of all the times you and God have done it together before.**

MOSTLY GIRLS

STEP 2

Ask for a couple of volunteers to help you perform a skit. Explain that you will play the role of a popular, good-looking guy in school. One of the volunteers will play the role of the most beautiful girl in school. The other girl will play the role of the smartest—and wisest—girl in school. Explain that you will perform the skit twice. The first time, you (the popular, good-looking guy) will talk to the beautiful girl and ignore the other one, even though both girls are vying for your attention. The second time, you will talk to the smart (and wise) girl and ignore the beautiful one. See how both girls react to being talked to and ignored. Afterward, ask your girls which version of the skit they think is most realistic. Ask: **Do you think most guys care about how wise a girl is? Why or why not? If not, what other benefits are there to being wise?**

STEP 4

Have your group members imagine that a new girl has arrived at school. She seems nice, and has indicated that she'd like to make friends. Ask your group members to make a list of five reasons or "obstacles" that might prevent them from becoming friends with this girl. You might throw out some examples like "My other friends might get jealous" or "I'm too busy." After a few minutes, have your group members read their lists. Use this activity to lead in to a discussion on building a relationship with God, and the barriers that can make this difficult.

MOSTLY GUYS

STEP 1

Begin the meeting dressed as "The Great Wise One"—perhaps wearing robe, fake beard, and turban. Say: **I am so wise, I know the answers to questions that haven't even been asked. Let me show you.** [NOTE: This is very similar to Johnny Carson's old "Carnac" routine.] Before the session, prepare several envelopes, each with a question sealed inside and three answers written on the outside. Hold up each envelope to your forehead, concentrate, and announce the three answers. Then open the envelope and read the question. This activity is designed to be humorous, and will work best if you include the names of your group members in the answers. For example, you might give the following answers: **Double-pump, two-handed reverse slam; Porky Pig; and** _____ (the name of a guy in your group who thinks he's pretty cool). You would then open the envelope and read: **What is a dunk, a chunk, and a punk?** Try to use enough questions so that each of your guys is mentioned (and poked fun at lightheartedly) at least once.

STEP 2

Focus on the key words *knowledge, insight,* and *judgment.* Ask: **How might these three things apply to someone who wants to become a good basketball player?** (Knowledge comes from listening to what the coach says in practice. Insight comes from watching how other basketball players play. Judgment comes from making decisions on the court.) Then ask: **How might these three things apply to someone who wants to improve his Bible study time?** (Knowledge comes from reading the Bible and listening to what other Christians say about it. Insight comes from asking, "What does this passage mean to me?" Judgment comes from applying the Bible to life situations.)

EXTRA FUN

STEP 1

To begin the session, play "Wisdom Bingo." Before the session, prepare several cards. Write the letters W-I-S-D-O-M across the top of each card. Under each letter, draw a vertical column of six boxes. Use increments of 12 for the numbers in each column (W = 1-12; I = 13-24; S = 25-36; D = 37-48; O = 49-60; M = 61-72). Write the appropriate numbers randomly on each card. Then prepare small slips of paper to "draw" during the game. For the most part, the game is played just like regular Bingo. (Of course, when someone covers a row of numbers, he or she should yell "Wisdom!") However, when someone calls out "Wisdom!" he or she hasn't automatically won the game. At that point, you will ask him or her a Trivial Pursuit question (allowing the player to choose the category). If the person answers it correctly, he or she wins. If not, he or she is out, and the game continues.

STEP 2

Have kids form teams. Explain that there are slips of paper with the letters W, I, S, D, O, and M written on them (one set for each team) hidden in six places around the church. You will use Bible verses as clues. These verses should tie in with the different hiding places ("I stand at the door and knock" [Revelation 3:20]— church entrance; "Sing to the Lord a new song" [Psalm 149:1]—choir loft, "I am the bread of life" [John 6:48]—kitchen; "Jesus was baptized too" [Luke 3:21]—baptistry; etc.) Give each team a clue to start with. Each hiding place should have six slips of paper (one for each team) that have one of the letters written on them, as well as six other Bible-verse clues (one for each team) that will help the teams find the next hiding place. The first team to return all six letters to you is the winner.

MEDIA

STEP 1

Using a VCR and monitor, show scenes (which you've pre-screened) featuring some of the following movie "wise men"—characters who share their "wisdom" with others: Ten Bears (*Dances with Wolves*), Obi-Wan Kenobi (*Star Wars*), Yoda (*The Empire Strikes Back*), Gandhi (*Gandhi*), Humphrey Bogart's ghost (*Play It Again, Sam*), Mr. Miyagi (*The Karate Kid*), and Gordon Gekko (*Wall Street*). Then discuss the scenes, using the following questions: **How are these "wise men" similar? How are they different? Which do you think are really wise? Why? If you were going to ask advice from a "wise man"—or woman—what would you want that person to be like?**

STEP 4

Show the following scenes from *The Wizard of Oz* on video. First, about two-thirds of the way through the film, Dorothy and her friends approach the fearsome, fiery Oz and ask for things they need (courage, brains, etc.). Ask: **Is this what it's like to ask God for wisdom? Why or why not?** Second, near the end of the movie, the all-too-human Oz presents the Scarecrow and others with substitutes for what they seek. Ask: **If the Scarecrow had asked for wisdom instead of brains, what do you think he would have gotten? Is this how God deals with requests for wisdom? Explain.**

SHORT MEETING TIME

STEP 1

Name some pairs of characters from TV shows. Have kids vote on which character in each pair is wiser. Here are some pairs you might use: Will (*Fresh Prince of Bel-Air*) or Martin (*Martin*); Roseanne Connor (*Roseanne*) or Dr. Quinn (*Dr. Quinn, Medicine Woman*); Bart Simpson or Lisa Simpson (*The Simpsons*); Commander Benjamin Sisko (*Deep Space Nine*) or Captain Jean-Luc Picard (*Star Trek: The Next Generation*). Afterward, ask: **How did you decide who was wiser? Are there different kinds of wisdom? What are wise people able to accomplish that others can't?**

STEP 3

Summarize yourself the definition of *proverb* and who Solomon was. Then ask the following questions, having kids look for answers in the accompanying passages. **Where does wisdom come from?** (Prov. 2:6.) **What are some benefits of wisdom?** (Prov. 3.) Read Proverbs 9:10. Explain that fearing the Lord is having a loving awe and reverence for Him. It includes knowing and obeying Him. To save more time, replace Steps 4 and 5 with the following. Read 2 Chronicles 1:1, 6-12. Ask: **What kind of relationship did Solomon have with God before he asked for wisdom? What did Solomon get? Why do you think God was so pleased?** To help kids consider why they need wisdom, have volunteers tell how they might have completed the sentence from verse 10: "Give me wisdom and knowledge, that I may ..." To close, have the group brainstorm at least eight areas in which kids might need wisdom (choice of colleges and careers, study habits, picking friends, getting along with parents, buying things, etc.). Then have each person list these in the order in which he or she feels the greatest need.

URBAN

STEP 1

To give Repro Resource 1 an urban slant, add the following question:

• A recent study in Boston found that gang members would be willing to give up selling drugs if they could be guaranteed to make how much money per hour?
a. $8-10
b. $12-17
c. $20-25
d. $26-30
(The answer is a.)

STEP 2

If your kids live in a world in which mere survival is an everyday concern, they may question the importance of striving after wisdom. So you'll need to help them recognize that wisdom can be beneficial to them in their daily lives. As a group, brainstorm a list of ways in which wisdom can help an inner-city teenager. Among other things, wisdom can help a young person sort out his or her future, allowing him or her to recognize which paths are "dead ends" and which lead to opportunity. Wisdom might also help a young person keep his or her head when faced with a difficult situation (like a gang confrontation). Wisdom might help a young person find a suitable mate in a society inundated with sexual immorality. After you've established some of the potential benefits of wisdom, lead in to a discussion on how to *gain* wisdom.

STEP 1

The questions on Repro Resource 1 are pretty obscure and trivial. It's not likely that your high schoolers will know more of the answers than your junior highers do. Therefore, a game based on this quiz might work well for a mixed group. Have kids form a circle with their chairs. Ask each quiz question one at a time. But instead of giving all four possible answer choices, give only two (the correct one and another one). Instruct kids to *physically* answer each question. They should move one seat to the left if they choose "A," and one seat to the right if they choose "B." After everyone has moved, give the correct answer. Those who answered correctly are still in; those who didn't are out. (And those who have someone sitting on their lap probably *wish* they were out!) Continue until only one person remains. Then crown him or her the "Wise Old Owl." (You might want to award him or her something scholarly, like a notebook or ruler.)

STEP 2

Ask each of your junior highers to make a list of situations he or she has faced (or is facing) that required some degree of wisdom. Their lists might include things like an important choice, a response to someone, an attitude change, etc. Ask each of your high schoolers to make a list of the costs they've "paid" in becoming wiser. Their lists might include things like friends who they think they're weird for making wise choices, a lack of popularity for not following the crowd, less free time, etc. After a few minutes, have the kids in each age group share their lists. Then ask your high schoolers to share whether or not they think the "costs" of their wise choices were "worth it."

STEP 1

Have your kids form pairs. Then distribute lists of questions for members of each pair to ask each other. The lists should include questions like "How many freckles do you have on your body?" "How tall will you be when you stop growing?" "What did you do on the afternoon of March 21, 1984?" "How many hairs fell out of your head the last time you used a hairbrush or comb?" Of course kids won't know the answers to these questions, but have them try to make educated guesses. Then have someone read aloud Matthew 10:30 to give kids a sense of the scope of God's knowledge. Briefly discuss whether knowledge and wisdom are the same thing. Ask: **If you knew the answers to all of the questions we asked earlier, would that make you wise?** (Not necessarily.) Point out that God is both ultimately knowledgeable and fully wise. Ask: **If you were all knowing, all wise, and all loving, wouldn't you want to give some of that wisdom to those you loved? God does. And that's partly what Proverbs is for.**

STEP 2

Ask group members to brainstorm some common sayings, phrases, or terms that mention wisdom. List these on the board as they are named. Kids may mention things like "Wise as an owl"; "streetwise"; "Early to bed, early to rise makes a man healthy, wealthy, and wise"; "wisdom teeth"; "wisecracks"; etc. After you've compiled a list, ask: **What do these phrases and terms suggest about the nature of wisdom?** (It comes with age; it involves humor; it is part of moderate living; etc.) Then explain: **As we look at the Book of Proverbs, we will discover what wisdom is really all about!**

DATE USED:

Approx. Time

STEP 1: *Who's the Wisest of Them All?* _____
❏ Extra Action
❏ Small Group
❏ Large Group
❏ Fellowship & Worship
❏ Mostly Guys
❏ Extra Fun
❏ Media
❏ Short Meeting Time
❏ Urban
❏ Combined Jr. High/High School
❏ Extra Challenge
Things needed:

STEP 2: *What Is Wisdom?* _____
❏ Heard It All Before
❏ Mostly Girls
❏ Mostly Guys
❏ Extra Fun
❏ Urban
❏ Combined Jr. High/High School
❏ Extra Challenge
Things needed:

STEP 3: *A Proverbs Primer* _____
❏ Extra Action
❏ Small Group
❏ Large Group
❏ Heard It All Before
❏ Little Bible Background
❏ Short Meeting Time
Things needed:

STEP 4: *Wisdom Blocks* _____
❏ Little Bible Background
❏ Mostly Girls
❏ Media
Things needed:

STEP 5: *Barrier Breakers* _____
❏ Fellowship & Worship
Things needed:

A Fool and His Happiness Are Soon Parted

YOUR GOALS FOR THIS SESSION:

Choose one or more

☐ To help kids identify different types of foolishness.

☐ To help kids understand the importance of avoiding foolish ways.

☐ To help kids evaluate their own ways to determine how wise or foolish they have been lately, and commit to seeking after wisdom.

☐ Other:_____
_____

Your Bible Base:

Selected Proverbs

Fooling Around

(Needed: Chalkboard and chalk or newsprint and marker, April Fool's novelties [optional])

OPTIONS

EXTRA ACTION

FELLOWSHIP & WORSHIP

MOSTLY GUYS

EXTRA FUN

MEDIA

SHORT MEETING TIME

EXTRA CHALLENGE

Before the meeting, write "A fool is . . ." on the board. As kids arrive, distribute chalk or markers and instruct them to write down how they would complete the sentence.

To get kids in the mood, you might want to bring in some typical "April Fool's" novelties—fake vomit, rubber noses, etc. While kids complete the sentence starter and examine the novelties, begin a discussion with some general questions about foolishness.

Ask: **What's the best April Fool's joke you've ever played or heard of?** Let kids share their stories. You may want to supplement their responses with the following ideas (from the author's college days): smearing black shoe polish on black toilet seats, putting Vaseline on doorknobs so that the doors can't be opened, and tying a rope between two opposing doors, so that neither can be opened.

Why do some people enjoy April Fool's pranks? Get a few responses.

When can a joke backfire, or do more harm than good? (When someone gets hurt, embarrassed, or made fun of.)

What is a fool, anyway? Read off some of the group members' responses from the board. Then point out that one dictionary definition of a fool is "a person lacking judgment or prudence." Some synonyms listed in the dictionary include idiot, imbecile, moron, and simpleton.

No one wants to be considered a fool. What kinds of people would kids your age say are most foolish? Why? Encourage a variety of answers. Some young people may say that kids who blow off school are foolish. Others may say that kids who don't party a lot are foolish. Some may say that kids who engage in "unsafe" sex are foolish. Others may say that virgins are foolish. Some may say that parents or other authority figures are fools.

What kinds of people do you think the Bible says are most foolish? Get responses from several group members. Then point out that the Book of Proverbs has a lot to say about fools. Much of the book contrasts wisdom and folly. That's what you're going to look at today.

Fool House

(Needed: Copies of Repro Resource 3, pencils)

Hand out copies of "Fool House" (Repro Resource 3) and pencils. Instruct group members to complete the sheet individually or in small groups. When everyone is finished, have group members share their responses.

Start by having kids call out some of the last names they came up with for each character. After group members have shared the names they came up with, suggest the following ones: Alexis Adulteress, Wanda Wise, Samantha Simple, Francis Fool, Molly Mocker, and Sally Sluggard. (The significance of these names will become more obvious in the next step.)

Next, have group members share their rankings. Obviously, kids will say that Wanda is the wisest; but how did they rank the rest? There's no one right way, but you might want to suggest the following order based on the severity or harmfulness of each: Wanda, Samantha, Sally, Francis, Molly, and Alexis.

Give group members a few minutes to explain why they ranked the characters as they did. Then move on to the Bible study, in which you'll look at some verses to describe each type of character.

Fool Proof

(Needed: Bibles, chalkboard and chalk or newsprint and marker)

Say: **In this session, we're going to be looking at different types of people described in the Book of Proverbs. These people include The Wise, The Simple, The Fool, The Mocker, The Adulteress, and The Sluggard.** List these names on the board as you mention them.

You'll study the first type of person—The Wise—as a group. Instruct group members to open their Bibles to Proverbs. Have them skim

OPTIONS

EXTRA ACTION

SMALL GROUP

LARGE GROUP

SHORT MEETING TIME

URBAN

JR.HIGH HIGH SCHOOL COMBINED

EXTRA CHALLENGE

through the book randomly, calling out any characteristics of a wise person they find. (This activity could also serve as a review of the first session.) Here are some characteristics your group members may find:

The Wise
• Fear the Lord (Prov. 1:7).
• Listen to instruction (1:8).
• Don't give in to sin (1:10).

After your group members have come up with several characteristics of The Wise, have them form teams to study the rest of the types of people listed on the board. Assign each team one or more of the types on the board, as well as the accompanying passages to look up. Instruct each team to answer these two questions:
• **What do these passages say about this type of person?**
• **What are two or three modern-day examples of someone exhibiting this type of behavior?**
Use the following information to guide your discussion of the activity.

The Simple (Prov. 1:22; 9:1-6, 13-18; 14:15, 18)
• *Description*—A simple person is someone who is easily persuaded or lacks good judgment. Other words for "simple" might include "gullible" or "naive." In many ways, all people start out as "simple" and have to choose whether they will follow the way of wisdom or the way of folly. Some simple people enjoy being simple, thinking ignorance is bliss.
• *Examples*—Someone who engages in immoral sexual activity, but doesn't realize it's immoral; someone who is curious about spiritual things and is willing to try anything, even cults.
Ask: **In Proverbs 9, both wisdom and folly call out to simple people. How are their invitations similar and different? Why do some people choose folly over wisdom?** (Both want simple people to come into her "house" or way of life. Wisdom has done more advance preparation. Wisdom demands leaving simple ways behind. Folly's feast consists of stolen water and food that is so shameful it can only be eaten in secret. Sinful pleasures might "taste" good for a moment, but they won't provide any lasting enjoyment.)

The Fool (Prov. 1:7, 22; 12:15-16; 13:19; 26:11; 28:26)
• *Description*—A fool is someone who knows the difference between right and wrong but deliberately chooses wrong. Fools don't want to be told how they should live. They shun other people's advice if it contradicts what they want to do. Fools repeat their foolishness (sin), even though they have enough knowledge or experience to know better.
• *Examples*—Someone who knows the dangers of drinking and driving, but does so anyway; someone who has read about the dangers of steroids, but chooses to use them anyway in order to look better.

Ask: **Can a smart person be foolish? If so, how? Why do some people deliberately choose to repeat "foolish" behavior?** (Intelligence, as measured by IQ or SAT tests, has nothing to do with whether someone is wise or foolish. Wisdom involves someone's willingness to learn God's ways and apply what's learned in daily life.)

As you talk about the repeat nature of foolishness, you might want to have kids compare Proverbs 26:11 with Proverbs 23:29-35. The verses in chapter 23 talk about one specific type of foolishness—alcohol abuse. It's a very accurate portrayal of drunkenness. Note the last part of verse 35, where the drunk wants to wake up only to have another drink. Harmful behaviors like drunkenness, sexual immorality, drug abuse, and the like can become addictive. These behaviors might give some short-term pleasure, but the cycle is extremely destructive as the person caught in it always needs to find a greater thrill or high in order to get the same level of pleasure. Give kids an opportunity to talk about addictions, and follow up outside of your group time with any who want to talk more about it.

The Mocker (Prov. 1:22; 13:1; 15:12; 21:24; 22:10; 29:8)
• *Description*—A mocker is someone who makes fun of others, especially those who are following wisdom. Mockers are arrogant and don't want to be corrected. They delight in putting others down. Because of their insults and their intent to cause harm, mockers cause quarrels and strife between others.
• *Examples*—Someone who teases others who choose not to drink; someone who enjoys putting down people of other races.
Ask: **Why would someone delight in mockery?** (It sets the person up in a position of superiority. His or her acquaintances might try to get on the person's good side so as not to become the brunt of his or her offensive remarks. The person's mockery might make him or her feel somewhat better about his or her own foolishness.)

The Adulteress (Prov. 2:16-19; 5:3-6; 6:24; 7:4, 5, 21-23; 22:14)
• *Description*—In Proverbs, the adulteress is depicted as an unfaithful wife intentionally trying to lead impressionable young men into her trap by seducing them. Though she can be awfully tempting, those who give in to her find death, not life. The adulteress can also be taken symbolically to represent any person who intentionally tries to get someone else to engage in immoral behavior, including, but not limited to, sexual immorality. In this sense, the adulteress could be an individual (male or female), or even a group. Note that Proverbs seems to be suggesting a progression in which each succeeding character is more dangerous. Someone starts out simple. He or she chooses whether to follow wisdom or folly. Those who choose folly become foolish. Those who are deeply into their foolish ways begin teasing or mocking those who aren't. Those who are most completely entrenched in their foolishness

actively try to recruit or trap others to join them in their sinful ways. Misery loves company.

• *Examples*—Obvious examples would include prostitutes and drug dealers. The list could also include peers who pressure others into engaging in immoral behavior, a guy pressuring his date to have sex, or even advertisers who try to "seduce" others into buying something they don't need.

Say: **Proverbs 2:19 says, "None who go to her [the adulteress] return or attain the paths of life." Does this mean that there's no turning back for someone who has committed adultery or other immoral behavior? Why or why not?** (Obviously, the rest of Scripture depicts a loving God who can rescue us from any type of sinful, immoral behavior. Yet anyone who deliberately and repeatedly chooses to give in to immoral behavior is playing with fire. It's not that God can't still save the person; it's that the person may get to a point where he or she no longer senses any need for God.)

The Sluggard (Prov. 6:6-11; 10:26; 13:4; 21:25; 24:30-34)

• *Description*—A sluggard is a lazy person who doesn't want to work for the things he or she craves. Others find such people very irritating. The sluggard appears many times throughout the Book of Proverbs and seems to be a special type of fool that the writers have singled out. Many times the sluggard is depicted in some type of humorous fashion.

• *Examples*—Someone who has the ability, but refuses to study in order to improve his or her grades; someone who refuses to work but would rather take advantage of someone else's generosity.

Ask: **Without naming names, who's the laziest person you know? Why do you think this person is so lazy?** Don't dwell very long on this. Try to get kids thinking about the source of laziness. For some, it's just a matter of taking advantage of others so that they don't have to work as hard. Ask kids to comment on Proverbs 10:26. Get them to comment on why lazy people can be so irritating.

What Kind of Fool Am I?

(Needed: Copies of Repro Resource 4, one of which is cut apart)

Before the session, you'll need to cut apart one copy of "What Kind of Fool Am I?" (Repro Resource 4). At this point in the session, distribute complete copies of Repro Resource 4 so that group members can see the six categories. Note that "The Adulteress" has been renamed "The Tempter" so as to include both genders. Ask for two volunteers to come forward. Have each volunteer draw one of the cards from the cut-apart copy of Repro Resource 4. You will set up a situation. Each volunteer will then answer questions that you and/or other group members pose as if he or she was the type of person indicated on the card. After several questions have been posed, see if group members can guess what type of person the volunteer is pretending to be. As time allows, ask for additional volunteers for each of the other situations.

Here are the situations and possible questions:

Situation 1: You have a major test at school tomorrow.
• **How did you study for the test?**
• **What is your strategy for passing the test?**
• **What did you say to your classmates after taking the test?**

Situation 2: Several kids are talking about the big party that's going to take place Friday night at the Johnsons'— while Mr. and Mrs. Johnson are out of town.
  • **Are you going to the party?**
  • **What are you saying about the party?**
  • **How do you feel inside as people are talking about the party?**

Situation 3: You're home alone and an R-rated movie you're not supposed to watch is showing on one of the cable channels.
  • **Do you watch it?**
  • **If so, why? If not, why not?**
  • **A friend calls just as you're deciding what to watch. What do you say to this friend?**

Feel free to come up with additional situations if you have time. Some possibilities might include sitting at the lunch table with a group of people making fun of the class "nerds" or talking with a group of friends about a classmate who is HIV-positive.

Some of your volunteers may have difficulty with this activity, because they may not know how to respond to some of the questions. That's OK. Let them struggle with it a bit. You want to get them thinking about what it would mean to be wise or foolish in a variety of situations. Getting them to think about this in a general sense will help prepare them to make specific application of the Scripture in their own lives.

Beyond Folly

(Needed: Copies of Repro Resource 4, pencils, scissors [optional])

Refer to the six types of people listed on "What Kind of Fool Am I?" (Repro Resource 4). Point out that an understanding of these people will help your kids get more out of the Book of Proverbs if they study it on their own in the future. Have kids cut apart the six cards on the sheet and write down the following lists on the back of each card:

The Wise—List one or more areas of your life in which you feel the need for more wisdom.

The Simple—List three advantages of seeking after God's wisdom in your life.

The Fool—List one or more foolish things you've done lately.

The Mocker—List one or more things you could say to someone who teases you for choosing wisdom over something foolish.

The Tempter—List three things that tempt you most, or three situations in which you feel most tempted.

The Sluggard—List any areas of your life in which you are especially lazy or could be lazy if you allowed yourself to be.

After kids have given some thought to these lists, have them get into groups of three to share their responses to at least one card. If your kids are comfortable praying together, let each group spend some time in prayer. If some kids aren't ready for that, you could say the closing prayer.

FOOL HOUSE

THE SETTING
A sorority party during pledge week at the University.

THE CHARACTERS
• **Alexis.** When the party is in full swing, she brings out some crack cocaine and all of the necessary paraphernalia to smoke it. She says that this is the *real* initiation ceremony—and all those who don't participate are fools.

• **Wanda.** Since she wants to be Alexis' friend, she's tempted to try it—but she knows that would be stupid. She says, "I'm not into that stuff," and leaves the party.

• **Samantha.** She's never tried crack and doesn't know much about it. She says, "I'll try anything once," thinking it might be something like a peace pipe.

• **Francis.** She's heard that crack is dangerous and should be avoided. She's gotten lectures about it at home, church, even school. She knows she's supposed to "just say no," but she wants to fit in, so she smokes it anyway.

• **Molly.** She smokes some herself. As she does, she gives Wanda a hard time about not joining in, calling her "little miss goody two-shoes" and some other names that can't be repeated here.

• **Sally.** Sally was supposed to attend the party, but she took a late afternoon nap and overslept. When she finally showed up, the party was over.

Give a last name to each character that describes her behavior. Try to use a word that starts with the same letter as her first name. Then rank the characters from 1 to 6, with "1" being the wisest and "6" being the most foolish.

	Rank
Alexis _____	_____
Wanda _____	_____
Samantha _____	_____
Francis _____	_____
Molly _____	_____
Sally _____	_____

What Kind of Fool Am I?

The Wise

The Simple

The Fool

The Mocker

The Tempter

The Sluggard

NOTES

EXTRA ACTION

STEP 1

Have kids compete to see who can look the most foolish. Provide orange slices with the rind still on them (for kids to hold in their mouths while smiling); Chiclets gum (to be used as big teeth that stick out); wax lips; Ping-Pong balls cut in half and markers (to make goofy eyeballs); and slices of bologna (to be used as tongues that hang out). Have hairbrushes and styling gel available for the truly foolhardy. Take Polaroid photos of contestants at their most foolish. Then post the photos for judging by the group or by a couple of impartial guests. Award a prize to the winner, and let kids keep their photos. Then ask: **Does a foolish person always look foolish? Explain.**

STEP 3

Have volunteers play the roles of five hospital patients—The Simple, The Fool, The Mocker, The Adulteress, and The Sluggard. They should keep their characters' identities secret, however. Have the actors take their places around the room, acting as their characters would, lying on "hospital beds" (short rows of chairs placed together). Tape a "chart"—a sheet of paper on which you've written Bible references from Step 3 of the session—to each bed. You will play the role of the wise old doctor who's taking interns (the rest of the group) on rounds through the ward. As you come to each bed, observe the "symptoms" of the patient and have interns describe them. Then have the interns read the verses and give a "diagnosis" (tell which type of person the patient is). Afterward, discuss the activity, using the questions from the session.

SMALL GROUP

STEP 3

Assign one of the characters on Repro Resource 3 to each of your group members. (Change the names and genders of the characters as needed.) Instruct each group member to write a summary of the events of the party (described on Repro Resource 3)—from the point of view of his or her character. For instance, "Alexis" might explain why she decided to bring out the crack pipe and how she felt about the other characters' reactions. "Wanda" might explain what she thought when she first saw the crack pipe and how she felt when she left the party. After a few minutes, have each person read his or her account.

STEP 5

Assign each group member one of the lists to tackle on his or her own. Make your assignments according to the characters you assigned in Step 3 (see above). For instance, you'll give "The Wise" assignment to the person who wrote from Wanda's point of view in Step 3; you'll give "The Simple" assignment to the person who wrote from Samantha's point of view; etc. Give group members a few minutes to work on their lists. When everyone is finished, ask each person to share at least one item from his or her list with the rest of the group.

LARGE GROUP

STEP 2

Have your kids form groups of six. Distribute copies of Repro Resource 3. Instruct group members to read the situation on the sheet. Then have each group come up with a new scenario based on a similar situation. However, instead of being tempted by crack cocaine, the people in the skit might be faced with drinking alcohol, sneaking into an adult party club, cheating on a test, vandalizing a building, spreading vicious rumors, etc. The characters in the new scenario may have different names (perhaps the names of the members of the group), but they should respond in the same way that the various characters on Repro Resource 3 responded. After a few minutes, have each group read aloud its new scenario.

STEP 3

Have kids form six groups. Assign each group one of the "types" of people listed in the session. Give each group a large sheet of newsprint and a black marker. Within each group, have members appoint "researchers" (to look up the Bible passages), "recorders" (to write down the information), and "relevance seekers" (to apply the information to modern-day situations). Have each group make a large poster, with the "type" of person printed at the top and the rest of the information written below. As time permits, group members may also draw pictures of types of people who fit their category. After a few minutes, have each group share its findings and display its poster.

STEP 2

If the "Fool House" scenario and the made-up names are too clichéd or hokey for your kids, try another option. Bring newspaper and magazine clippings about risky activities (car racing, missionary work, running for office, starting a business, drug dealing, drug use, being a police officer, riding an amusement park ride, drinking alcohol, making fun of spiritual things, joining a gang, working as a telephone solicitor, teaching in the inner city, sexual promiscuity, buying a lottery ticket, etc.). Have kids try to arrange the clippings in order of the foolishness involved in taking the risks—from least foolish to most foolish. Allow no more than five minutes for this. Then discuss the difficulty of comparing some risks, and ask kids to explain why they felt certain activities were more foolish than others.

STEP 5

"Heard it all before" kids are likely to be mockers who think themselves wise. They'll probably resist the self-criticism called for in the session's conclusion. Instead, have them form pairs. Explain that one partner is wise, and the other is a mocker. The wise partner will try to walk across the room. The mocker can force him or her to stop every few seconds and take a step backward by mocking him or her. The wise person may then resume walking. Eventually the wise partner will make it across the room. When all of the wise partners reach the other side of the room, reveal that you neglected to mention an important fact: The mockers' side of the room was on fire. The mockers may have been clever "wiseguys," but the wise people made it to safety. Use this to illustrate the fact that in order to make progress at anything, including a relationship with God, it's necessary to stop mocking and start moving.

STEP 2

Kids with little Bible background aren't likely to come up with last names like "Adulteress," "Mocker," and "Sluggard" for the characters on Repro Resource 3. In fact, they may have a hard time even understanding the assignment. So rather than having kids work on the sheet individually or in small groups, go through the information as an entire group. Bring six people to the front of the room. Assign each person one of the identities on Repro Resource 3. (Change the genders and names of the characters as necessary.) Read the information on the sheet, directing the actions of each character as you do. For instance, when you read that Wanda "leaves the party," you might escort the person playing Wanda out the door of your room. Afterward, have your six "actors" stand in front of the group. Then have the rest of your group members rank them from 1 to 6 according to who was wisest.

STEP 5

If your group members don't have much experience applying biblical principles to their lives, they may have some problems coming up with personal lists for each card on Repro Resource 4. Instead, you might want to brainstorm some items for each list as a group. For instance, for "The Wise," you might ask: **What are some areas in which kids your age may feel they need more wisdom?** List group members' responses on the board. Once you have a sizable list for each category, have group members choose the items that apply to them and write them on their cards.

STEP 1

Have your group members brainstorm a list of the various things God has given us to help keep us from being fools. List the items on the board as group members name them. The list might include things like the Bible, parents, natural intelligence, school, other Christians, godly advice columnists, etc. Then lead the group in a brief prayer of thanks to God for His goodness and love, and for "arming" us to recognize and avoid the wily ways of the world.

STEP 5

Have your kids form groups of three. Instruct each group to write its own proverb about being foolish and wise in ways that pertain to modern-day situations. ("My son, give not yourself to an abundance of television; for in the multitude of shows, there is foolishness.") After a few minutes, have each group share its proverb.

STEP 2

After group members complete Repro Resource 3, point out that all of the characters on the sheet are female. Ask: **If this story were about a guys' frat party, how might some of the characters' actions be different?** Depending on the guys your group members know, your girls may say that if the characters had been guys, probably none of them would have done what Wanda did. Or they may say that more than one of them would have overslept and missed the party like Sally did. Briefly discuss how guys and girls might respond differently to situations like the one on Repro Resource 3.

STEP 5

After your group members complete their lists, have them sit together in a circle. Hand a candle (or flashlight) to one of the girls. Ask her to share something from one of her cards that she would appreciate prayer for. Then have her pass the candle to the person on her right. That person will then pray for the first girl and share something from one of *her* cards. Then she will pass the candle to her right, and so on. Continue until everyone in the circle has shared. Then as you wrap up the session, point out that making wise decisions involves supportive friends.

STEP 1

Continue the discussion on foolishness by asking your group members to name some foolish things that high school guys sometimes do. If your guys are reluctant to respond, suggest things like unwise sexual behavior (going further than you know is right), drinking, smoking, cheating, fighting, etc. Briefly discuss what makes each action unwise, focusing particularly on the negative consequences of each one.

STEP 4

Put together or purchase a video "highlight" clip of foolish moments in sports history. (For instance, you might show Michigan's Chris Webber calling time out at the end of the 1993 NCAA basketball championship game—when his team didn't have any time outs left.) You could show clips of poor decisions in football games, baseball games, motorbike racing, downhill skiing, etc. Afterward, point out that most of us have "20-20 hindsight." In other words, it's easy to look back on our past actions and recognize the foolish choices we made. However, at that point, it's often too late to escape the consequences. Emphasize that we need to seek wisdom from God to *prevent* ourselves from making foolish choices.

STEP 1

Begin the session with a "fish toss." You'll need a large, greased (perhaps with Vaseline), whole fish in an appropriately sized bucket. You'll also need a Nerf football in the bucket and a large bedsheet. Ask two volunteers to hold the bedsheet so that it forms a "net" about six feet off the ground. Explain that one person will stand on one side of the net and toss the item in the bucket over the net. The rest of the group members will stand on the other side of the net and try to catch the object. The person who catches the object gets a point and becomes the next thrower. To demonstrate, pull the Nerf football out of the bucket and toss it over the net. The person who catches it will become the first thrower. Then subtly discard the football and let the thrower discover the actual object he or she will be throwing—the greased fish. Use this activity to lead in to a discussion on being "fooled."

STEP 5

Set up a "Folly's Olympics." Schedule "events" to illustrate how frustrating life becomes when normal things are made difficult because of unwise actions. As you describe the events initially, make them seem simple: running through a row of chairs, drawing a picture of a vase of flowers, eating soup, wrapping a package, etc. However, when it's time for kids to actually compete, introduce a "twist" for each event. The people who run through the row of chairs will have their hands and feet tied together. The people who draw a picture of the vase of flowers will be blindfolded. The people who eat soup will have to use a fork. The people who wrap a package will be wearing mittens. Feel free to add your own ideas as well. Afterward, discuss how much more difficult life can be when we don't act wisely.

STEP 1

Show some video scenes (which you've screened yourself beforehand) in which the late Peter Sellers plays two very different kinds of "fools." First, show a slapstick scene featuring the bumbling Inspector Clouseau (*A Shot in the Dark, Return of the Pink Panther, The Pink Panther Strikes Again,* or *Revenge of the Pink Panther*). Then play a segment of *Being There,* in which Sellers portrays the mentally slow gardener, Chance, who knows only what he's seen on TV—but is taken as a genius by the rich and powerful. Afterward, ask: **In what sense is each of these characters a fool? Is one funnier than the other? Why? Are those who think Chance is wise actually fools themselves? Why or why not? How are some people able to "fool" others into thinking they're wise? Can you think of any examples among famous people today?**

STEP 5

Play a contemporary Christian song about commitment, such as "Who's on the Lord's Side" by Petra. Discuss how the six types of people described in the session might react to the song. For example, the Mocker might laugh at the idea of being a "fanatic"; the Sluggard might agree that commitment is good, but be too lazy to follow through; the Wise person might be encouraged to consider how committed to Christ he or she really is. Close by asking kids to think about which point of view is closest to their own.

STEP 1

Replace Steps 1 and 2 with a shorter opener. Give the group an assignment like rearranging chairs. Then leave the room. What the group won't know is that beforehand you've secretly prepared five kids to play these roles while you're gone: a simpleton (who pretends not to understand and keeps setting up the chairs incorrectly), a fool (who keeps deliberately messing up the chairs), a mocker (who only criticizes what others are doing), a tempter (who tries to lure workers away with refreshments), and a sluggard (who refuses to do anything). After a few minutes, return and discuss what happened.

STEP 3

Instead of having everyone skim the Book of Proverbs, have one team study The Wise just as other teams study the other characters. Limit the number of references as follows:
The Wise—Proverbs 1:7-10; 10:1, 5, 8, 14;
The Simple—9:1-6, 13-18; 14:15, 18;
The Fool—12:15, 16; 13:19; 26:11; 28:26;
The Mocker—1:22; 21:24; 22:10;
The Adulteress—2:16-19; 7:21-23;
The Sluggard—6:6-11; 10:26; 21:25.
To save more time, combine Steps 4 and 5 as follows. Using a copier that makes enlargements, prepare bigger versions of the cards on Repro Resource 4. (If you can't do that, make signs on poster board.) Post these at intervals around the room. Read the Ten Commandments (Exod. 20:3-17) aloud, one at a time. After each one, have kids stand under the card that they think represents the attitude most kids at school would have toward that commandment. For example, kids might mock one commandment; they might agree with another, but be too lazy to follow it. Let volunteers explain their "stands." To close, have all group members crowd under the "Wise" card and think of one commandment they'll work harder to obey this week.

STEP 3

Point out that the end of the Book of Proverbs (31:10-31) gives an insightful description of a wife of noble character. Explain that the passage is written in the form of an acrostic poem, in which each letter of the Hebrew alphabet is used as the first letter of one of the lines of the poem. As a group, create your own acrostic poem about wisdom, using the letters of the alphabet—in order—as the first letters of the lines of the poem. See how many letters you can use. Here's a brief example to get you started:

Acquiring wisdom should be an everyday goal; it keeps the mind active and brings peace to the soul.

Believing in God's wisdom will strengthen you daily, when gangs all around you are makin' you crazy.

STEP 4

Add the following situation to your discussion of Repro Resource 4:
Situation 4—A fight breaks out in school. You saw the whole thing happen, so you know who started it and what happened.
• **Would you try to break up the fight?**
• **If so, how would you do it? If not, what** *would* **you do?**
• **After the fight, when the principal is looking for witnesses to tell what happened, what would you do? Why?**

STEP 2

Have your kids form groups. Make sure that each group contains both high schoolers and junior highers. Assign one of the "types" of people listed on Repro Resource 3 (Alexis, Wanda, Samantha, etc.) to each group. Once a group is assigned a "type," instruct each member of the group to describe an experience in his or her life in which he or she acted in a way that the "type" of person assigned to the group might have acted. For example, if a group was assigned "Alexis," group members would need to think of a situation in which they thought of something to do that wasn't right and tried to pressure others into doing it. Encourage the high schoolers in each group to respond first to give junior highers an idea of what you're looking for.

STEP 3

As you go through the list of the various "types" of people described in Proverbs, ask (for each "type"): **Would you say this type of person is more likely to be a junior higher or a high schooler? Why?** For instance, some kids may say that "The Simple" are more likely to be junior highers because junior highers are more gullible and naive than high schoolers are. Other kids may say that "The Fools" are more likely to be high schoolers because high schoolers have enough experience and knowledge to know what things are wrong, but do them anyway. Of course, this activity will probably stir up a debate between the two age groups, but it may be interesting to hear whether group members associate themselves or other people with each "type" of person.

STEP 1

After agreeing on a definition for "fool," ask: **What kinds of people does the world say are foolish?** Answers will probably vary, and may include things like drug users, Christians, people who turn the other cheek, etc. Have someone read aloud I Corinthians 3:19; 4:8-10. Then ask: **What does the world consider to be the benefits or fruits of wisdom?** (Wealth, power, prestige, honor, fame, status, possessions.) **What does Paul consider to be the fruits of wisdom?** Get responses from several group members.

STEP 3

As you go through the "types" of people listed in the session, ask volunteers to describe ways in which they've fallen prey to the snares of the Simple, the Fool, the Mocker, the Adulteress, and the Sluggard. If possible, try to get *specific* answers (instead of responses like "Sometimes I make fun of other kids at school"). To insure that you get specific, honest answers, you may want to have kids write their responses anonymously on slips of paper. Then you could collect the slips and read each one aloud. Afterward, as a group, brainstorm some suggestions for avoiding the snares of each "type" of person in the future.

DATE USED:

Approx. Time

STEP 1: *Fooling Around* _____
- ❑ Extra Action
- ❑ Fellowship & Worship
- ❑ Mostly Guys
- ❑ Extra Fun
- ❑ Media
- ❑ Short Meeting Time
- ❑ Extra Challenge
Things needed:

STEP 2: *Fool House* _____
- ❑ Large Group
- ❑ Heard It All Before
- ❑ Little Bible Background
- ❑ Mostly Girls
- ❑ Combined Jr. High/High School
Things needed:

STEP 3: *Fool Proof* _____
- ❑ Extra Action
- ❑ Small Group
- ❑ Large Group
- ❑ Short Meeting Time
- ❑ Urban
- ❑ Combined Jr. High/High School
- ❑ Extra Challenge
Things needed:

STEP 4: *What Kind of Fool Am I?* _____
- ❑ Mostly Guys
- ❑ Urban
Things needed:

STEP 5: *Beyond Folly* _____
- ❑ Small Group
- ❑ Heard It All Before
- ❑ Little Bible Background
- ❑ Fellowship & Worship
- ❑ Mostly Girls
- ❑ Extra Fun
- ❑ Media
Things needed:

Hold Your Tongue!

YOUR GOALS FOR THIS SESSION:

Choose one or more

☐ To help kids see what the Book of Proverbs says about proper speech.

☐ To help kids understand how our words are a reflection of our true "heart condition."

☐ To help kids think about their own speech patterns and name specific ways to apply the Proverbs they have studied.

☐ Other:_____
_____

Your Bible Base:

Various Proverbs that deal with the way people should speak to one another

STEP 1

You Can Say That Again

(Needed: Copies of Repro Resource 5, pencils, paper)

O P T I O N S

EXTRA ACTION

SMALL GROUP

LARGE GROUP

MOSTLY GUYS

EXTRA FUN

SHORT MEETING TIME

EXTRA CHALLENGE

As kids arrive, don't let anyone talk. Give each person a pencil and a copy of "Fill in the Blanks" (Repro Resource 5) to complete. As kids are working, you should fill in a copy of the Repro Resource with the correct words that appear below. After kids have made their guesses as to how to complete each proverb, collect and shuffle their sheets—along with the one you filled out.

Then give each group member a blank piece of paper and instruct him or her to number it from 1 to 10. Read off three or four of the more plausible responses to the first saying (including the correct one) and have kids write down which one they think is correct. Then shuffle the papers and read off a few possibilities for the second phrase. Continue until you've gone through all 10 phrases.

Then read through the correct answers and see who completed the most phrases correctly originally, who guessed the most correct answers after hearing them read, and who got the most people to vote for their made-up answers. Don't reveal the source of each proverb (listed in parentheses) until later.

Here are the correct answers (in capital letters):

1. An enemy will AGREE, but a friend will ARGUE (Russian proverb).
2. When WORDS are many, SIN is not absent (Prov. 10:19).
3. Don't judge a man by the words of his MOTHER, listen to the comments of his NEIGHBORS (Yiddish proverb).
4. RECKLESS words pierce like a sword, but the TONGUE of the wise brings healing (Prov. 12:18).
5. Many a man's TONGUE has BROKEN his NOSE (Anonymous).
6. An ANXIOUS heart weighs a man down, but a KIND WORD cheers him up (Prov. 12:25).
7. Words have WINGS and cannot be RECALLED (Anonymous).
8. A wise man's HEART guides his MOUTH (Prov. 16:23).
9. SPEECH is the mirror of the SOUL. As a man SPEAKS, so he is (Publius Syrus).
10. A GOSSIP separates close FRIENDS (Prov. 16:28).

Hand the Repro Resources back to their rightful owners. Then ask: **What do all of these proverbs have in common?** (They all deal with some aspect of people's speech.)

If you had to choose just one of these sayings to memorize, which would you choose, and why? Let kids share their favorite ones, or ones that have special meaning to them. Ask for some specific examples of how some of these proverbs are true.

How many of these sayings would you say are from the Bible? Have kids circle the numbers of the sayings they think are from the Bible. Then have kids indicate their answers with a show of fingers. Congratulate all those who held up five fingers. Ask them to identify which of the sayings are from the Bible. All of the even-numbered ones are from the Book of Proverbs. The others may be true, but they aren't from the Bible.

STEP 2

Word Power

(Needed: Bibles, chalkboard and chalk or newsprint and marker)

Ask: **How many of you have heard the saying, "Sticks and stones may break my bones but names will never hurt me"?** Ask for a show of hands.

Have you ever used this statement before? If so, under what circumstances? If not, when might someone use it? (The saying is usually used by children who are trying to prove to other children that being teased or called a name doesn't hurt.)

Do you think the saying is true? Why or why not? (While it's true that words probably won't cause physical harm, they can be very painful.)

Assign the following verses to various group members: Proverbs 11:9; Proverbs 12:18; Proverbs 16:24; and Proverbs 18:21. Have them read the verses in succession.

Then ask: **What can we conclude from these verses? Are words good or bad?** (The key thing to see from these verses is that words are very powerful—for good or for bad.)

Say: **Let's make two lists to show the types of words that can hurt or heal.** Draw two columns on the board. Label one "Hurt" and the other "Help."

Then say: **Give me some examples of the types of words— not the words themselves—that can really hurt.** Group members may suggest things like gossip, insults, coarse joking, teasing, lies, etc. List these on the board as they are named.

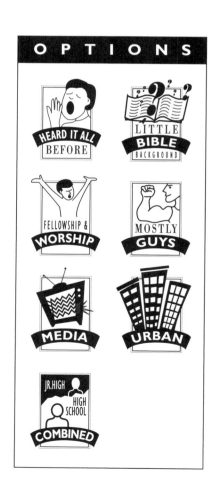

OPTIONS

HEARD IT ALL BEFORE

LITTLE BIBLE BACKGROUND

FELLOWSHIP & WORSHIP

MOSTLY GUYS

MEDIA

URBAN

JR. HIGH HIGH SCHOOL COMBINED

Ask: **Can the truth ever cause harm?** (Possibly, if it's told in such a way as to purposely upset someone, or if it's told insensitively.)

Give me an example of a time when you were really hurt by something someone said. Let a few kids share. Be prepared to share an example of your own first.

Now give me some examples of the types of words that can help or heal. Group members may suggest things like apologies, compliments, words of encouragement, etc. List these on the board as they are named.

Then say: **Give me an example of a time when someone's words really made you feel better.** Let a few kids share. Again, be prepared to share an example of your own first.

If you put all of the hurtful words you hear in a week on one side of a scale and all of the helpful words you hear in a week on the other side, which side would weigh more? You might want to physically demonstrate this by having kids move to one side of the room or the other to symbolize their answer.

To those who feel they hear more hurtful things in a given week, ask: **Why do you think so many people use hurtful words? How do you respond when someone says something hurtful to you?** Get a few responses.

To those who feel they hear more helpful words in a given week, ask: **Who are you most likely to hear positive words from?** Get a few responses.

Then say: **Let's think about a scale again. But this time, weigh all of the words *you* spoke last week. Which side would weigh more: the hurtful words or the helpful words?** Let kids move around if you choose to have them demonstrate their answers this way.

Then ask: **When are you most likely to use hurtful words?** Get a few responses.

If somebody invented a pill people could take every morning that would cause them to speak only helpful words to one another, would you want to take it? Why or why not? How would your life be different if everybody took this pill? How would your life be different if only you took this pill? Let kids speculate.

Point out that such a pill doesn't exist, but that the Bible is full of "good medicine" concerning how we should speak. Even if other people don't take the Bible's medicine, that's no reason we shouldn't.

STEP 3

Speaking of Proverbs

(Needed: Bibles, copies of Repro Resources 6, copies of Repro Resource 7, pencils, chalkboard and chalk or newsprint and marker)

Say: **I've got good news and bad news. First, the bad news: The Book of Proverbs doesn't tell us *what* to say, so we're on our own when it comes to choosing our words. But here's the good news: Proverbs has a lot to say about *how* we should say things. So while it won't put words in our mouth, it will give us some principles for how we should speak.**

Hand out copies of "The Proverbial List of Proverbs to Paraphrase" (Repro Resource 6). This sheet contains 18 short passages for kids to look up and paraphrase. If you have a lot of time let kids work individually, in pairs, or in small groups to paraphrase all 18 proverbs. Otherwise, divide the passages evenly among individuals, pairs, or small groups, making sure that someone is paraphrasing each passage.

When kids are done paraphrasing, hand out copies of "I Don't Wanna Be Like Mike" (Repro Resource 7). This sheet will give kids a chance to demonstrate how well they understand the verses.

Read (or have kids act out) the first conversation (between Mike and his dad). Then have group members answer these four questions:

1. What is Mike's basic problem in this situation?

2. Which of the verses you just looked up might apply to this situation? Some of the verses may apply to more than one situation. For example, Proverbs 16:23 applies to all four.

3. How might these verses help Mike if he were to apply them in the future?

4. What words would have been more appropriate for Mike to use in his response?

Follow this procedure for each conversation on Repro Resource 7. Use the following to aid your preparation and discussion. Keep in mind, however, that this is just one way of looking at each conversation. See what your kids come up with before sharing anything here.

Conversation #1 (Mike and Dad)

1. Mike's basic problem is that he's lying. He's also trying to use flattery to distract his dad from the real issue.

2. Verses that might apply include Proverbs 14:5; 16:13; 24:26; 26:23-28.

3. These verses all talk about the value of honesty. [NOTE: You don't need to convince your kids that "honesty is the best policy"; instead, ask them why it's sometimes hard to be totally honest.]

4. Obviously, Mike should have said where he really was. [NOTE: In case any of your group members wonder, Mike was watching a movie that his folks told him not to see.]

Conversation #2 (Mike and Mom)

1. Mike's basic problem is that he assumes the worst before he knows what his folks want to talk about. Instead of being calm, he jumps to the wrong conclusion.

2. Verses that might apply include Proverbs 12:16; 15:1; 17:27; 18:13; 25:15.

3. These verses talk about the value of using restraint before speaking. They also talk about the value of speaking gently and without anger.

4. Mike could have avoided a lot of grief if he had said something like, "Sure, what did you want to talk about?" [NOTE: Incidentally, Mike's parents had read a review of the movie Mike wanted to see, had a change of heart, and wanted to let him know that it's OK for him to see it.]

Conversation #3 (Mike and Mandy)

1. Mike's basic problem is that he keeps saying the wrong things. He isn't choosing his words very carefully.

2. Verses that might apply include Proverbs 10:20, 32; 15:23; 25:11.

3. These verses talk about the value of choosing our words carefully, treating them like choice silver or gold. If Mike had thought a little more about using fitting words, he probably wouldn't have come off as being so offensive.

4. Maybe he shouldn't have commented on the outfit at all, unless he really liked it. If so, he could have said something like, "You look good in that" or "That's a cool outfit. Is it new?"

Conversation #4 (Mike and Mrs. Applegate)

1. Mike's basic problem is that he says too much (not to mention the fact that he's being a sluggard—but that's another session).

2. Verses that might apply include Proverbs 10:19; 11:12; 13:3; 17:28.

3. These verses talk about the value of few words. Mike only makes things worse by going on and on about the teacher's rule. He also gets a jab in at the teacher, which certainly won't help things.

4. Maybe Mike shouldn't have said anything at all. If he felt compelled to say something, he probably should have apologized for not having the paper done on time.

Ask: **Which of the four conversations do you relate to most? Why?** Get a few responses.

You can summarize what Proverbs says about *how* we should speak by writing the following on the board:

Our words should be
- Honest
- Calm
- Apt (or carefully chosen)
- Few

Say: **Our words are more likely to be honest, calm, apt (or carefully chosen), and few if we take some time to weigh them carefully before speaking. I'm sure you've all heard this before, but if you think before speaking, you'll save yourself a lot of grief. But what does it mean to think before speaking? How do we do that?**

STEP
4

The Heart of the Matter

(Needed: Paper, pencils)

Read Proverbs 16:23 together. See how kids paraphrased it earlier. Then explain: **This is a key verse because it tells us that if our heart is in the right place, our words will be too. Instead of focusing on our words, we should focus on our hearts to see if they are right with God. If something's out of whack on the inside, then it only stands to reason that our words will often be inappropriate too.**

O P T I O N S

MOSTLY GIRLS

EXTRA CHALLENGE

I'm going to give you a little "heart test" that you can complete privately. Have kids use the back of one of the Repro Resources to write their responses. **Number your papers from 1 to 10. Answer each question with one of the following responses: "A lot," "Sometimes," "Seldom," or "Never."**

1. How often do you repeat a juicy rumor you've heard about someone else?

2. How often do you swear or make off-color remarks?

3. How often do you put someone down in order to make yourself feel better?

4. How often do you twist the truth in order to avoid negative consequences?

5. How often do you respond to someone without really listening to what the person is saying?

6. How often do you flatter someone without really meaning what you say?

7. How often do you say something about another person behind his or her back that you wouldn't say to his or her face?

8. How often do you betray a friend's confidence?

9. How often do you speak out of anger rather than out of love?

10. How often do you think about stuff like this at church, but then forget about it as soon as you leave?

After kids have written their responses, say: **If you answered "A lot" or "Sometimes" to any of these questions, then you might want to ask God to point out ways you can improve in these areas. If you answered "Never" to every question, then either you're not being honest or you should be leading this session, because you're a lot further along than I am!**

Hold Your Tongue

(Needed: Bibles)

To close the session, have each group member choose one thing he or she will do this week in response to what you've talked about today. Some kids might make a commitment to do something about one area of his or her speech habits. Others might choose a relevant proverb to memorize or apply. Give kids a moment to think of what they want to say.

Add a twist to the activity before kids actually share. Have them "hold their tongues" as they talk. Explain that this exercise should remind them to always think before speaking. For the sake of fairness, you should go first. If your group is large, have kids form teams of four to six to share together.

As you close in prayer, you might want to read aloud Psalm 139:23-24 and/or Psalm 19:14, asking God to search us and point out to us ways in which our words can be more pleasing to Him.

OPTIONS

SMALL GROUP

FELLOWSHIP & WORSHIP

EXTRA FUN

JR. HIGH HIGH SCHOOL COMBINED

FILL IN THE BLANKS

Complete each saying with words that you think make the most sense. Either try to guess what each proverb actually says, or make up something that might fool someone else into thinking it's the real saying.

1. An enemy will _____,
but a friend will _____.

2. When _____ are many, _____ is not absent.

3. Don't judge a man by the words of his _____, listen to the comments of his _____.

4. _____ words pierce like a sword, but the _____ of the wise brings healing.

5. Many a man's _____ has _____ his _____.

6. An _____ heart weighs a man down,
but a _____ _____ cheers him up.

7. Words have _____ and cannot be _____.

8. A wise man's _____ guides his _____.

9. _____ is the mirror of the _____.
As a man _____, so he is.

10. A _____ separates close _____.

The Proverbial List of Proverbs to Paraphrase

Please paraphrase these particular proverbs. In other words, put them into your own words.

Proverbs 10:19

Proverbs 10:20

Proverbs 10:32

Proverbs 11:12

Proverbs 12:16

Proverbs 13:3

Proverbs 14:5

PROVERBS 15:1

Proverbs 15:23

Proverbs 16:13

Proverbs 16:23

Proverbs 17:27

Proverbs 17:28

Proverbs 18:13

Proverbs 24:26

PROVERBS 25:11

Proverbs 25:15

Proverbs 26:23-28

I DON'T WANNA BE LIKE MIKE

Write down some Proverbs (chapter and verse) from "The Proverbial List of Proverbs to Paraphrase" that Mike should take to heart in each situation.

Proverbs to Apply

Conversation #1
DAD: Where have you been?
MIKE: I was studying at Tom's house.
DAD: Is that so? Tom's mom just called, wondering if Tom's been over here. Do I detect a lie?
MIKE: Dad, you are so clever. Nothing gets past you. I hope that someday I'll be just as good a dad as you. Well, I've gotta run.
DAD: I don't know where you have to run—because you're grounded.

Conversation #2
MOM: Mike, your father and I would like a word with you.
MIKE: What did I do now? I can't believe you guys. Here I am just minding my own business, and you get on my case. I can't believe how suspicious you guys are. When are you going to start trusting me and treat me like an adult?
MOM: Boy, are you edgy. Maybe this isn't a good time to tell you what we wanted to say.

Conversation #3
MANDY: Hi, Mike.
MIKE: Hey, Mandy. Say, is that a new outfit? It's really interesting.
MANDY: What's that supposed to mean?
MIKE: I mean it's unique—one of a kind.
MANDY: Are you saying it's weird?
MIKE: No, I just admire your courage for wearing it.
MANDY: I've gotta go.
MIKE: Where?
MANDY: Home to change.

Conversation #4
MRS. APPLEGATE: Turn in your papers before you leave. If yours isn't finished, turn it in Monday. I'll dock you one letter grade for each day it's late.
MIKE: I had every intention of finishing the paper, but something came up that was completely beyond my control and I didn't get it done. I think it's unfair to dock me when you don't even know the circumstances that resulted in its being late. You're not even taking into account the fact that I turned in two of the last three papers on time. Besides, you didn't say you'd lower our grade if it was late, so I don't see how you can make up new rules as we go along here. I wish you'd be a little more considerate of our needs for a change.
MRS. APPLEGATE: Someday you'll thank me for this. See you Monday, Mike.

STEP I

Instead of using Repro Resource 5, play "Weighing Your Words." Collect 26 flat, smooth stones or blocks in widely varying sizes and weights. On the front and back of each object write a letter of the alphabet—with different letters on the front and back of any one object. Put the objects in a box. Bring them, along with a bathroom scale, to the meeting. Have kids form two teams. The first team will dump the objects on the floor and, in one minute, try to form the *heaviest* word it can, using the letters that are showing on the objects. Using the scale, weigh the word the team comes up with. Then give the other team a chance. Play as many rounds as you have time for. The team with the most verbal poundage at the end of the game wins. Use this as an introduction to the idea of weighing our words—being careful about what we say.

STEP 3

Have two volunteers practice the conversations from Repro Resource 7. Meanwhile, divide the Repro Resource 6 verses among the rest of the group. Give each person (other than the two actors) a marker and a sheet of poster board for each verse he or she has. Each person should write his or her paraphrase on the poster board. As the first conversation is acted out, each person with a verse that applies should run behind the actors and hold up the sign so the group can see it. Have your actors replay the conversation until all applicable verses have been shown. After discussing briefly how the verses apply, repeat the process with the other conversations.

STEP I

Instead of having kids work on Repro Resource 5 individually, work on it together as a group. And instead of filling out the sheet according the instructions, use it for a "Madlibs" game. You will ask group members to supply you with words, giving them only the part of speech you're looking for (noun, verb, adjective, etc.). The first word kids call out for each blank is the word you will write down. The parts of speech you'll look for to fill in Repro Resource 5 are as follows: (1) verb, verb; (2) plural noun, noun; (3) noun, noun; (4) adjective, noun; (5) noun, past-tense verb, noun; (6) adjective, adjective, noun; (7) noun, past-tense verb; (8) noun, noun; (9) noun, noun, plural verb; (10) noun, plural noun. After you've filled in all of the blanks, read back what group members have come up with. (Chances are you'll get sentences like "Many a man's turtle has punched his shoelaces.") Then read and discuss the correct proverbs.

STEP 5

As you wrap up the session, try a memorization activity to help kids remember some of the relevant information from the session. On the board, write the references for several of the proverbs you studied in this session (Prov. 10:19; 11:9; 12:18, 25; 16:23-24, 28; 18:21). See how many of the verses group members can memorize together. Then, rather than having the group recite the verses in unison, have members recite the verses one word at a time—with kids taking turns saying each word. You might want to award a prize for each verse the group successfully recites.

STEP I

After you go through Repro Resource 5, have kids form groups of four to six. Instruct each group to come up with its own proverb about the "tongue" or being careful of what we say. You might want to reread a couple of the proverbs from Repro Resource 5 to give the groups an idea of what you're looking for. Encourage group members to come up with short proverbs that are witty, clever, and/or humorous. The proverbs should also apply to the lives of kids today. After a few minutes, have a spokesperson from each group stand and recite his or her group's proverb. Then have group members vote on which proverb was best. Award prizes (perhaps tongue depressors) to the winning group.

STEP 3

Have kids form groups of six. Assign each group one of the situations on Repro Resource 7. Explain that two members of the group will act out the assigned situation. The other four members will then each answer one of the questions from the session regarding the situation ("What is Mike's problem in this situation?" "Which of the verses [from Repro Resource 6] might apply to this situation?" "How might these verses help Mike if he were to apply them in the future?" "What words would have been more appropriate for Mike to use in his response?"). Give the groups a few minutes to work. When everyone is finished, have each group present its situation and responses.

STEP 2

Kids may resist the idea of being careful about words, thinking that so much self-control will take the fun out of life. Use the following questions to introduce the idea of thinking before speaking. Have kids answer with the first reply that comes to mind. (1) **Is the Pledge of Allegiance sung more often at baseball games or football games?** (It isn't sung at all.) (2) **Do more people go to lunch at 11:30 a.m. or 12 a.m.?** (11:30; 12 a.m. is midnight.) (3) **In what country did the wall between North and South Berlin fall?** (None; the wall was between East and West Berlin.) (4) **Who was President of the U.S. when Sherlock Holmes was alive?** (Sherlock Holmes was never alive; he was fictional.) (5) **If S is the symbol for the element known as sulfur, what is the symbol for the element known as salt?** (Salt is a compound, not an element.) Point out that just as blurting out an "obvious" answer may cause us to flunk a quiz, blurting out the first angry or sarcastic words we think of can wreck relationships. Weighing our words can protect us as well as others.

STEP 3

Skip the "good news, bad news" paragraph. Your kids probably don't *want* anyone to tell them what to say; they want freedom to express themselves. Since most of the session's emphasis is on what *not* to say, take a breather and affirm the freedom God gives us to say things in our own individual styles. Encourage kids to be as creative as possible in their Proverbs paraphrases and in their suggestions for what Mike should have said. In Step 5, have kids compete to see who can come up with the most creative way to communicate the sentiments of "Have a nice day" or "May the road rise to meet you; may the wind be always at your back" in their own words.

STEP 2

Rather than having your kids look up the verses from Proverbs and try to interpret what they're saying, try another activity. Have your kids form teams. Instruct each team to think of as many fictional stories and real-life situations as possible in which words have a powerful effect. For instance, God created the universe by speaking it into existence. A state governor can stop an execution by granting a pardon to the condemned person. In the movie *The Day the Earth Stood Still*, the heroine must say certain words to prevent the world from being destroyed. After a few minutes, have each team share its list. Use this activity to lead in to the discussion on which types of words are good and which are bad.

STEP 3

Kids with little Bible background may have difficulty paraphrasing the passages on Repro Resource 6 by themselves or in a small group. So choose eight of the passages to work on as a group. (The following passages apply best to Repro Resource 7, so you might want to consider using them: Prov. 10:19; 10:32; 12:16; 15:1; 15:23; 16:13; 17:28; 26:23-28.) Read each passage aloud. Then ask three group members to explain (in their own words) what they think it means. After all three have shared, have the rest of the group vote on which explanation makes the most sense—or suggest ways to combine the three definitions to create a new one. Write each passage and its agreed-upon paraphrase on the board for use later in the session.

STEP 2

After pointing out that "Sticks and stones may break my bones but names will never hurt me" is not necessarily true, focus on the flip side of the statement. Explain that if words have the power to hurt, they also have the power to encourage. Organize a brief "complimentfest" in which group members mingle around, giving "pick me up" compliments to each other. Emphasize that the compliments don't have to be "major" ("You're the smartest girl I've ever known"). Instead, they should focus on "minor," everyday things ("That joke you made last week about Daniel in the lions' den was really funny"; "I saw you playing basketball after school yesterday; you've got a good jump shot"). Afterward, have volunteers share some other examples of when words made them feel better.

STEP 5

As you wrap up the session, lead your group members in singing a couple of hymns that deal with the "tongue" or the words that come from our mouths. Among the hymns you might consider are "O for a Thousand Tongues to Sing" and "Take My Life" (focusing on the second verse: "Take my voice and let it sing . . .").

STEP 3

Ask: **How many of you know what the "10-second rule" is?** If your girls don't know, encourage them to make up a plausible-sounding possibility. Then explain that the 10-second rule applies to how we speak. Before we say something that maybe we shouldn't, we should count to 10 and decide what effect our words might have. Give your group members a chance to practice this. One at a time, have each girl come to the front of the room, close her eyes, and count to 10. When she opens her eyes, she should describe everything she sees in a positive, nice, non-cutting way. (For instance, she may comment on the ugly—or, rather, "practical"—wallpaper.) Give each of your group members a chance to "practice."

STEP 4

Have your group members sit in a circle. Write on a piece of paper, "Did you hear about Matilda? I heard she got caught _____." [NOTE: If you have a girl named Matilda in your group or know of a girl named Matilda in the area, use another name.] Pass the paper and pencil to the person on your right. Give her 15 seconds to add to the rumor or create a new one involving Matilda. Then have her pass the paper to the person on her right, who will continue the process. Encourage the girls to keep their rumors lighthearted and humorous. When the paper comes around to you again, read aloud the rumors your girls came up with. Afterward, ask: **Do you think girls are more likely to gossip than guys are? Explain. What are some situations in which gossip typically occurs? How can a person stop gossip before it occurs?** Encourage most of your group members to respond to these questions.

STEP 1

Point out that although there are a lot of ways that the tongue can do damage—through unclean talking or joking, backbiting, cutting down others, etc.—it can also be very helpful to others and to us. To demonstrate this, have your guys compete in a bubble gum bubble-blowing contest. Give each of your guys a piece of gum. Allow one minute for the contestants to chew the gum and get it into prime bubble-blowing shape. Then call the contestants to the front of the room one at a time and give them 30 seconds to blow a bubble as big as possible. You will serve as judge for the event. After everyone has had an opportunity to blow a bubble, declare a winner and give him a pack of gum as a prize.

STEP 2

Say: **"Sticks and stones may break my bones, but names will never hurt me." How many of you believe that's true?** Probably many of your guys will raise their hands or indicate that they think it's true. Chances are that name-calling *does* affect them as much as it does anyone else; however, they're afraid to admit that they can be hurt by "simple words." If several of your guys raise their hands, say: **Wow, you guys must be pillars of strength. When I was your age, I remember that names hurt a lot.** If possible, share an experience from your youth in which you were hurt by being called a name. Then discuss why guys try to pretend that they're unaffected by names.

STEP 1

Have kids form teams. Give each team three pieces of poster board, several colored markers, and a sheet of paper on which you've written three proverbs or short sayings. Among the proverbs/sayings you might use are "The early bird gets the worm"; "Early to bed, early to rise makes a man healthy, wealthy, and wise"; "A stitch in time saves nine"; etc. Instruct the teams to illustrate each of their assigned proverbs/sayings on the individual sheets of poster board. For instance, one team might draw a bird—wearing a watch that reads "4:30 a.m."—pulling a worm out of a hole (to illustrate "The early bird gets the worm"). After a few minutes, have each team display its posters while the rest of the group tries to guess what proverbs/sayings are being illustrated.

STEP 5

As you wrap up the session, organize a game to illustrate that our mouths can (and should) be used positively. Have kids form two teams (dividing up guys and girls evenly on each team). Instruct each team to line up guy-girl-guy-girl for the old "pass-the-Lifesaver-on-a-toothpick" contest. Distribute toothpicks and instruct kids to put them in their mouth. Then give the first person in each line a Lifesaver candy. When you say, **Go**, he or she will put the Lifesaver on his or her toothpick and then "transfer" the candy (without using his or her hands) to the toothpick of the next person in line. If, during a transfer, the Lifesaver falls to the ground, the team must start over with a new piece of candy. The first team to successfully pass its Lifesaver to the end of the line wins. You might want to award prizes to the winning team.

STEP 2

During the week, videotape about 20 seconds of a positive, warmhearted children's TV character (Barney the Dinosaur or Mister Rogers, for example) talking. Then videotape about 20 seconds of a sarcastic TV character (like Murphy Brown or Bud Bundy [*Married with Children*]) putting someone down. Follow this with 20 more seconds of a kindly children's TV character, then 20 more seconds of a sarcastic one. At this point in the session, play the whole tape. Contrast the helpful and hurting words and their effect. Ask: **Are children the only ones who need to be built up instead of put down? Why do you suppose so much comedy today is based on criticizing people? If everyone gave up putting people down, would we all have to talk like** [name of kindly children's TV character you showed]**? Why or why not?**

STEP 3

In place of Conversation #4 on Repro Resource 7, play one or two secular rap songs on tape or CD (after first listening to them yourself). Ask: **Which verses might apply here? Are the words honest? Calm? Carefully chosen? Few?** (Some rap songs [and songs in other styles] tend to be the opposite—boastful, agitated, reckless, and repetitive.) Point out that some rap music gets away with making statements that some listeners might like to make, but can't. Ask: **What do you think the author(s) of Proverbs would say about people who are careful with their words but enjoy listening to musicians, actors, and comedians who aren't?**

STEP 1

Replace Steps 1 and 2 with the following opener. Have kids stand in a circle, facing outward, so that no one can see anyone else's back. Tape to each person's back a sign that reads "OK." But say: **I'm taping a sign to your back. Yours says either "OK" or "Weird."** Then have everyone turn to look at the back of one group member, who doesn't get to turn around. Kids shouldn't say what the person's sign says, but can say "Oh" or "Hmm." Do the same with another group member, and then another. Afterward, ask kids how they felt. Talk about the power of words—how they can hurt. Then let kids remove their signs and see that they're all "OK." Talk about the power of words to help. Ask: **Do you hear more hurtful or helpful words in a week? Why? How does that affect you?** Then go to the end of Step 2, asking the questions about the hypothetical pill that could cause everyone to say only helpful words.

STEP 3

Skip Repro Resource 6. Instead, have kids form three teams. Assign Team A the first conversation from Repro Resource 7 and these references: Proverbs 14:5; 16:13; 24:26; 26:23-28. Assign Team B the second conversation and these references: Proverbs 12:16; 15:1; 17:27; 18:13; 25:15. Assign Team C the third conversation and these references: Proverbs 10:20, 32; 15:23; 25:11. Skip the fourth conversation and its references. Instruct each team to look up its assigned verses, act out its conversation for the rest of the group, and explain how the verses relate. Skip Step 5. Close in silent prayer, letting kids talk to God about the way they talk.

STEP 2

The saying "Sticks and stones may break my bones, but names will never hurt me" hits close to home with urban kids, who probably face the threat of "sticks and stones" (violence) more often than most other kids. So for an urban youngster, being called a name actually may be the lesser of two evils—when you consider the alternative. But still, names can hurt. Have kids form small groups. Instruct the members of each group to come up with a list of names and insults that they hear every day at school or on the street. Ask them to focus on words or insults that are used specifically by urban young people. (They should *not*, however, list any expletives or vulgarities.) After a few minutes, have each group share its list. Then discuss which names and insults seem especially hurtful and which seem (relatively) "harmless." Ask kids to explain their reasoning.

STEP 3

Give your urban teens an opportunity to paraphrase, using hip-hop slang, some of the proverbs listed on Repro Resource 6. Have kids form groups of three or four. Assign each group one (or more) of the proverbs on the sheet. Instruct each group to read its assigned passage and then restate it, using words and phrases that they're comfortable with. After a few minutes, have each group share its paraphrase. Afterward, have kids vote by applause on which paraphrase was the "hippest-hoppest" version. Here's an example from Proverbs 10:19: "Too much talkin' means sin is somewhere frontin', but those who cap their lip are b-b-bumpin' on the wise tip."

STEP 2

Have your junior highers and high schoolers make a list of as many put-downs and cutting remarks as they can think of that they've heard in school lately. (Keep them clean.) After a few minutes, have each person share his or her list. Write the put-downs and remarks on the board as kids share them, making a high school list and a junior high list. After all of the group members have shared, compare the high schoolers' list with the junior highers'. Do you notice any trends among each age group? Are one group's remarks more vicious and cutting than the other's? If so, why do your kids suppose that is? After you've discussed the differences between the two lists, go through each remark on the lists, asking your group members how the person to whom the remark was directed may have felt about it.

STEP 5

It would be nice to end this session with a time of affirmation in which group members use their words to compliment and encourage each other. Unfortunately, in a mixed group, your kids may be hesitant to do much face-to-face complimenting. (High schoolers especially may feel uncomfortable about being "extra nice" to junior highers.) So give your kids an opportunity to share "anonymous" compliments. You'll need several valentines (the kind little kids exchange at school). Make sure the valentines are friendship-oriented, and do not include romantic sentiments. Distribute the valentines. Instruct each person to prepare a valentine for every other group member, writing a heartfelt compliment for the person who will receive it. After a few minutes, collect the valentines and then distribute them to the appropriate people.

STEP 1

Once your group members have completed the proverbs on Repro Resource 5, spend some time discussing why each proverb is true and brainstorming some situations in which the truth of each proverb is proved. For instance, for #1, you might ask: **Aren't friends supposed to agree with us and enemies disagree?** (Not necessarily. If a person is wrong about something, his or her enemies won't care. The person's friends, however, *will* care, and will seek to correct him or her—even if it means arguing with him or her.) **Name a situation in which an enemy would agree with someone and a friend would argue.** As time allows, go through all 10 proverbs.

STEP 4

After going through the 10 questions in the session, have your group members each create a "code of ethics" for their speech habits (based on the questions themselves and the proverbs you covered in the session). Explain that the code should be as specific as possible ("I will not . . ."; "When I hear other people violating this code, I will . . ."). After a few minutes, have volunteers read their codes to the rest of the group. Then encourage kids to keep their codes in a place where they'll see them often in the coming week. Have them keep track of how well they follow their codes and report back next week.

DATE USED:

Approx. Time

STEP 1: *You Can Say That Again* _____
❑ Extra Action
❑ Small Group
❑ Large Group
❑ Mostly Guys
❑ Extra Fun
❑ Short Meeting Time
❑ Extra Challenge
Things needed:

STEP 2: *Word Power* _____
❑ Heard It All Before
❑ Little Bible Background
❑ Fellowship & Worship
❑ Mostly Guys
❑ Media
❑ Urban
❑ Combined Jr. High/High School
Things needed:

STEP 3: *Speaking of Proverbs* _____
❑ Extra Action
❑ Large Group
❑ Heard It All Before
❑ Little Bible Background
❑ Mostly Girls
❑ Media
❑ Short Meeting Time
❑ Urban
Things needed:

STEP 4: *The Heart of the Matter* _____
❑ Mostly Girls
❑ Extra Challenge
Things needed:

STEP 5: *Hold Your Tongue* _____
❑ Small Group
❑ Fellowship & Worship
❑ Extra Fun
❑ Combined Jr. High/High School
Things needed:

The Meaning of Life

Choose one or more

☐ To help kids get a basic grasp of the main themes of Ecclesiastes.

☐ To help kids understand how meaningless life is apart from God.

☐ To help kids evaluate how meaningful various things are to them and concentrate more on areas that really matter.

☐ Other:_____

_____

Your Bible Base:

Selected portions of Ecclesiastes

STEP 1

Is There a Flaw in Murphy's Law?

(Needed: Copies of Repro Resource 8, pencils)

Arrange to have something go wrong just as your session is about to begin. Maybe the electricity could go off, or you could "lose" your teaching materials, or another group could come and demand use of your room—anything out of the ordinary. After dealing with your temporary crisis, explain that it is a good example of "Murphy's Law."

Ask: **How many of you have heard of Murphy's Law? If so, what is it?** (Murphy's Law states that "If anything can go wrong, it will.") As group members respond, hand out copies of "Murphy's Law" (Repro Resource 8) and pencils.

Say: **Give me some examples of how you've seen Murphy's Law at work lately**. Get a few responses.

As you look over these other "laws," which ones can you relate to? Why? Let kids share for a while.

At the bottom of the sheet there's a place for you to coin your own version of Murphy's Law. Let's see what you can come up with. Give kids a minute or two to come up with some type of law or rule and a title for it. The first word in the title should be the person's name—last or first—and the second should be some other word like law, observation, theory, hypothesis, etc. Have some volunteers share their ideas.

Then ask: **What do all of these statements have in common?** (They all are from a negative or pessimistic view of life.)

How many of them would you say are true all of the time? Kids will probably point out that most of these statements are true sometimes, but not all of the time. It may *seem* like they are true all of the time, but that doesn't mean they are.

Do any of the "laws" on the sheet sound familiar? If so, where have you heard or seen them before? See if your group members recognize that several of the laws are from the Bible. Can they guess which ones? It's not too hard to figure out, but we've made it easy for you to tell. All of the ones starting with the letters A through F are from the Book of Ecclesiastes. Explain that you'll be looking more closely at Ecclesiastes today. Point out that upon first reading, some people think the book is depressing.

Say: **Today we're going to see why such a "pessimistic" book is included in the Bible.**

A Real Downer

(Needed: Bibles, paper, pencils, chalkboard and chalk or newsprint and marker)

Since Ecclesiastes is probably unfamiliar territory to most of your group, it would be ideal to read the whole book together. If that's not possible, assign kids to read aloud the following sections (in order):

- Ecclesiastes 1:1-11
- Ecclesiastes 1:12-18
- Ecclesiastes 2:1-11
- Ecclesiastes 2:15-23
- Ecclesiastes 4:1-4
- Ecclesiastes 4:7-8
- Ecclesiastes 5:10-17
- Ecclesiastes 6:1-9
- Ecclesiastes 6:10-12
- Ecclesiastes 8:14-17
- Ecclesiastes 9:3-6
- Ecclesiastes 9:11-12
- Ecclesiastes 11:8-10
- Ecclesiastes 12:1, 6-8
- Ecclesiastes 12:9-14

Ask group members to read the passages in their most depressing, "woe-is-me" voices. Instruct those who are listening to write down any key words or phrases they hear multiple times.

Afterward, ask: **How do you feel after hearing these verses?** Point out that the passages are not very uplifting. In fact, some say they're downright depressing. If your group members read only the passages listed previously, then they skipped over some of the more positive sections like Ecclesiastes 3:1-22 and 4:9-12.

From what we read, who do you think wrote these words? Have kids review Ecclesiastes 1:1, 12-16; 2:4-9; 12:9. These verses all suggest that the author is King Solomon. However, it's also possible that someone wrote it at a later date as if it were Solomon speaking.

Assuming Solomon wrote these words, how does it make you feel to know that one of the wisest and richest people who ever lived felt this way? If no one mentions it, point out that how rich, good-looking, or smart we are is no guarantee of our happiness.

OPTIONS

EXTRA ACTION

SMALL GROUP

LARGE GROUP

LITTLE BIBLE BACKGROUND

FELLOWSHIP & WORSHIP

SHORT MEETING TIME

JR.HIGH HIGH SCHOOL COMBINED

EXTRA CHALLENGE

Why do you think such depressing words are contained in the Bible? The answer to this question will become clearer after taking a closer look at some of the phrases that are repeated. So allow group members to offer their opinions, but hold off on answering this question right away.

Of the verses that we just read, were there any that surprised you or that really made you stop and think? If so, what were they?

What are some of the key words or phrases that appear multiple times in these verses? See what kids wrote down as they listened to the verses being read. Also let them look at the passages again and call things out.

Use the following information to supplement group members' responses. The reference in parentheses is the first verse in Ecclesiastes in which the word is mentioned. You might want to write the information on the board as you share it.

- "Meaningless" (1:2)—This word appears well over 30 times in Ecclesiastes.
- "Under the sun" (1:3)—This phrase appears about 30 times in the book.
- "Work," "toil," "labor" (1:3)—These words appear over 25 times.
- "God" (1:13)—This word appears almost 30 times.
- "Chasing after the wind" (1:14)—This phrase appears at least nine times.
- "Eat and drink and find satisfaction" (2:24, 25)—Variations of this phrase appear at least six times.

STEP 3

A Meaningless Exercise

(Needed: Bibles)

Say: **Let's take a closer look at some of these phrases to help us better understand the book.**

What are some of the things the writer of Ecclesiastes says are meaningless? Have kids skim the verses and call things out as they find them. Among the answers group members might come up with are "everything" (1:1; 12:8), "all the things that are done under the sun" (1:14), "pleasure" (2:1), achievements (2:11), "being wise" (2:15), "work" (2:17), pain and grief over work (2:23), people who work hard but aren't content with what they have (4:7-8), loving money (5:10), not being able to enjoy one's wealth and possessions (6:2), a roving appetite (6:9), "righteous men who get what the wicked deserve" and vice versa (8:14), "everything to come" (11:8), and "youth and vigor" (11:10).

Have you ever felt "everything" was meaningless? If so, when? Why did you feel that way? When might someone feel that way today? What would your life be like if you felt everything was totally meaningless? Use questions like these to get kids thinking about what the author of Ecclesiastes might be saying.

Knowing what you know about the rest of the Bible, how would you complete this sentence: "Everything is meaningless when . . ."? Group members may give responses like "Everything is meaningless when you don't have Jesus in your life" or "Everything is meaningless when you try to live your life apart from God" or "Everything is meaningless when you try to do things on your own." You might want to point out that Matthew 16:26 is a great New Testament counterpart to this statement. Matthew 16:26 tells us that nothing is accomplished if a person gains the whole world, but loses his or her soul.

Read a few of the "under the sun" references from Ecclesiastes 1:3, 9, 14; 2:11, 17; 8:17. Then ask: **Where exactly is this place "under the sun"?** If no one mentions it, point out that the phrase is probably referring to earth. Verse 8:17 is the key. God is over and above His creation. We can't comprehend what He has done. So if we keep God out of the picture, things will be meaningless. God isn't confined to a place "under the sun."

What is the phrase "chasing after the wind" referring to? (Any meaningless, futile activity.)

O P T I O N S

SMALL GROUP

FELLOWSHIP & WORSHIP

MOSTLY GUYS

MEDIA

URBAN

EXTRA CHALLENGE

What are some things people do that amount to nothing more than wind chasing? (Acquiring more and more things, only to leave them behind when they die; watching a lot of television shows; etc.)

Read the following passages in quick succession: Ecclesiates 2:24-25; 3:12-13, 22; 5:18-20; 8:15; 9:7.

Then ask: **What are these verses saying?** (The most a person can expect out of life is to eat, drink, and enjoy his or her work. These things are gifts from God.)

Is the writer of Ecclesiastes saying that all there is to life is eating, drinking, and working? (No. He's saying it is a gift from God to be able to enjoy life. Viewing things from this side of the cross, we know how much more God has in store for us. The writer of Ecclesiastes didn't have this same view.)

Is the writer saying it's OK to party all the time? If not, what is he saying? (No. He's saying to enjoy life, not to overindulge ourselves.)

Does Ecclesiastes 12:13 add anything to our understanding of the book? If no one mentions it, point out that this verse is the summation of the matter: Life lived apart from God (under the sun) is totally meaningless. The only possible conclusion for someone who keeps God out of the picture is despair. But there's another alternative: to live for God. Those who fear God and keep His commandments will find enjoyment in their daily lives, not to mention the afterlife.

Say: **A preacher once said that the Bible is the cradle of Christ and, like the manger, it has some straw in it. This preacher once said that the Book of Ecclesiastes is some of the straw that needs be be thrown out. Given the little we've looked into it today, would you tend to agree or disagree with this statement?** If no one mentions it, suggest that it's very dangerous to start discarding parts of the Bible. Maybe instead of throwing Ecclesiastes out, we should seek to learn what we can from it. Maybe it's there to get us thinking about what life is really all about and how senseless it is without God.

STEP 4

Vanity Plates

(Needed: Copies of Repro Resource 9, pencils)

Hand out copies of "License to Talk" (Repro Resource 9). Let group members work in pairs to complete the sheet. Each license plate represents a type of person who echoes some of the sentiments expressed in Ecclesiastes. Kids are to think about what they would say to each person. After a few minutes, ask volunteers to share their responses. If you have time, ask kids to speculate on what kind of car each license plate might be seen on.

Use the following information to guide your discussion as necessary.

I C I BUY (I see, I buy)
What might this plate tell you about the person who chose it?
(The person probably likes to shop and probably has a lot of money— or a large credit card debt.)
What might you say to this person to get a conversation started? What questions could you ask this person to get him or her thinking about what really matters in life? (Why do you like to shop so much? What's the last thing you bought that really brought you lasting happiness?)
Ask: **What's the last thing you bought in order to make yourself happy? How do you feel about that thing now? What's something you really want to buy right now? How much happiness will that thing bring you in 10 years?**
Get several responses.

I PARTY
What might this plate tell you about the person who chose it?
(The person enjoys a good time. Maybe the person enjoys drinking. Maybe the person sells Tupperware.)
What might you say to this person to get a conversation started? What questions could you ask this person to get him or her thinking about what really matters in life? (What's the greatest party you've ever been to? What was so great about it? Are there ever times when you don't feel like partying? If so, when?)
Ask: **Why do you think some kids are really into partying? What's going through their minds before, during, and after the party? What was going through your mind at the last party you went to? Why were you there?** Get several responses.

MAKE LUV

What might this plate tell you about the person who chose it?
(The person probably enjoys having sex. Maybe the person advocates a "free love" value system. Maybe the person is a peace activist.)

What might you say to this person to get a conversation started? What questions could you ask this person to get him or her thinking about what really matters in life? (Why did you feel compelled to put that message on your license plate? What does it mean to "make love"? What's the connection between love and sex? Do you think most people find lasting fulfillment in sexual relationships?)

Ask: **Do you think people who are sleeping around are happier than those who aren't? Why or why not? If sex doesn't give people lasting fulfillment, why are so many people having sex outside of marriage?** Get several responses.

ALL WORK

[NOTE: You might want to point out that this person's other car says "NO PLAY."]

What might this plate tell you about the person who chose it?
(The person probably feels like he or she works too much. The person is probably working hard to get ahead.)

What might you say to this person to get a conversation started? What questions could you ask this person to get him or her thinking about what really matters in life? (What kind of work do you do? Why do you work so hard? What would happen if you didn't work so hard? Do you enjoy your work?)

Ask: Why do you think some people are workaholics? Do you think you could become a workaholic? Why or why not? How important do you think work is to your parents? Why? Get several responses.

Summarize: **The Book of Ecclesiastes has something to say to all of these people. It was written for anyone who questions what life is all about or who's seeking fulfillment in some way that doesn't involve God. Even in Bible times, people were looking to things like materialism, sex, drinking, and work to find fulfillment in life. The bottom line is that life has no meaning if it's lived apart from God. All of these things might bring temporary pleasure, but in the scope of a lifetime, they mean nothing apart from God. That's what the Book of Ecclesiastes is all about.**

STEP 5

A Lot on Your Plate

(Needed: Bibles, paper, markers, scissors, license plate [optional])

Continue with the vanity-plate idea by having kids create their own vanity plates. These plates should convey some type of positive message about what really matters in life. Give kids a supply of blank paper and markers. If possible, try to use paper that is roughly the same size and shape as an actual license plate. You could even photocopy a real license plate and then "white out" the letters and numerals. The idea is to have kids make their plates look as real as possible.

Here are a few examples that we came up with. Don't share them unless your kids are having trouble coming up with their own.

GOD IS
HES RISN
JOHN 316
NEW LIFE
I MATTER
ASK ME 1

After a few minutes, ask group members to share their creations.

Then say: **Pretend that you're 70 years old and you're looking back on your life. What things in your life right now will still matter then? What things will seem totally unimportant?** Get a few responses.

Then ask: **How can you get your friends who don't have a relationship with Jesus to see that a life lived apart from God is meaningless?** Get several responses.

Close the session in prayer, thanking God for bringing real meaning to our lives. Psalm 90 offers many parallels to the Book of Ecclesiastes and may serve as a fitting prayer—especially verse 12.

Murphy's Law

Murphy's Law: If anything can go wrong, it will.

Henning's Corollary: Nothing is ever as easy as it looks.

Grocke's Gripe: Everything takes longer than you think.

LeFever's Lesson: Everything goes wrong at once.

Quartermain's Commentary on Murphy's Law: Murphy was an optimist.

Adair's Axiom: Everything is meaningless.

Nagle's Theory: If it ain't broke, it will be soon.

Parker's Principle: If it's raining, it must be the weekend.

Brinkman's Observation: There's nothing new under the sun.

Irwin's Rule: When riding your bike, it's always uphill and against the wind.

Jackson's Finding: If you paid full price, it will go on sale tomorrow.

Cook's Comment: All things are wearisome.

Duckworth's Dilemma: What is twisted cannot be straightened.

Kwon's Creed: The other line always moves faster (unless you switch to it).

Edington's Eulogy: Of making many books there is no end.

Mephibosheth's Message: When called upon to read the Bible out loud, your passage will have a lot of difficult names to pronounce.

Forsyth's Finding: Much study wearies the body.

Ogleby's Lament: All the good ones are already taken.

Develop your own law, corollary, rule, axiom, theorem, observation, principle, or whatever along the lines of Murphy's Law. Give it a fancy title too.

LICENSE TO TALK

Sometimes vanity plates say a lot about the person who chose them. Here are some actual vanity plates that have been spotted on the highway. Answer the questions for each one.

What might this plate tell you about the person who chose it?

What might you say to this person to get a conversation started? What questions could you ask this person to get him or her thinking about what really matters in life?

What might this plate tell you about the person who chose it?

What might you say to this person to get a conversation started? What questions could you ask this person to get him or her thinking about what really matters in life?

What might this plate tell you about the person who chose it?

What might you say to this person to get a conversation started? What questions could you ask this person to get him or her thinking about what really matters in life?

What might this plate tell you about the person who chose it?

What might you say to this person to get a conversation started? What questions could you ask this person to get him or her thinking about what really matters in life?

STEP 1

Before the session, buy or make a piñata. Don't put any prizes or candy inside. (If you bought one with goodies in it, perform surgery and take them out.) Hang the piñata from the ceiling or a tree. Don't let kids know the piñata's empty. To start the meeting, blindfold the kids and let them take turns trying to smash the piñata with a broom handle. After several minutes, tear the piñata open to reveal that nothing's inside. Tie this into the view that life is a difficult, meaningless attempt to find our way in the dark—with no reward at the end.

STEP 2

Have group members line up. Tie each person's arm and leg to the next person's arm and leg, chain-gang style (but with crepe paper or yarn, not chains). Then get the group trudging around the room, singing either "That's the sound of the men working on a chain gang . . ." or the "Yo-ee-oh" chant of the Wicked Witch's castle guards in *The Wizard of Oz.* Kids must keep up, but not go too fast. Anyone who breaks the chain will be re-tied and become leader of the singing or chanting. Kids must carry Bibles. Call out the 15 Ecclesiastes references; each person must read one in a "woe-is-me" voice. Let several kids read different passages simultaneously to save time.

STEP 2

To accentuate the content and mood of the Book of Ecclesiastes, introduce the Bible study in your most depressed, subdued, couldn't-care-less-one-way-or-the-other voice. Say: **Since most of you probably aren't familiar with Ecclesiastes, I guess we might as well read some of it.** (Yawn.) **Well, maybe not. All it talks about is how everything is meaningless, so why even read it? Who really cares?** Stand in a spaced-out, comatose-like state for a few seconds. Then say: **Actually, I guess I probably should read this to you guys, since that's my job. So, if you feel like it, open up your Bibles . . .** Open your Bible slowly, and start lethargically thumbing your way through it—until it just "slips" out of your hand. Stare at it on the floor for a few seconds. Then "snap out of it" and shift back into your normal, excited-youth-worker mode! Ask: **Do you ever feel that way about life sometimes? Kind of like a slug? Asking, "Who really cares?"? The writer of Ecclesiastes describes life as being "meaningless"—if you try to live it without God. Let's see what he says.** Assign group members the passages from Ecclesiastes to read. Then answer the accompanying questions as a group.

STEP 3

To introduce the idea of chasing after the wind, stage a quick contest. You'll need a hand-held, battery-operated fan; a box of facial tissues; and a stopwatch. Have kids take turns seeing how long they can keep a tissue afloat, using just the wind power from the fan. Each contestant may move around the room as much as necessary, but may not touch the tissue with any part of his or her body or allow the tissue to touch the floor.

STEP 1

If your group is too unwieldy to cover Repro Resource 8 together, try a different opening activity instead. Briefly explain the concept of Murphy's Law and read some of its variations from Repro Resource 8. Then have kids form groups of six. Announce that the members of each group will compete to see who can come up with the most variations of Murphy's Law. Have the members of each group stand in a circle. Explain that one person will start the contest by giving his or her first variation ("If you run a red light, a police car will be sitting at the intersection."). The person to his or her right will go next, and so on around the circle. If a person cannot come up with a new variation in 10 seconds, he or she is out. Continue until only one person remains in each group. If you have enough time, you might assemble the winners from each group and have them compete for the "grand championship."

STEP 2

Have kids form teams of four. Ask each team to come up with a song passage that illustrates the feelings and/or principles of the Ecclesiastes verses. The teams may use existing songs or come up with their own (perhaps changing the lyrics to a current popular song). For instance, one team might use "Bohemian Rhapsody" by Queen ("Nothing really matters/Anyone can see/Nothing really matters/Nothing really matters to me"). Another might use "Dust in the Wind" by Kansas ("All we are is dust in the wind/Dust in the wind/Everything is dust in the wind"). After a few minutes, have each team perform its song, using any choreography or enhancements it thinks might make the presentation more entertaining. You will judge the acts as though they're in a talent show, and award prizes to the winning team.

STEP 1

The Book of Ecclesiastes is perfect for jaded kids. It reflects the views of one who's tried practically everything and found it wanting. Instead of using Repro Resource 8, have teams improvise satirical skits in which an always sunny "positive thinker" tries to look on the bright side as he or she is (1) being robbed; (2) undergoing brain surgery without anesthesia; (3) being executed for a crime someone else committed; or (4) taking the driver's road test when nothing is going right. Then ask: **Do you just "keep smiling" when life seems rotten? Why or why not? What do you think is a more realistic attitude?** Point out that Ecclesiastes makes no effort to cover up the parts of life that seem meaningless and miserable.

STEP 5

Kids may question whether life without God is meaningless, especially if they know happy non-Christians. Acknowledge that life without God may not feel pointless—and that the Christian life may not always feel great. Then play an audiotape of a non-English language being spoken. See whether kids can figure out what's being said. Ask: **Were these words meaningless?** (Only to someone who doesn't understand them.) **Could you get any meaning out of them if you didn't understand the language?** (Maybe a little, if there was visual content or a few familiar words.) **If you did understand the words, would you understand everything the speaker meant?** (Not necessarily.) Point out that in a similar way, the meaning of life is garbled when you aren't on speaking terms with God. Even if you do speak His "language," you don't necessarily understand everything that happens in this world. But life makes a lot more sense when you can communicate with its Creator.

STEP 2

Kids who aren't familiar with biblical principles may be confused by the "everything is meaningless" discussion. After all, if work (especially homework) and achievements are meaningless, why bother doing anything? Help your kids see that Ecclesiastes refers to these things as meaningless *in the context of eternity*. To help make this point, try to find some news stories about people who were buried with their prized possessions (a Cadillac, jewelry, etc.) when they died. If you can't find such stories, point out that the pharaohs of ancient Egypt were buried with vast riches, servants, and even pets. Briefly discuss the axiom, "You can't take it with you." Then ask: **Do you think there's any similarity between the statements "You can't take it with you" and "Everything is meaningless"? Explain.**

STEP 4

Kids with little Bible background—and with considerable worldly background—may not be able to easily dismiss the philosophies represented by the vanity plates (on Repro Resource 9) as "meaningless." Give these kids a chance to voice their opinions. Ask for four volunteers to play the roles of the people who own the plates. Encourage each one to explain why he or she places such an emphasis on the activity represented by the plate—and why life might seem "meaningless" without that activity. After all of the volunteers have shared, use their specific comments as a reference as you go through the questions on Repro Resource 9.

STEP 2

To brighten the mood of the group after going through the "meaningless" passages in Ecclesiastes, have your kids brainstorm a list of the *meaningful* things God has given us. Write group members' suggestions on the board as they're named. The list might include things like our relationship with Him, our relationship with other Christians, and our eternal future. After a few minutes, pause for a time of silent prayer so kids can thank God for the meaningful things in their lives.

STEP 3

Ask: **Do you think our meeting together every week is "meaningless"? Why or why not?** It is hoped that most of your group members will agree that your meetings are *not* meaningless. If so, ask each person to name one thing about your meetings that are meaningful to him or her. Encourage *specific* answers, not responses like "I like the people here." The affirmation that comes from this activity should increase the level of fellowship among your kids.

STEP 4

Some of the priorities expressed by the vanity plates may hit home with your group members. Give your girls an opportunity to share their feelings about these priorities—in a non-threatening way. Say: **Let's say one of these plates belongs to your best friend. How would you defend her if someone started making fun of her plates?** Encourage most of your group members to respond. If possible, try to cover all four plates.

STEP 5

Rather than having your girls come up with their own vanity plates, call each of them sometime before the meeting and ask her to bring three things that describe or define her life. For instance, one of your girls might bring a musical instrument (or music book), a pair of basketball shoes, and a cross-stitch pattern to show that she spends a lot of time practicing music, playing sports, and making crafts. As you wrap up the session, have each of your girls present and explain the things she brought in. Then point out that having hobbies and working toward career and personal goals is not necessarily wrong— as long as we realize that they cannot compare in importance to the "meaningful," eternal things of God.

STEP 1

Rather than going through Repro Resource 8, ask each of your guys to describe one of the worst days he ever had—a day in which everything seemed to go wrong. You might want to start the activity by describing one of *your* worst days. After everyone has shared, ask: **How many of you guys know what Murphy's Law is?** If no one knows, explain what it is. Then read some of the variations from Repro Resource 8— including "Everything is meaningless." Ask: **Do any of these statements sound like things you'd find in the Bible? They are.** Then move into Step 2.

STEP 3

Ask your guys to name some of their favorite male athletes. Then ask: **What is it that motivates these guys and gives their professional lives meaning? Is it money? Fame? Their friends and family? A competitive nature? The desire to win? The desire to be the best?** Ask your guys which of these motivations they think are admirable and which aren't. Use this discussion to introduce the topic of the meaninglessness of "everything."

STEP 1

At the end of Step 1, have kids form two teams. Announce that the teams will be competing in a "meaningless relay." Use cones or some other kind of markers to make a "track" around your meeting room. Explain that when you say, **Go,** the first member of each team will start jogging around the track. However, the two contestants will be running in *opposite* directions. After one lap, they'll tag the next person in line, who must skip around the track. The next person must hop; the person after that must gallop; the person after that must crawl backward; the person after that must do somersaults around the track; etc. Toward the end of the competition, just as kids are starting to get excited about winning, stop the race. Point out that it really doesn't matter who wins the race because, according to the Bible, everything is meaningless.

STEP 5

Wrap up the session with a "nostalgia party." Play some music that was popular when your group members were in third or fourth grade. You might even want to have group members bring in their baby pictures and stage a "guess the identity" contest. During the party, ask your group members to look back on their (brief) lives so far and identify things that were meaningful and things that were meaningless. If you don't think your kids would be comfortable sharing these things aloud, have them write their responses anonymously on sheets of paper. After a few minutes, collect the sheets and read some of the responses aloud. Then lead in to the activity in the session in which the kids, pretending to be 70 years old, look back at what is meaningful and meaningless in their lives now.

STEP 1

Instead of using Repro Resource 8, rent the video of the movie *City Slickers*. Play the scene early in the film in which a disillusioned Mitch Robbins (Billy Crystal) tells his son's classmates about the meaningless lives they can expect. The speech begins with "Value this time in your life, kids, because this is the time in your life when you still have your choices. . . ." It ends with "The eighties, you'll have a major stroke, and you end up babbling with some Jamaican nurse who your wife can't stand, but who you call Mama. Any questions?" Ask: **What questions would you want to ask if you were in that class? How do you feel about this view of life? Why do you think this character feels this way? Do you think people get more optimistic or more pessimistic as they grow older? Why?** Note that you're going to look at a remarkably similar picture of life—in the Bible, of all places.

STEP 3

Sometime during this step, play a bleak, lamenting song like "The River" by Bruce Springsteen. Ask: **How is this song like the Book of Ecclesiastes? Does it offer any hope at all?** During Step 4, play a "searching" song like "River of Dreams" by Billy Joel. Ask: **What is this person searching for? What are the chances of finding it apart from God?** At the beginning of Step 5, play an upbeat but realistic contemporary Christian song like "Called to Hope" by Geoff Moore and the Distance. Ask: **What reasons for hope does this song give?**

STEP 1

For a shorter opener, try the following activity. Have kids form pairs. Give each pair a pencil, a separate eraser, and a sheet of poster board. Each pair should put its poster board on the floor and kneel nearby. At your signal, one partner in each pair will write a passage from Ecclesiastes (you choose which one) on the poster board, while the other partner erases it as it's written. The first pair to write and erase its passage wins. Don't award a prize, though. Note the pointlessness of what kids just did—rushing and working, and then ending up with the same blank sheets they had in the beginning. Ask: **Does life ever seem that way? Which parts of a typical day seem most pointless to you?**

STEP 2

Skip most of this step—except to read just one or two of the fifteen passages listed, explain the authorship of Ecclesiastes, and note the six often-repeated phrases and words mentioned at the end of the step. In Step 3, instead of having kids skim the fifteen passages for "meaningless" things, assign kids to look for them in some or all of the references listed in the second paragraph of Step 3. Of the "under the sun" passages listed in the fifth paragraph of the step, skip 1:3, 9, 14. Of the passages listed in the eighth paragraph, read only 2:24-25.

STEP 1

Urban variations of Murphy's Law probably should reflect more serious situations than paying full price for something. Use the following statements in your discussion of Repro Resource 8:
• **The Poverty Pit: Once you're down, you stay down.**
• **Godfather Pacino's Realization: Just when you think you're out, they pull you back in.**
• **The Ultimate End: You're better off dead.**
• **Urban Baseball Treatise: You can't win for losing.**

STEP 3

Because many urban kids have done without "things" for most of their life, their goal may be to acquire as many possessions as possible when they get older. So calling material possessions "meaningless" may not make sense to them. You may want to approach the topic from another direction. Ask: **What are some of the wrong methods that people use to get money?** (Stealing from or robbing others, selling drugs or guns, selling their bodies in prostitution, etc.) **Would you be willing to use one or more of these methods to get money? Why or why not?** It's likely that at least some of your kids will say that having money is not worth the risks associated with the methods you named. Point out that similarly, having material possessions is not worth risking your relationship with God. Compared to the gifts God has in store for us, material possessions are worthless.

STEP 1

Rather than distributing copies of Repro Resource 8, simply explain what Murphy's Law is and read a few variations from the sheet. Then distribute paper and pencils. Instruct your high schoolers to work together to come up with some more variations of Murphy's Law ("If you accept a part-time job, a better-paying one will become available the next day."). Instruct your junior highers, on the other hand, to work together to come up with *positive* variations of Murphy's Law ("If it's raining, there's something to do inside," or "If you paid full price for something, you'll get a bigger refund if you return it."). After about five minutes, see which group came up with the most variations.

STEP 2

Explain that a certain key word and a certain key phrase are each used over 30 times in the Book of Ecclesiastes. Have your high schoolers and junior highers compete to see which group can figure out what word and phrase you're talking about—simply by scanning the Book of Ecclesiastes in their Bibles. Make sure all group members have the same translation, preferably the NIV. The first group to write the correct word ("meaningless") and phrase ("under the sun") on a piece of paper and bring it to you is the winner. You may want to award prizes to the winning group. Use the activity to lead in to your study of Ecclesiastes.

STEP 2

As you go through the seemingly depressing sections in Ecclesiastes, challenge your group members to counter each downbeat passage with another Scripture passage that emphasizes the joy of serving the Lord and the happiness and fulfillment that come from living a Christian life. For instance, someone might counter Ecclesiastes 1:1-11 with Philippians 4:4-7.

STEP 3

Have your group members compare some of the "meaningless" passages in Ecclesiastes (1:1, 14; 2:1, 11, 15, 17, 23; 4:7-8; 5:10; 6:2, 9; 8:14; 11:8, 10) to Paul's comments in Philippians 3:2-11. Ask: **How are the things that Paul called "loss" and "rubbish" similar to the things the writer of Ecclesiastes called "meaningless"? How are they different?**

DATE USED:

Approx. Time

STEP 1: *Is There a Flaw in Murphy's Law?* _____
- ❑ Extra Action
- ❑ Large Group
- ❑ Heard It All Before
- ❑ Mostly Guys
- ❑ Extra Fun
- ❑ Media
- ❑ Short Meeting Time
- ❑ Urban
- ❑ Combined Jr. High/High School

Things needed:

STEP 2: *A Real Downer* _____
- ❑ Extra Action
- ❑ Small Group
- ❑ Large Group
- ❑ Little Bible Background
- ❑ Fellowship & Worship
- ❑ Short Meeting Time
- ❑ Combined Jr. High/High School
- ❑ Extra Challenge

Things needed:

STEP 3: *A Meaningless Exercise* _____
- ❑ Small Group
- ❑ Fellowship & Worship
- ❑ Mostly Guys
- ❑ Media
- ❑ Urban
- ❑ Extra Challenge

Things needed:

STEP 4: *Vanity Plates* _____
- ❑ Little Bible Background
- ❑ Mostly Girls

Things needed:

STEP 5: *A Lot on Your Plate* _____
- ❑ Heard It All Before
- ❑ Mostly Girls
- ❑ Extra Fun

Things needed:

A Matter of Time

TIME TO BE BORN	TIME TO DIE	TIME TO PLANT	TIME TO UPROOT	TIME TO WEEP	TIME TO LAUGH	TIME TO MOURN	TIME TO DANCE

YOUR GOALS FOR THIS SESSION:

Choose one or more

☐ To help kids see that God is in control of all things.

☐ To help kids understand how different life is when they really believe that God is in control of everything that happens.

☐ To help kids affirm that God has set eternity in their hearts and wants them to share eternity with Him

☐ Other:_____

Your Bible Base:

Ecclesiastes 3:1-14

A Time to Get Started

(Needed: Copies of Repro Resource 10, pencils, dictionary [optional])

To begin the session, pass out copies of "It's about Time" (Repro Resource 10) and pencils. This sheet lists in one column 10 different time spans (from one second to one lifetime). In another column, 10 different events are listed. Group members are to match the events with the appropriate time span. Kids may work in pairs or small groups to complete the sheet.

If you want to use the activity as a mixer, divide the group in half. Cut apart one or more copies (depending on the size of your group) of Repro Resource 10. Distribute the time span slips among one half of the group; distribute the events slips among the other half. Then give the kids a few minutes to pair up with the appropriate partner.

The correct answers are as follows:

- In one second/Eight million blood cells die within the average adult human
- In one minute/Forty-seven Bibles are distributed worldwide
- In one hour/A pig can run eight miles
- In one day/The average person laughs twenty times
- In one week/775 new books are published in the U.S.
- In one month/The average person cries one time
- In one year/The average person grows four new eyelashes
- In one decade/The average person's head sheds 247,520 hairs
- In one quarter-century/The average person takes 250 million breaths
- In one lifetime/The average person's heart beats 2.5 billion times

Afterward, ask: **Did any of these numbers surprise you? If so, which ones?** Let kids briefly share anything that they found interesting. It is pretty amazing to think that the human body generates millions of new blood cells every second. It's also interesting to note that people typically laugh 600 times more often than they cry.

Let's say some alien race got their hands—or tentacles, or whatever—on this sheet. If these aliens didn't know anything else about earthlings, what would they learn from this sheet? This is kind of a wild question that may or may not work for your group. If it works, have some fun with it. If it doesn't, hurry on to the next question and blame it on us. Some things the aliens might learn are that humans are complex creatures, that we read a lot, that we like to laugh, and that we keep track of time in strange ways.

Today we're going to be looking at time and how we should view the passing of time in our lives. Each of us is given only so much of it. So, before we go any further, what exactly is time? You might want to bring in a dictionary and read the definitions listed there. One definition is "the measured or measurable period during which an action, process, or condition exists or continues: duration; a continuum which lacks spatial dimensions and in which events succeed one another from past through present to future."

Say: **Back in the 1970s, a guy named Jim Croce recorded a song called "Time in a Bottle." Ironically, he died in a plane crash shortly after recording it. If time were available in a bottle, how much do you think people would be willing to pay for it?** Get a few responses.

A Time to Think

(Needed: Bibles, paper, pencils, chalkboard and chalk or newsprint and marker)

Distribute paper (save a tree by using the back of Repro Resource 10) and pencils. Have group members write down their answers to the following nine questions:

1. What do you think you'll be doing 10 seconds from now?
2. What do you think you'll be doing 10 minutes from now?
3. What do you think you'll be doing 10 hours from now?
4. What do you think you'll be doing 10 days from now?
5. What do you think you'll be doing 10 weeks from now?
6. What do you think you'll be doing 10 months from now?
7. What do you think you'll be doing 10 years from now?
8. What do you think you'll be doing 10 decades from now?
9. What do you think you'll be doing 10 centuries from now?

Afterward, have kids share some of their answers. Then ask:

Which answers are you least certain about? Which ones are you most certain about? Kids will probably be least certain about what they'll be doing in 10 years. Pay particular attention to how kids answered questions 8 and 9. Obviously, we'll all be dead and gone

by then, but did any kids mention anything about their ultimate spiritual destiny? This is a concept you'll want to revisit later in the session.

Ask: **When it comes right down to it, how much control do you have over what happens in your life? Would you say you have total control, a lot of control, some control, very little control, or no control?** Let kids debate this for a while. There's no easy way to answer the question. In some ways, we have a lot of control over our actions and the choices we make. But on the other hand, we can't control a lot of things—nature, other people, time itself.

How does the passing of time make you feel? Chances are, many young people don't give it much thought. But they're probably aware that "older people" keep commenting on how quickly time goes by. With a question like this, you're starting to get closer to the crux of the issue. When we stop to think about it, we see that a lifetime comes and goes very quickly. If kids have trouble talking about this, ask them how they feel about getting older—much older. How do they think their parents feel about it? Why do some people dread getting older?

A Time to Study

(Needed: Bibles)

Say: **When we start thinking about time and the future, we can get pretty philosophical about it. That's exactly what happens to the writer of Ecclesiastes in the third chapter**.

Have kids turn to Ecclesiastes 3. Read aloud verses 1 through 14. If possible, stay together as one group to discuss the following questions. If your group is too large for that, feel free to photocopy these questions for any other discussion leaders.

The first eight verses talk about there being a time and a season for everything. Which of these things do people have the least control over? (Certainly a time to be born [vs. 2]. Most people also have no control over the time of their death [vs. 2]. Individuals may feel they have no control over times of war [vs. 8].)

Which ones would you question as to whether there's ever a proper time for? (Possibly a time to kill [vs. 3], a time to scatter or gather stones [vs. 5], a time to tear [vs. 7], a time to hate and a time for war [vs. 8].) Point out that there are two interpretations as to what it means to scatter or gather stones. Some think it refers to building

a house or tearing one down. Others see it as a reference to military action—scattering stones to ruin an enemy's field, or gathering stones to prepare the way for a leader, as seen in Isaiah 62:10. Let kids offer suggestions for when it might be appropriate to hate or kill. Instead of getting hung up on issues like capital punishment or euthanasia, help kids remember that the author is painting a picture of our lives and pointing out that all things are within God's control and happen according to His divinely appointed timetable. This becomes much clearer in verse 14.

Do you see any progression in the first eight verses, or any logical order to these pairings? (The passage starts with the most momentous events in our lives—birth and death [vs. 2], then covers other activities and events in our lives, including creating and destroying things [vss. 2-3], human emotions [vs. 4], friends and enemies [vs. 5], material possessions [vss. 6, 7], and human relationships [vss. 7-8]. It's hard to imagine an area of life that's not covered.)

How would you answer the question in verse 9? Why do you suppose the writer is raising this question now? (The simple truth is that all of our toil is for nothing if we have no lasting relationship with God. The writer is probably talking about more than one's job. Toil might be referring to all of the effort put into life. When life is over, it might seem that it's all been for nothing. The writer raised the same point in Ecclesiastes 1:3. It's as if the writer is looking at the entire scope of life and wondering what he's been working so hard for all of these years.)

Have someone read again Ecclesiastes 3:10-11. Then ask: **What is the "burden" God has laid on people? How can something beautiful be burdensome?** If no one mentions it, point out that even though life can be beautiful, people will never be satisfied with created things because God has given us a hunger for eternal things. Even though we want to understand how it all fits together and what the future holds, we'll never fully understand God's ways here. To those who think about this hard enough, it can be a terrible burden—especially those who haven't found eternal life through Jesus.

What evidence is there that God has "set eternity" in people's hearts? (People of very diverse cultures throughout history have held some belief in a higher power and the hope of some type of eternal existence—that there's more to life than what we experience here on earth. Even with tremendous scientific advances, most people still cling to belief in a higher power. People also want to know what the future holds and understand how things work. People also have some sense of right and wrong—a moral conscience—that suggests that some truths are eternal. When God made us in His image [Gen. 1:27], He gave us a degree of likeness to Him. We are made for eternity, but our sin interrupted the unblemished relationship humans had. Nevertheless, we can live with God because of Christ.)

Who do you think would be least likely to agree with the writer's comments in verses 12 and 13 that there's nothing

better in life than to be happy, do good, eat and drink, and find satisfaction in our toil? (Probably people who aren't content with their lot in life. Some "religious" people might question whether there's more to life than this. The passage may seem self-centered, especially if the "do good" part is translated "enjoy the good" as some Bible versions render it.) Point out that we have to keep in mind that the writer of Ecclesiastes didn't know about God's plan and the grace He would extend through Jesus. [See 2 Tim. 1:10.]

Verse 14 is a great verse. What does it tell us about the things God does or allows to happen in our lives? (All of God's actions are permanent [they last forever]; they are complete [nothing can be added]; they are secure [nothing can be taken from them]; they are purposeful [so that we'll revere or worship Him].)

How does it make you feel to know that God is in total control of everything that happens? If no one mentions it, point out that the fact that God's control *should* make us feel secure and trusting. But in reality, we often lose sight of what it really means, and we end up fretting over things, especially the future.

STEP 4

A Time to Apply

(Needed: Bibles, chalkboard and chalk or newsprint and marker)

Ask your group members to call out terrible things that have happened in their lives or in the lives of other people—things like the death of a loved one, illness, loss of a job, natural disaster, etc. Write these things on the board as they are named.

Then ask: **What might someone who doesn't have faith in God say about a list like this?** (Perhaps that it proves He doesn't exist—otherwise, He wouldn't allow such terrible things to happen.)

What might someone who does have faith in God say about a list like this? (There's no way we'll ever understand why all of these things happen. But just because God allows them to happen doesn't mean He doesn't exist.)

Next, have group members list some of the biggest fears young people face as they look to the future—things like major decisions and responsibilities (like college, career, and marriage), being a victim of a violent crime, war, AIDS and other terminal diseases, etc. Write these things on the board as they are named.

OPTIONS

LARGE GROUP

HEARD IT ALL BEFORE

LITTLE BIBLE BACKGROUND

MOSTLY GIRLS

MEDIA

URBAN

JR. HIGH / HIGH SCHOOL COMBINED

Then ask: **What might someone who has no faith in God say about this list?** (Life is pretty frightening. How am I ever going to make it? What's the point, anyway?)

What might someone who does have faith in God say about a list like this? (Life is pretty frightening, but I know God is in control of all that happens to me. With that in mind, I can face the future, and I don't have to worry about what will happen.)

Finally, have group members list some of the things Christians hope for—things like heaven, eternal life, reuniting with loved ones, being with Jesus forever, etc. Write these things on the board as they are named.

Then say: **Some people might look at a list like this and call it "wishful thinking." Is it?** (Wishful, no; hopeful, yes. There is a difference. Christians believe in these things through faith in what God has promised. There are really only two logical conclusions a person can come to about the future—hope or despair. If God isn't in the picture, there's really no reason for hope.)

We've been talking a lot about eternity. What exactly is eternal life? You may need to point out that it's much more than the continuation of time forever. Look up John 17:3 together. Ask kids to comment on how this verse expands our view of eternal life. In it, we see that eternal life involves knowing Jesus. It's something we can begin experiencing here and now—and forever. Encourage any kids who haven't seriously considered a relationship with Jesus to talk with you more about it after the session.

A Time to Commit

(Needed: Bible, copies of Repro Resource 11, pencils)

Distribute copies of "The Bad and the Beautiful" (Repro Resource 11). This is an exercise in structured journaling, a written prayer activity that should help kids focus on the central message of Ecclesiastes 3. Have kids work individually to complete each sentence on the sheet. Then spend some time in prayer, allowing individuals to share what they've written. This would probably work best if you have several people share one section at a time. You could read aloud the words on the sheet and then pause for kids to read aloud what they've written. Be prepared to read some of your own responses too. To close the prayer time, read Psalm 93 or I Timothy 1:17.

OPTIONS

FELLOWSHIP & WORSHIP

MOSTLY GUYS

EXTRA FUN

IT'S ABOUT TIME

Match each event (in the right column) with the amount of time it takes for that event to happen (in the left column).

In one second

The average person cries one time

In one minute

The average person grows four new eyelashes

In one hour

A pig can run eight miles

In one day

The average person laughs twenty times

In one week

Forty-seven Bibles are distributed worldwide

In one month

775 new books are published in the U.S.

In one year

The average person's head sheds 247,520 hairs

In one decade

Eight million blood cells die within the average adult human

In one quarter-century

The average person takes 250 million breaths

In one lifetime

The average person's heart beats 2.5 billion times

The BAD AND the Beautiful

He has made everything beautiful in its time. He has also set eternity in the hearts of men; yet they cannot fathom what God has done from beginning to end. . . . I know that everything God does will endure forever; nothing can be added to it and nothing taken from it. God does it so that men will revere him (Ecclesiastes 3:11, 14).

Thank You, Lord, for the beautiful things in life like . . .

Thank You also for the certainty that You are still in control, even when really bad things happen like . . .

Help me to keep trusting in You even though I'm not sure about . . .

Augustine said, "You have made us for yourself, and our hearts are restless until they find peace in you."

Lord, thank You for setting eternity in my heart. Help me . . .

EXTRA ACTION

STEP 1

You'll need one or more watches (the kind with hands) for this game. Each watch should have a knob on the side for setting the time. You'll also need stick-on labels, each big enough to cover a watch face. Have kids form groups. Instruct each group to stand in a circle. Cover the watch faces with labels; give each group a watch. Make sure the knob is pulled out so that the time can be reset. At your signal, members of each group will pass the watch back and forth across their circle. Each person who receives the watch must turn the dial forward or backward to randomly reset the time before passing it to someone else. When you call, **Time,** kids in each group will guess what time the watch says. Then pull off the labels to see whose guess was closest. Play as many rounds as you have time for (no pun intended). Then award a prize to the best guesser in each group. Use this activity to lead in to the last two questions in Step 1.

STEP 3

Assign kids an action to go with each activity mentioned in Ecclesiastes 3:1-8 (hugging themselves for "embrace," hopping on one foot for "dance," etc.). Have group members stand in a wide-open space. Call out the "times" from the passage at random (**Time to plant! Time to search!**), pausing for just a few seconds after each one. Any person who doesn't recall and perform the correct action after an instruction is out. Do this, increasing the speed, until you're down to one or two winners. Afterward, ask: **Do you ever feel that there isn't enough time to do everything that needs doing? How does this relate to verses 9-14?**

SMALL GROUP

STEP 1

At the end of the step, sit with your kids in a circle on the floor. Place an empty soft-drink bottle in the middle of the circle. Announce that you'll be playing "Spin the Bottle" (or, more specifically, a version of the game appropriate for a church youth group). After the bottle is spun, the person to whom it points must share one thing he or she would do if given an "extra bottle of time" (say, one year's worth). For instance, one group member might dedicate the entire year to becoming a guitar virtuoso. Another might use the extra time to see as many movies as possible. Another might take a year's worth of naps. Continue until all of your group members have shared at least once.

STEP 2

In a small group, it's likely that your group members know each other fairly well. With this in mind, you might want to turn the prediction activity into a game. After kids have written their nine answers on a sheet of paper, collect the sheets. Then read aloud the responses one at a time and see if kids can guess who wrote what. The first person to correctly identify who wrote a particular response gets a point. The person with the most points at the end of the game is the winner. Use the questions in the session to discuss the activity.

LARGE GROUP

STEP 1

Try a large-scale "Beat the Clock" contest as an opener for your large group. Have kids form teams. Give each team an assignment to complete some kind of stunt within one minute. Here are some stunts to consider:

• Team members, with their arms tied behind their back and their legs tied together, must get 10 inflated balloons into a clothes basket.

• Team members, while wearing oven mitts, must arrange a deck of cards in a certain order.

• Team members, while blindfolded, must locate and stack a certain number of blocks.

If possible, try to have an adult volunteer (equipped with a stopwatch) observing each stunt. After a minute, have the teams rotate and try a new stunt. The team that successfully completes the most stunts within a minute is the winner. Use this activity to lead in to a discussion of how we should view the passing of time in our lives.

STEP 4

Have kids form groups of four to six. Distribute several newspapers and news magazines to each group. Instruct each group to find articles that illustrate some terrible things that happen to people (loss of a loved one, natural disaster, etc.). Then have each group brainstorm what a person who has faith in God and a person who doesn't have faith might say about these terrible occurrences. Continue by having the groups list some of the biggest fears young people face as they look to the future. Then have each group answer the questions that follow in the session. After several minutes, have each group summarize its findings for everyone else.

STEP 3

Looking at Ecclesiastes 3:1-8, kids may think, "So there's a time for everything. So what?" Help kids see that God has *preferred* times for these things, and that we need to think about the right and wrong times for them. Ask: **Which verse from the passage might encourage a radio "shock jock" to clean up his act?** (Verse 4—Some things shouldn't be laughed at.) **Which verses might be used to encourage recycling?** (Time to keep [vs. 6]; time to mend [vs. 7].) **Which verse summarizes the debate over how Christians should act toward AIDS victims?** (Time to embrace, time to refrain [vs. 5].) **How can we decide the right times for these things?** (By praying and considering what else the Bible says on these subjects.) Note that this passage's purpose is not to tell us when to do these things. Other Scripture passages help with that. For example, Matthew 25:31-46 could help Christians decide how to react to AIDS victims.

STEP 4

For jaded kids and those who struggle with doubts, Steps 4 and 5 may sound like shallow, wishful thinking. If you think your kids will need more help with the question of God's control in a world filled with tragedy, you can either skip these steps—or be prepared for more in-depth discussion. You may want to plan an additional session, using a resource like *When Kids Ask Sticky Questions* (Cook). Instead of calling for commitment in Step 5, read Ecclesiastes 3:15-17, which implies that God will deal with this world's injustices. Instead of demanding that we ignore what's going on and be happy anyway, He promises to make things right—in His time. You may want to end with silent prayer, encouraging kids to express their feelings to God about this.

STEP 3

Kids with little Bible background may wonder about the relevance of Ecclesiastes 3:1-14 in today's society. After all, probably very few of them have experienced a time to scatter or gather stones. So as a group, decide which of the events listed in the passage are easy to understand today and which aren't. Replace the ones that are hard to understand with other events kids face in their daily lives ("A time to study and a time to goof off," "A time to get some exercise and a time to rest," etc.). Then brainstorm some scenarios in which an event is done "out of time." For example, what if someone *laughed* when it was time to *weep* (perhaps at a funeral)? What if someone *tore down* when it was time to *build* (perhaps at a construction site)? If your group members enjoy performing, have them act out some of the scenarios. If not, just have them describe what the results might be.

STEP 4

If your kids don't have much Bible background, they may have had their view of eternity colored by media portrayals of heaven, hell, and the afterlife. So it might be helpful to spend a few minutes going through the "basics" of what the Bible says about such topics. A helpful resource for this is *Unseen Mysteries* in the Custom Curriculum series. Focus specifically on Sessions 3 and 4, which deal with what the Bible says about heaven and hell. Don't spend too much time on this. Give kids just an overview of what eternity will be like.

STEP 1

As your group members arrive, give each of them a slip of paper made out in the form of a blank check. It should have the current date on it; but other than that, all lines should be left blank. Explain: **This is a blank check. It's good for one thing—and that's whatever you want. If you could run out now and buy one thing you've always wanted, what would it be? Write the item on your check. On the line labeled "amount," write "Free." Then sign your name at the bottom.** Have kids pair up. Instruct them to share with their partners what they wrote and why. After a few minutes, say: **Now let's suppose you've all just found out that you're going to die in exactly one week. If you could, would you trade the item on your check for an extra year of life? How about an extra month? An extra week? An extra day?** Have your group members share their responses with their partners. Then, as a group, discuss why time is so important to us.

STEP 5

As you wrap up the session, lead your group members in singing (or reviewing the lyrics of) a couple of hymns that deal with eternity or God's eternal nature. Among the hymns you might consider is "Amazing Grace" ("When we've been there ten thousand years . . ."). If your group members are reluctant to sing, play a recording of "The Hallelujah Chorus" ("He shall reign forever and ever . . ."). Afterward, have each group member try to describe eternity in a way a five year old could understand. However, he or she may not use the word *forever* in his or her description.

STEP 2

In a group of mostly girls, you might want to consider using questions that are more specific than the ones listed in the session. For instance, you might ask: **How many of you think you'll be married 10 years from now? Where do you think you and your husband will live 10 years from now? How many kids do you think you'll have 10 years from now? What do you think your career will be 10 years from now?** Distribute paper and pencils. Instruct your group members to briefly sketch out their "ideal life" for the next 10 years. After a few minutes, ask several volunteers to share what they wrote. Then introduce the topic of how much control we have over our lives.

STEP 4

Have your group members refer to the "ideal life" sheets they created in Step 2 (see the option above). Ask: **What if some unexpected tragedies invaded your ideal life? For instance, what if one of your children died due to complications at birth? Or what if your marriage turned out to have some serious problems, and you and your husband separated? How would you deal with these issues? Would your faith in God make any difference in the way you responded?** Acknowledge that the future can be frightening. However, if we know that God is in control of all that happens, we don't *have* to worry about the future—even though sometimes we may forget that.

STEP 2

Before the session, rent a radar gun (a device that tells you how fast something is moving) from your local batting cage or sporting goods store. You'll also need to bring in several mattresses (and any other "cushioning" material you can find) and three hard rubber balls (about the size of baseballs). Set up your room so that guys will be throwing at the mattresses. You (or another volunteer) will stand off to the side of the throwing lane, clocking the speed of your guys' pitches with the radar gun. Allow each guy three pitches, so he can gauge how fast he's throwing. Before his last pitch, he must predict the speed of the throw. If he's exactly right on his prediction, give him a prize. Afterward, ask your guys how much control they think they had over the speed of their pitches. Then ask them how much control they think they have in other areas of their life.

STEP 5

Ask your guys to respond honestly to the following questions. Ask: **How hard is it for you to accept the fact that you're not in control of your own life? Explain. Do you ever wish that you could take control of your life away from God for a while so that you could do some things that you think are best? If so, what areas of your life would you most like to control?** Have someone read aloud Romans 8:28. Then ask: **Why is this sometimes hard to believe?**

STEP 1

Begin the session with a variation of the game "Telephone." Have your kids form two teams. Instruct the members of each team to sit in a line, facing forward. Give the person at the back of each line a sheet of paper and a pencil. Instruct him or her to draw something—perhaps an elephant (but do it quietly so that no one else can hear what you say). Give the person 10 seconds to draw; then have him or her pass the paper and pencil to the person in front of him or her. The next person will then continue the first person's drawing, not knowing what the picture is supposed to be. Continue until everyone has had a chance to draw. Then have each team hold up its finished picture while you announce what it was *supposed* to be. Afterward, ask: **What would have been a quicker and more time-efficient way to get this picture drawn?** (Have one person draw it according to instructions.) **What are some ways people waste time in their everyday lives?** Get responses from several group members.

STEP 5

As you wrap up the session, prepare a time capsule. Ask your group members to bring in items that represent the current era (e.g., a T-shirt with the logo of a popular brand of athletic apparel on it, a videotape of TV shows that are currently popular, audiotapes of music that is currently popular, etc.)—things that are likely to become "dated" in a few years. Also have kids write out Bible verses that speak of the promises of God—which *don't* change over time (particularly those that deal with His promise to us of eternal life). Place these verses in the time capsule as well. If possible, try to "bury" the time capsule somewhere in your church—perhaps in that messy storage closet. Put a note in there to the youth group of 20 years from now.

STEP 1

Show a time-travel scene from one or more of the following videos: *Time after Time, Time Bandits, Bill and Ted's Excellent Adventure, Star Trek IV, The Philadelphia Experiment,* one of the *Back to the Future* films, etc. Be sure to screen the scenes for appropriateness first. Then ask: **What kinds of things usually happen in time-travel movies? How about in movies that show a character being frozen and then thawed out in the future—like *Demolition Man, Sleeper,* and *Forever Young?* What appeals to you about being able to free yourself from the grip of time? What doesn't?**

STEP 4

Rent the video of *Dead Poets Society.* Show the trophy case scene (after first screening it yourself) about 10 minutes into the film, in which John Keating (Robin Williams) teaches his *"Carpe diem"* ("Seize the day") philosophy. Ask: **How is this philosophy like the philosophy in Ecclesiastes 9:7? How is it different? How could it lead to a meaningful life? How could it lead to selfishness or ignoring God?**

STEP 1

Skip Step 1. For Step 2, bring a VCR remote control. Announce that this high-tech device can alter time, fast-forwarding whole youth groups into the future. Have the group "travel" into the future by the increments mentioned in the session's nine questions. For example, point the remote, push "Fast Forward," and say: **We have now traveled 10 seconds into the future. What are you doing?** Kids should pantomime what they expect to be doing then, and at each of the other eight intervals as you announce them. Have volunteers explain their actions. Then discuss as instructed in the session.

STEP 3

Instead of using the first three questions in Step 3, condense the discussion of Ecclesiastes 3:1-14 by asking this: **Do you think these things happen at the "right" times in most people's lives? Why or why not? How could we do a better job of doing things at the right times?** Then move into the session's discussion of verses 9-14. To save more time, skip the last question in Step 3 and go directly to the last question in Step 4. In Step 5, instead of instructing kids to fill out Repro Resource 11, work your way around the circle (or up and down rows) as each person chooses one of the first three incomplete sentences on the sheet and completes it out loud.

STEP 2

Give each group member a paper plate and a marker. On the plate, kids should create a "life clock." Explain that for this exercise, you will assume that group members will live 72 years. So group members should write multiples of 6 on the clock face in place of the numbers (1-12) that normally go there. In place of "1," kids should write "6" (representing 6 years of age); in place of "2," they should write "12" (representing 12 years of age); in place of "3," they should write "18" (representing 18 years of age); and so on, until they reach 72. Have kids mark the spot on the clock that represents their age now; then have them shade in the area back to 12 o'clock, representing the years they've already lived. On the rest of the clock, have kids write near the appropriate numbers the things they foresee themselves doing at that age. (For instance, they might write "Graduate from college" near 21.) After a few minutes, have volunteers display and explain their clocks.

STEP 4

If you think your kids might be reluctant to share some of the terrible things that have happened to them, their families, or people they know, try another approach. Show scenes (which you've screened beforehand) from movies like *Boyz N the Hood, New Jack City, Menace 2 Society,* etc. that show the effects of urban violence. Then ask: **What might someone who doesn't have faith in God say about tragedies like these? What might someone who *does* have faith in God say about them?**

STEP 2

As a group, brainstorm a list of things that have been created for the purpose of saving time. Your list might include microwave ovens, dishwashers, remote controls, computers, fax machines, fast-food restaurants, etc. After you've listed the items on the board, stage a mini-debate. Have your junior highers argue that the things on the list have made our lives better because they've freed up time for us to spend on other activities. Have your high schoolers argue that the things on the list have made our lives worse because they've caused us to become lazy and impatient. After the debate, discuss how much control we actually have over time and the things in our lives.

STEP 4

Have kids prepare for a game of musical chairs. As much as possible, try to have junior highers standing next to high schoolers for the game. Explain that this version of musical chairs will not include music. Instead, kids will walk around the circle until a designated junior higher yells, "Stop!" At that point, a mad scramble for the chairs will ensue. The person who does not get a seat is out, and the game continues. [NOTE: Your junior highers could all gain an advantage if they planned a strategy with the designated person for when he or she will yell "Stop!" For instance, the person might give a signal (e.g., a cough) just before he or she yells.] Your high schoolers may complain that the junior highers have an unfair advantage because they're in control of what happens. Regardless, let the game continue until you have a winner (who *should* be the designated junior higher). Afterward, say: **This game may not have been very fair, but it can serve as a reminder to us that we have very little control over our lives—especially the timetable of our future.**

STEP 2

Distribute paper and pencils. Instruct your group members to write down everything they can remember that they did yesterday. They should be as specific as possible as they list items. Explain that in addition to the "major" events, you're looking for things as minute and insignificant as "I waved at Mark on my way to English class" or "I asked my mom what's for dinner." After a few minutes, collect the papers. Explain to your kids that you'll refer to the sheets later in the session. Later, at the end of Step 4, read some of the lists aloud. As a group, determine which of the items on the lists might have "eternal significance." Certainly things like reading the Bible (or going to youth group meetings) might have eternal significance. But what about things like hanging out with friends, watching TV, or playing video games? Afterward, ask: **How much of our time should be spent doing things that have eternal significance? Explain.**

STEP 3

One of the most intriguing parts of the Ecclesiastes 3 passage is the phrase "He [God] has . . . set eternity in the hearts of men." Explore this concept further with your group. Ask: **How has God set eternity in our hearts? If God has set eternity in our hearts, why do we need the Bible? Why can't some people recognize what God has set in their heart? What "proof" is there that we have eternity in our hearts?**

DATE USED:

Approx. Time

STEP 1: *A Time to Get Started* _____
- ❏ Extra Action
- ❏ Small Group
- ❏ Large Group
- ❏ Fellowship & Worship
- ❏ Extra Fun
- ❏ Media
- ❏ Short Meeting Time
Things needed:

STEP 2: *A Time to Think* _____
- ❏ Small Group
- ❏ Mostly Girls
- ❏ Mostly Guys
- ❏ Urban
- ❏ Combined Jr. High/High School
- ❏ Extra Challenge
Things needed:

STEP 3: *A Time to Study* _____
- ❏ Extra Action
- ❏ Heard It All Before
- ❏ Little Bible Background
- ❏ Short Meeting Time
- ❏ Extra Challenge
Things needed:

STEP 4: *A Time to Apply* _____
- ❏ Large Group
- ❏ Heard It All Before
- ❏ Little Bible Background
- ❏ Mostly Girls
- ❏ Media
- ❏ Urban
- ❏ Combined Jr. High/High School
Things needed:

STEP 5: *A Time to Commit* _____
- ❏ Fellowship & Worship
- ❏ Mostly Guys
- ❏ Extra Fun
Things needed:

Unit Two: Too Tough?

Talking to Kids about the Tough Teachings of Jesus

by Paul Borthwick

I was in the middle of a conversation with a friend when several large portions of my old Bible fell out of its cracked binding. My friend lunged to save them as they fell. Without thinking, I quipped, "That's all right. They were problem texts anyhow."

We laughed because we both knew of tough passages in Scripture which we would rather do without.

In preparing for messages or Bible studies, we've all probably come across very difficult passages (either tough ones to apply or difficult ones to understand), and thought to ourselves, *I really wish that Jesus hadn't said that.*

But if we truly believe that we should teach the "whole will of God" (Acts 20:27) and that "all Scripture is God-breathed" and is profitable for growth (2 Tim. 3:16), then we cannot shrink away from the tough texts—whether they're addressing doctrinal issues or lifestyle convictions.

One thing we need to remember before we start is that following Jesus is difficult. We would all like an instant Christianity that's "as easy as 1-2-3" to understand, but this is not the life of faith. Following Jesus is described in the Bible with images of running a marathon or wrestling in a fight. Tackling tough issues and texts is simply part of the discipline of discipleship.

Foundation for Success

The best foundation to build upon as we start this series is honesty. We do not need to pretend that these are texts that we have mastered and that cause no problems for us. Instead, we should feel free to admit that these are difficult questions, and then illustrate that point with the questions we personally bring to the texts. For example:
- How can we flee from lust in an X-rated society in which almost every TV program, movie, or song seems laced with sexual innuendo?
- When I ask in faith for something, why doesn't Jesus respond as He promised?
- How can I keep from worrying when life seems out of control?
- Does following Jesus really mean loving enemies who have hurt me deeply, rejected me, or belittled me?
- What if I enjoy the thought of being rich? Does this disqualify me from being a Christian?

I once thought that working with young people meant protecting them from these tough texts and difficult issues. I suppose I thought, *My job is to get them grounded in the faith; later in life they can think about these things.*

But as we studied the Bible together, the tough issues were too prevalent to be avoided. If I tried to dodge the issues, group members knew that I was being selective in what Scripture I applied to our lives.

I came to the conclusion that integrity demanded that I address these tough texts. No matter what their ages, the young people in our groups need to know that following Jesus is a rigorous challenge.

Proceed with Caution

As we teach these tough texts, there are two pitfalls to avoid. First, we need to be careful not to ridicule other people's interpretations of these texts. We can explain our differences with others in the Christian tradition without belittling those who adhere to other views.

For example, in trying to understand the extreme and literal application of the passage about "selling all and giving it to the poor," I made some jokes about what I thought was the weird lifestyle of those who had taken vows of poverty for Jesus. For the young people in our ministry who were from Roman Catholic families, this seemed like an unnecessary criticism of some heavily committed people, and my ill-timed humor caused me to lose credibility as a teacher.

The same loss of credibility may occur if we mock the faith healers who have different interpretations of the text about "Ask, and it will be done for you" or the believers who understand "Love your enemies" as a command for total pacifism.

Remember, our goal is to help group members understand the texts as they affect their lives—not to excuse ourselves from grappling with the texts by ridiculing those who we think may have misapplied or overapplied them.

Second, we need to be careful not to talk at group members. Instead, we should talk *with* them. This reflects the basic foundation of honesty. When we engage in the study of texts that we do not understand, some of us have a tendency to resort to impersonal lecturing.

We report on the various ways that the church has understood these texts in the past. We get our explanations out of commentaries, and in so doing, we communicate to group members that we are seeking to understand the texts intellectually without really caring about what it means in our lives.

If we're unclear or insecure about the meaning of these texts, no scholarly lecture or commentary quotations will hide this from our group members. Instead, they will see us as being afraid to deal with the real meaning of the texts. It's far better to let group members know that we are fellow learners with them, striving to understand what these hard teachings of Jesus say to us today.

Building for Effectiveness

To effectively address the tough teachings of Jesus covered in this book, you'll need to emphasize and/or demonstrate three principles: grace, mercy, and empathy.

(1) Grace. In a discussion in our group about selling everything and giving to the poor, we began talking about some of our church-supported missionaries who, in the eyes of our group members, were the most vivid illustration of this passage.

One group member asked about Dr. Bob, a missionary doctor who had left what was obviously a lucrative practice to go work in central Africa. As the group members talked, I realized that they were under the impression that Bob had made this "once and for all" decision without a struggle, and that he never thought about returning to the United States to increase his earning power.

I knew something of the struggles that missionaries like Bob went through, so I explained to the group members that obeying the command was not a "once and for all" issue but rather a lifetime process. Did Bob ever struggle with that decision? Indeed! Had he thought about a return to the States? Often!

In teaching that text, I realized that it was my job to emphasize the grace of God in obeying His commands. I needed to remind group members that Jesus will give us grace to obey these commands. In a time when group members were feeling that the Christian life was far out of their reach, I pointed them to the fact of God's grace—where He commands, He also will empower to fulfill.

(2) Mercy. When you tackle the the tough teachings ahead of you in this book, you'll discover that many group members have already failed. Lustful thoughts may already be a daily occurrence. Worrying? Some will have already established life patterns built on anxiety and stress. Love your enemies? For some group members, hate has anchored itself deep in their souls.

As a result, we need to emphasize mercy. Our teaching of these tough commands should be intertwined with what one person calls the "Gospel of the second chance." Group members can respond to these texts more effectively if they understand forgiveness and the freedom we have as Christians to get back up after we fail.

Haddon Robinson's essay entitled "A Little Verse for Losers" helped me emphasize this mercy with group members. In this essay, Robinson recalls the story of Jonah, who responded to a hard command of God by going the opposite direction from God's command.

With an emphasis on mercy, Robinson points the reader to Jonah 3:1: "And the word of the Lord came to Jonah a second time." This "verse for losers" reminds us that God, in His great love, did not give up on Jonah—and He will not give up on us. This is a truth we all need to hear in the context of these tough commands.

(3) Empathy. When I embark on the study of texts like these, I do better if I think of myself as a "fellow struggler" rather than the teacher. With the "fellow struggler" perspective, I am free to share out of my own life.

I learned this lesson from an 84-year-old Christian leader who was leading a men's seminar at our church one summer day. As a young Christian, I was wrestling with the meaning of Jesus' teaching in the Sermon on the Mount about lustful thoughts and adultery in the mind. I could not seem to succeed in obeying this text.

The aged veteran started the seminar. In response to some of the scanty summer attire of women around the church, he prayed, "Lord, deliver me from lustful thoughts." At that moment, I realized, *I can listen to this guy; he knows what I'm going through.* He presented himself as a fellow struggler rather than an accomplished veteran.

So empathize. When the study covers "Sell all and give to the poor," pray honestly before group members, "Lord, You know that I am coming to this passage with the desire to rationalize it away. Help me to hear Your voice." Admit the struggle with anxiety. Confess the difficulty in loving enemies.

Such empathy allows group members to see us as real people who are genuinely battling with the application of these tough texts.

Into the Fight

In the weeks ahead, this study will take you into texts that you might rather tear out of your Bible and throw away. Instead of taking the easy route, accept the challenge of teaching these tough sayings of Jesus. It may not be easy—but neither is following Jesus.

Paul Borthwick is minister of missions at Grace Chapel in Lexington, Massachusetts. A former youth pastor and frequent speaker to youth workers, he is the author of several books, including Organizing Your Youth Ministry *and* Feeding Your Forgotten Soul: Spiritual Growth for Youth Workers *(Zondervan).*

What's the Toughest Thing Jesus Said?

The images on these two pages are designed to help you promote this course within your church and community. Feel free to photocopy anything here and adapt it to fit your publicity needs. The stuff on this page could be used as a flier that you send or hand out to kids— or as a bulletin insert. The stuff on the next page could be used to add visual interest to newsletters, calendars, bulletin boards, or other promotions. Be creative and have fun!

Of all the hard sayings of Jesus, which one do you find most difficult?
a. Don't look at anyone lustfully.
b. You can have enough faith to move mountains.
c. Don't worry about anything.
d. Love your enemies.
e. Sell everything you have and give it to the poor.
f. All of the above!

For the next few weeks, we'll be tackling some of Jesus' toughest teachings in a new course called *Too Tough?* It won't be easy, but it'll be worth it!

Who:

When:

Where:

Questions? Call:

Unit Two: Too Tough?

Have you heard the latest?

Was Jesus joking?

Use your head.

Have a heart.

Take courage.

Write your own message in the signal.

Are Sexual Thoughts Always Sinful?

YOUR GOALS FOR THIS SESSION:

Choose one or more

☐ To help kids distinguish between lust and normal sexual thoughts.

☐ To help kids understand that the Bible condemns lust, but it doesn't condemn sex or sexual thoughts.

☐ To help kids choose behaviors that will lead them away from lust to purity and respect of others.

☐ Other:_____

_____

Your Bible Base:

2 Samuel 11:1-5
Matthew 5:27-30
1 Thessalonians 4:7
Hebrews 4:15-16

The Great Cover-Up

(Needed: Several rolls of elastic bandage)

Divide group members into two teams. Give each team several elastic bandages—the kind you would use for wrapping a sprained ankle. Before explaining the game, ask each team to choose a volunteer.

Then give the following instructions: **When I say "Go," start winding the bandage around your volunteer, covering him or her up as much as possible. Go!**

While kids are wrapping their team members, call out expert advice on how to do the job (over, under, around, through the legs, and so on). When one team has finished, evaluate the cover-up job. If the other team isn't too far behind, allow it to finish. Then judge between the two teams.

Announce which team pulled off the best cover-up, applaud the winning team, and let your volunteers unwrap themselves.

Then say: **Ever since Adam and Eve sewed together the fig leaves, people have covered themselves up in varying stages, hoping to prevent sexual temptation. Unfortunately, covering up temptation doesn't make it go away.**

The Fine Line of Lust

(Needed: Index cards prepared according to instructions, tape, chalkboard and chalk or newsprint and marker)

Before this session, write the following items on separate index cards:
- Ads
- Music videos
- Cable stations
- Romance novels
- Magazines like *Playboy* and *Playgirl*

- R-rated movies
- NC-17 movies
- Adult movies
- Thong bathing suits
- Topless sunbathing
- Trashy TV movies
- Swimsuit issue of *Sports Illustrated*
- Hunk-a-month calendars

Depending on the maturity of your group members, you may want to separate guys and girls into two groups for better discussion. Some kids might feel more comfortable talking about these issues in this "safer" atmosphere.

[NOTE: Kids might ask you about other sexual matters that concern them: masturbation, wet dreams, and so on. If so, you'll need to decide whether or not to sidetrack this discussion of Jesus' tough teaching on lust and tackle these other issues.]

Say: **Although God created us with sexual desires, He placed restrictions on how we express those desires. So what's the deal? How do we know what's right or what's wrong?**

Hand out the index cards to various kids. You'll also need a roll of tape on hand. Draw a line down the middle of the board. Point to one side of the line and say: **Anything we put on this side of the line is OK. We don't have any problems with this stuff. But when we cross the line** (drag your finger across the line on the board), **the stuff on this side is wrong and makes us uncomfortable.**

One at a time, ask each group member to read aloud his or her card. As a group, decide on which side of the line each item belongs. Encourage group members to explain their reasons for why one thing is OK and another thing isn't. If group members can't agree on something, ask them to vote on it, and go with the majority decision. No matter how much you may disagree with a decision, let it stand. When a decision has been reached, the group member with the card will tape it to the appropriate side of the board.

Choose one of the items group members put on the "OK" side of the line and ask: **Is there any way this item might cross the line and become wrong?** (Yes. For example, some romance novels are "soft porn" in disguise. Or a guy might start obsessing about the models in a *Sports Illustrated* swimsuit edition, which might lead to unhealthy fantasies and unfulfilled desires.)

Explain: **There's a fine line between positive sexual desires and negative desires. But how do you know when you've crossed that line? While on earth, Jesus talked about that line; but instead of making things easier, He seemed to make them more difficult to understand.**

STEP
3

What's Love Got to Do with It?

(Needed: Bibles, chalkboard and chalk or newsprint and marker)

OPTIONS

SMALL GROUP

HEARD IT ALL BEFORE

LITTLE BIBLE BACKGROUND

FELLOWSHIP & WORSHIP

MOSTLY GIRLS

JR. HIGH / HIGH SCHOOL COMBINED

EXTRA CHALLENGE

Say: **A lot of Jesus' teachings are tough to understand and even tougher to practice—like the one we're going to talk about in Matthew 5:27-30.** Have group members turn to the passage in their Bibles. Ask a volunteer to read it aloud.

Then say: **Look at verse 28 again: "Anyone who looks at a woman lustfully has already committed adultery with her in his heart." And the same thing goes for a woman looking lustfully at a man.**

What's your first reaction to this teaching? (It's unrealistic; it's unreasonable; it's too rigid.)

You might want to explain what Jesus was doing in His Sermon on the Mount. Because of the hypocrisy of the Pharisees, Jesus set a higher standard for His followers and elevated the Ten Commandments. Not only was murder wrong, but so was getting angry with someone. Not only was adultery wrong, but so were lustful thoughts. The Pharisees obeyed the law externally, but it was all a sham because they broke the commands internally.

What makes this teaching tough? (It seems impossible to keep! You could drive yourself crazy trying to figure out what is or isn't a lustful thought. Besides, what does the word "lust" mean anyhow?)

Before we go any further, let's define our terms. Lust is usually forbidden or unchecked sexual desire. It's a craving or intense desire or need. It doesn't necessarily have anything to do with love.

Let's look at David's example. He was the greatest king Israel ever had, an ancestor of Jesus, and a man after God's own heart. But he had a problem with lust. Turn back in your Bibles to 2 Samuel 11:1-5 and look at the opening scene of this made-for-TV story.

Give group members a chance to read the passage. Then ask: **Where did David go wrong?** (He gave in to sexual temptation. He let his sexual desires get out of hand and went after Bathsheba.)

David was also in the wrong place at the wrong time. According to verse one, King David probably should have been off to war as expected instead of hanging around the palace.

What could David have done to prevent his temptation from becoming lust and eventually becoming sin? Use the following ideas to supplement group members' responses.

- *Pray about the temptation.* David, the author of many moving prayers and psalms, should have prayed when he saw Bathsheba. Then he should have left the temptation zone.
- *Become accountable to someone you trust.* David probably had many advisors he trusted. He could have gone to one of them to talk about his temptation.
- *Get a wife.* This isn't a solution to lust. Some people think that being married solves lust problems, but it doesn't. According to 2 Samuel 3:2-5, David had at least six wives. Yet he still gave in to his lust.

Ask: **Why doesn't being married solve the problem of lust?** (Even if you're married, you can be attracted to others. They may seem more attractive, more tender, more fun than your spouse.)

- *Get a life.*

Ask: **Before David was king, he was a skillful warrior. What was he doing in this passage?** (*Not* going to war with his troops [see 2 Sam. 11:1]. Some people think that David gave in to his sexual temptation because he was bored. He wasn't doing what he was supposed to do—to lead the battle.)

Ask: **Do you think it was wrong for David to feel tempted?** After several group members have expressed their opinions, have them turn to Hebrews 4:15-16. Ask a volunteer to read the verses aloud.

Then say: **Can you see the difference between the temptation to sin and sin itself? It wasn't wrong for David to feel the sexual pressures, but it was wrong for him to give in to the pressure and sin. At some point he crossed the line between temptation and sin, fueled by his lust.**

Have group members form teams of three or four. Instruct each team to compare the story of David and Bathsheba and the Hebrews 4:15-16 passage with the tough teaching of Jesus in Matthew 5:28.

Say: **As a team, come up with a one- or two-sentence summary of Jesus' command in Matthew 5:28.** (For example: Anyone who looks at someone and is consumed with thoughts of having sex with that person has already committed adultery. The temptation isn't wrong, but thinking about it all of the time, making plans to do it, giving in to it, and committing a sin is wrong.)

When teams have finished, have them read their summaries. You'll probably hear some recurring themes such as being consumed with sex, giving in to the desire, or feeding a lustful thought until it becomes an act.

Summarize: **A sexual thought comes and goes, but a craving grows and consumes you. And just as adultery wrecks a** marriage, lust destroys relationships because you're treating people as objects or a collection of body parts.

Handled well, sex can be a wonderful part of a lifelong commitment in marriage. Handled badly, it can lead to a lifetime of loneliness, frustration, and guilt.

Lustbusters

(Needed: Copies of Repro Resource 1, pencils, Bibles, poster board prepared according to instructions, marker)

Before the session, you'll need to draw four continuums (i.e., horizontal or vertical bars) on a piece of poster board. At the left end of each continuum, write, "OK Zone"; in the middle write, "Warning Zone"; and at the right end, write, "Danger Zone."

Distribute copies of "Lustbusters" (Repro Resource 1) and pencils. Give group members a few minutes to read through the situations.

Explain: **For each situation, you'll need to decide whether the person is in the "OK Zone," and doesn't have a problem with lust; whether the person's in the "Warning Zone," and is headed for trouble; or whether the person is in the "Danger Zone," and has big problems with lust.**

When everyone is finished, hold up the poster board with the continuums on it. Say: **I'm going to start shading in this first bar for Denise. Yell for me to stop when you think I've reached the right zone for her.** Do this for each character on Repro Resource 1.

Each time someone shouts stop, stop; then ask if everyone agrees or whether should you keep going. When the majority of your group members tell you to stop, do so and ask them why the person belongs in that particular zone.

Have group members form teams of two or three to complete the bottom section of Repro Resource 1. Encourage them to list as many specific actions as they can think of that lead to and away from lust. Use the following suggestions to supplement group members' ideas.

Things that may lead to lust:
- Thinking of people just as bodies
- Looking at and reading pornography
- Daydreaming about having sex with certain people
- Watching a lot of TV
- Being obsessive about looks and outward appearance

- Thinking of sex as a way to gain acceptance or someone's love
  Things that may lead away from lust:
- Being interested and active in all kinds of activities
- Handling feelings in positive ways such as journal writing or talking to people you trust
- Having some sort of valuable focus or goal for your life
- Developing healthy relationships with all kinds of people
  When the teams are finished, have each one share and explain its list.

You Can Do It

Say: **Regardless of what you see in the movies or on TV or hear in pop music, you can—with God's help—resist sexual temptation.**

Ask group members to pair up with a friend of the same sex. Instruct them to tell their partners about a time they successfully resisted sexual temptation. You might ask the following questions to get them started.

- **Have you ever walked away from a display of sexually explicit magazines?**
- **Have you ever refused to respond to someone's sexual advances?**
- **Have you ever played basketball or done something else when you started to fantasize sexually?**
- **Have you ever decided not to hang out with a certain person who talks about sex a lot?**

After a few minutes, call the group back together. Read aloud I Thessalonians 4:7: "For God did not call us to be impure, but to live a holy life."

Explain: **Because God called us to be pure, He will help us overcome sexual temptation and sin.**

Close the session in prayer, thanking God for creating sex and asking Him to help your group members handle their sexuality in appropriate ways. Invite anyone who needs to talk with you privately after the session to do so.

OPTIONS

SMALL GROUP

LITTLE BIBLE BACKGROUND

FELLOWSHIP & WORSHIP

EXTRA FUN

MEDIA

EXTRA CHALLENGE

Lustbusters

D E N I S E likes to hang out at the pool in the summer—mostly to look at guys, flirt a little, and get lots of sun. Denise likes to "rate" guys and make comments about their looks. She and her friends make sure they look super-good in their suits, so they diet and do whatever else it takes to look good.

S T E V E doesn't have a life, except for cable TV. He likes to watch the adult channels on weekends. He also has a stash of *Playboy* magazines that he looks at a lot. Steve wonders why he has so much trouble talking with girls. After all, he thinks about them all the time—well, actually, he thinks about their *bodies* all the time.

K A R E N ' S parents are in the process of a divorce, and she feels lonely and rejected. If she had a boyfriend, she'd probably do anything to hang on to him. Fortunately, she's making a lot of friends in youth group and at school. She also spends a lot of time with a couple from church who are youth sponsors.

C R A I G is always on the go. He plays basketball and runs track. His next-door neighbor is showing him how to repair cars. Craig has a girlfriend, but they don't seem to have the problems resisting sex that other couples do. It does bug him when his friends keep asking when he and his girlfriend are going to "do it," but Craig hasn't given in to the pressure.

THINGS THAT MAY LEAD TO LUST

_____

_____

_____

_____

_____

_____

THINGS THAT MAY LEAD AWAY FROM LUST

_____

_____

_____

_____

_____

_____

NOTES

STEP 1

A particularly active group may be too antsy to stand by and watch as other team members do the bandage-wrapping activity. Another option in such cases is to let the group split into two-person teams. Provide each pair with a roll of toilet paper and instructions for one person to wrap the other as completely as possible. To keep anyone from taking too much time, you might want to establish a time limit at the beginning. When everyone is finished, let anyone "model" who wishes to do so. Then determine which team(s) did the best job. (You may also want to have a camera on hand. Usually the ones who get wrapped up don't have much of an opportunity to see the others clearly.)

STEP 4

With a bit of modification, the scenarios on Repro Resource 1 can be made into skits. Divide into teams and let each team bring Denise, Steve, Karen, and Craig to life. Team members can act as friends, parents, or other people in the lives of the central character. As kids act out the scenes, they are likely to add revealing comments or actions that reflect similar situations they or their friends have experienced in real life. When they finish, you can make the same applications by determining whether each person is in the "OK Zone," "Warning Zone," or "Danger Zone." But in this case, based on how the characters were portrayed in the skits, group members might also be able to make specific recommendations as to what the characters could do differently to stay in the "OK Zone."

STEP 3

As you discuss Matthew 5:27-30, assign a "body part" (eye, hand, foot, ear, etc.) to each group member. Then ask questions about lust—nothing embarrassing or too personal, but specific enough to require honest responses. For example:
Eyes—**Have you seen any TV shows or movies this week that focused on the sexual aspects of one of the characters? Have you looked at any magazines or catalogs that featured scantily clothed people as an attempt to turn you on or sell you something?**
Hands—**Have you picked up *Playboy* or a similar magazine this week? Did you pop a video that you knew contained nudity in your VCR?**
Feet—**Did you go to any R-rated movies this week? Did you go to any parties in which a lot of sexual activity was taking place?**
Ears—**Did you listen to any jokes that demeaned the opposite sex? Did you listen in on any 1-900 phone lines?**

Each time someone admits to involvement in one of these activities, "cut" him or her off from the rest of the body. After you "lose" several members, ask: **Could you blame your problem on some other body part?** (Point out that if we go somewhere we don't belong, we usually end up seeing what we shouldn't see, doing what we shouldn't do, and hearing what we shouldn't hear.) Ask: **Which is worse: eliminating a problem area or letting it keep getting the rest of the body in trouble?** (The best option is to keep the body part, but eliminate its lustful activities.)

STEP 5

Have kids answer the questions as a group rather than in pairs. Kids may be uncomfortable discussing lust in a group; but it's important for them to begin to open up to each other. Point out that if they can't even *discuss* the topic, they won't be able to effectively *help* each other.

STEP 1

After the opening exercise, emphasize the importance of the subject you're about to discuss. Use the most recent statistics you can find about sexual activity and attitudes, but customize it for your group. Suppose you have 25 guys and 25 girls. Rather than explaining that surveys show that 54 percent of high schoolers have had sex, you might say: **If this were an average group, 27 of you have already had sex. If you were all seniors, 36 of you** (72 percent) **would be sexually active. Two of you** (4 percent) **would have a sexually transmitted disease.** (Source: Centers for Disease Control, January 1992). Here are some additional observations collected from 19,958 readers of *Sassy* magazine (October 1992):
• 67 percent of girls have told a guy "I love you" without meaning it. (Only 15 percent of guys said they had done the same to girls.)
• 62 percent of guys have stereotyped a girl as a slut because of the way she dressed.
• 91 percent of guys said it wouldn't bother them if a girl they liked thought they were virgins.
• 63 percent of guys and 68 percent of girls have turned down offers of sex with someone they liked.

STEP 2

Rather than filling out index cards with the activities listed in the text, get group members involved in the process. Have each person give you a reason why some people *might* be led to lust. Explain that you're just looking for general problem areas, not personal ones. You might even want to make an elimination activity out of this. When someone is unable to come up with a new idea, he or she is out. Continue until you have just a few people left. Then jokingly applaud them for being the ones in your group who know the most about lust. Write the suggestions on index cards as they are named. Then discuss on which side of the line each one should go.

STEP 2

Announce that you've discovered a device that cures people of lust. Then hand out blindfolds (or sunglasses with the lenses covered with dark paper). Have kids put them on. Ask: **How effective do you think this device will be in fighting lust? Why?** As a group, develop a list of situations in which people should consider wearing these devices. Examples might include looking at magazine racks, watching cable TV, walking past adult videos at the video store, etc. Ask: **If a device were developed that really stopped lust, how well do you think it would sell? Why? Who do you think would buy it? Who do you think would protest it?** Questions like these might get kids thinking about the subject in new ways. They might see that some people don't want to get rid of lust because they enjoy it too much.

STEP 3

The story of David and Bathsheba is used a lot to deal with the topic of lust—as it should be. But if your group members don't seem to think they have anything else to learn, let them recreate the story in a variety of ways. One group might try to bring the story into a twentieth-century setting. Another might attempt to tell the story from a gender-reversal point of view. (Don't girls lust too?) It's one thing to *know* the facts of this story, but it may take a bit of creative writing to get your kids past the facts to deal with the mind-sets and emotions of the characters involved.

STEP 3

Matthew 5:27-30 is a difficult passage for trained theologians to deal with—much less students without much Bible background. Before you even begin to deal with it, let group members do an impromptu skit. One person should play the CEO of a large company. Other people, two at a time, should come into the CEO's office. One person in each pair should accuse the other of a serious offense—and have the proof to back up his or her accusations. In the first pair, perhaps the offender has been embezzling money from the company. Another person might have gotten the company into serious tax trouble. Another could be running his own business using the CEO's company's resources (copier, paper, supplies, stamps, etc.). Have the CEO decide in each case what should happen to the offending employee. (Firing? Arrest? Both?) Then shift to the passage in Matthew and discuss how people are even more important than companies, so Jesus wants us to do whatever it takes to keep us from harming ourselves and/or others.

STEP 5

As a summary of everything you've discussed, you might need to replace the discussion of personal resistance of temptation with one centered on exactly why lust (or even sexual activity) is such a big deal. If your kids are more attuned to secular culture than biblical truth, some of them may not have ever been taught that lust and premarital sex are wrong. Be sensitive to this possibility. If you suspect some of your group members need a bit more grounding before they can get serious about making personal commitments in resisting sexual temptation, close with a question-and-answer period. Be ready with some basic Bible texts that will help kids work through their questions (Gal. 5:19-23; Eph. 5:1-14; Phil. 4:8-9; I Thess. 4:1-12; etc.).

STEP 3

One reason lust is such a potentially dangerous sin is that people don't usually like to talk about their sexual feelings—or even admit them to themselves. As you discuss lust openly in your group, try to plan ahead for the future when your kids aren't *in* the group. Have kids form teams of three with the people (of the same sex) in the group they know best. Ask them to commit to becoming "lust-escape partners." Explain that any time someone is feeling particularly vulnerable to lustful thoughts, he or she should be able to call one or both of his or her partners. If possible, the partners should try to do something together (jogging, shopping, etc.). If not, they can at least talk for a while until the person is able to "change the channel" of the thoughts going through his or her head. Partners might even pray for each other during these times—and on a regular basis. Explain that it may seem strange at first to call someone up and say, "I'm feeling a bit lustful right now. Would you like to talk?" But this is a better option than acting on one's lustful thoughts. Many people choose to call 1-900 numbers. Challenge your kids to call a friend instead.

STEP 5

It's sometimes difficult to discuss sexual issues with teenagers without making sex sound horrible or evil. You might consider ending the discussion of lust with a "Celebration of Sex" ceremony. Challenge kids to think of all the reasons they can be thankful for sex at this point in their lives. (The reason they're here today is because their parents had sex; it's a wonderful gift of God that they can look forward to when they get married; etc.) Also have them express thanks for acceptable sexual activities during adolescence (hand holding, good-night kisses, talking with a date in a romantic setting, etc.). Do everything you can to affirm the good and right things about sex (in the proper context) even as you agree to take a hard stand against lust and improper sexual activity.

MOSTLY GIRLS

MOSTLY GUYS

EXTRA FUN

STEP 3

As you discuss Matthew 5:28, before talking about David, ask your group members to define the word *lust*. Ask: **Is lust the same thing as having sexual desires? What about sexual thoughts? Why or why not?**

STEP 4

After the continuums are marked for the situations on "Lustbusters" (Repro Resource 1), refer back to the character of Steve. Ask your girls whether they think they have a responsibility toward guys like Steve. Ask: **If Steve were a part of our group, what might you do to help him? Should you just avoid him until he changes his ways? Why or why not?** As a group, discuss girls' influence on and responsibility toward guys. Ask: **What do you think about girls' dressing in ways that make them feel good because of the attention they might receive from the guys? Is it just the guys' problem if the style of dress influences their thoughts?**

STEP 1

Bring in some bath towels and soap. Say: **I thought we might need these later on. Can anyone guess why?** If no one guesses, explain that you're going to be talking about sex, and you thought group members might need to take cold showers after the session. Point out that you're going to talk specifically about lust. It shouldn't be hard to get guys talking about the subject, especially if there aren't any girls around. Ask: **How often do you think most guys think about sex? Why? What percent of the average guy's sexual thoughts would you say are "lustful"? How old were you when you had your first intense sexual thoughts? How did you feel at the time? Why do you think God gave us such strong sexual desires?**

STEP 2

A favorite justification among many guys for their lusting is that they wouldn't lust if girls dressed more modestly. So while you have a group of guys together, discuss this. Ask: **To what extent are girls responsible for the things you think about them?** Moderate the discussion to encourage a lot of different opinions, but don't comment immediately on statements that are made. After a while, when you're ready to move on, ask: **What can you do to keep certain girls from dressing the way they do?** (Nothing.) **Where can you live so that you won't see girls dress in provocative ways?** (Not many places.) **So is it OK for you to go right on lusting as long as there are girls who choose to wear short skirts or thong bathing suits?** (Obviously not.) Help your guys see that while they're seldom, if ever, responsible for how other people dress, they are *always* responsible for how they relate to other people. Consequently, we *never* have the right to blame others for our lust problems. The only reason we look and lust is because we choose to. And the only way to prevent it is to choose not to look.

STEP 2

Traditionally, guys are more outspoken about issues of lust and in admitting their involvement in lustful thoughts and expressions. It can be argued that the problem is just as prevalent among girls, but that they usually remain less open about it. Since girls probably receive more stares and comments than guys do, at least at this stage in life, give them an opportunity to turn the tables. Have the guys compete in a beauty contest. One option is to make it a "blind" contest in which the guys roll up their pants legs and hold their bare legs out from under a partition or blanket. No one should be able to tell whose leg is whose. Girls can then vote for #3, #7, or whomever. You should monitor the contest, and make sure this remains a fun activity for everyone. Afterward, discuss how the guys liked being the targets of attention based entirely on their physical attributes rather than intelligence, personality, or other positive features. Also point out how, if we aren't careful, teasing and "just for fun" comments can get out of hand, leading to hurt feelings, damaged self-image, lust, and other harmful results.

STEP 5

Explain (tongue in cheek) that sometimes we don't begin to deal with lust quickly enough because we don't recognize it. Explain that you want all of your group members to show the others what a lustful expression looks like. They should use facial expressions only—no other body language. Perhaps you might go around the room, one at a time, and let kids try to appear lustful. Or you might have group members sit in a circle and simultaneously make their lustful faces. Have some fun with this. But then make a serious point that while you're having fun and laughing hard, it's hard to act genuinely lustful. That's an important thing to remember the next time you need to break out of a lustful mood. Stop thinking so much in sexual terms and go have some *real* fun with someone.

STEP 2

As you consider sources of potential lust, turn on a television set and begin to flip through the channels (or watch some video clips you've recorded earlier). Have kids try to identify anything that might be intended to arouse sexual thoughts. Listen for sexual jokes, comments, double entendres, etc. Evaluate the dress and body language of the characters. Examine the relationships of the characters. Even if you don't find any terribly offensive examples while doing this, you are likely to at least jar the memories of your group. Ask: **What are some things you've seen on TV lately that you're glad we didn't see as a group right now?** Challenge group members to think of music videos, cable shows, dating shows, 900-number ads, and so forth.) **Do you think you build up an immunity to these kinds of things, or do you think that over time they are likely to have a bigger influence on you than you might think?**

STEP 5

By now, you've discussed that certain magazines are common sources of lustful thoughts. Some people use the print media to make a lot of money by having millions of people lust over naked (or near-naked) models. So spend some time before you close thinking about how you might be able to *discourage* people from lusting. Create your own magazine to do this. Give it a title, decide on some key articles for the first issue, design a cover if you wish, and determine what regular columns and features it would need. (If your group is a bit more "spotlight oriented," let them do a pilot for a new TV show that would serve the same purpose. It should be good enough to be on against *Studs* and *Love Connection* and still hold viewers' attention.)

STEP 1

One way to condense the session is to focus on the personal application. Most young people don't need a lot of convincing that lust is a problem they must deal with. One shortcut is to do the activity in Step 1 and then skip Step 2. When you get to Step 3, start by reading Matthew 5:27-30 followed immediately by 2 Samuel 11:1-5. Before discussing anything else, ask: **How could David have followed Jesus' instructions to "gouge out" an eye that offended him?** Let kids come to the conclusion that, rather than actually poking out his eye, David could simply have turned around and walked the other way. It would have been that easy. But he gave in to his lustful thoughts and his life was never the same. Then move on to Steps 4 and 5, trying to help kids see how they can "turn around" rather than give in to their own lustful thoughts.

STEP 2

Perhaps you prefer to focus more on the Bible study aspects than the personal applications. If so, begin the session with Step 2. Then go through Step 3 as written. Be sure everyone understands the various Bible texts: Matthew 5:27-30; 2 Samuel 11:1-5; and Hebrews 4:15-16. Step 4 can be eliminated. But if you do have time, brainstorm suggestions for the bottom of Repro Resource 1—things that may lead to lust and things that may lead away from lust. This can easily be used as a transition between Step 3 and Step 5.

STEP 2

Tape a 10-foot line on the floor. Have all of your group members stand side by side on one side of the line. Then choose a volunteer to stand on the other side of the line. The object of the activity is for the volunteer to see how many times he or she can step over the line and back without being pulled over completely by the rest of the group. Each time the person jumps over the line and back, he or she gets a point. (To get a point, the person must have both feet on the other side of the line before he or she jumps back.) The rest of the group members must try to prevent the person from jumping back over the line. However, they may not reach across the line to grab him or her. Set a one-minute time limit. Then ask for other volunteers to try it. You might want to award a small prize to the person with the most points. Use the activity to introduce a discussion of how "crossing the line" with lust can be dangerous.

STEP 4

If you have an advanced, mature group of kids, you might want to use the following situation in conjunction with Repro Resource 1: **James is a 15-year-old church youth who says he does not have a lust problem. But he frequently buys *Hustler* and *Playboy* to assist him when he masturbates. One of his friends knows what he does and has tried to confront him, but James's response is, "There's nothing wrong with this. After all, it's safer than sex and better than getting AIDS. I'm not hurting anybody."**

STEP 3

It can be difficult to deal with junior highers when you get into sexual issues. You know that some of them are already dealing with issues like lust and other sexual temptations, but others may still be enjoying some degree of innocence that you don't want to shatter. So when it comes to forming discussion teams, try to group your kids according to experience. Try to keep the younger ones together while those you know are dealing with sexual issues talk among themselves. This kind of grouping should also help kids feel more comfortable. (The last thing you want is for one of your kids to feel inferior because he or she is in a group in which everyone else seems to be more sexually aware—which he or she might interpret as "experienced"—than he or she is.)

STEP 4

To help target temptations that are particularly hard for younger teens to overcome, do a skit. You (or one of your group members) should assume the role of an unscrupulous advertising executive. Your client manufactures condoms especially for high school students. As a ruthless ad person, your idea is to do whatever it takes to get junior highers sexually active by the time they get to high school, which will then benefit your client. (If nothing else, this activity should reveal the thinking behind some of the ads your kids see in magazines.) You should then have your staff (the students) advise you on the best strategies they could recommend to encourage junior highers to have sex. What you are likely to get in response are the temptations that most affect your group members. Afterward, explain that many junior highers might not be having sex simply because the right opportunity hasn't come along yet. Make sure your kids are willing to fight off lustful thoughts for the right reasons—not simply because they have nothing to worry about yet.

STEP 3

As you discuss Jesus' command to avoid lust, ask: **How do you think Jesus avoided lust? After all, He was followed around by many appreciative women whom He had healed or helped in some way. Prostitutes anointed His feet with perfume and used their hair to dry them. The Pharisees tried to trip Him up by bringing before Him a woman caught in adultery—who was possibly still naked. Jesus had a human body, just like the rest of us. How do you think He kept from lusting after all of these women?** After some discussion, kids should realize that Jesus never judged people on outward appearance. Rather, He saw past the physical aspects of people and saw them as spiritual children of His heavenly Father. We can do the same thing. It's hard and it takes a lot of practice, but we'll form stronger friendships as we are able to get past the outer (sexual?) attractions to other people and truly care about them as fellow, struggling, human beings.

STEP 5

As you deal with the ways that people try to avoid lusting after others, challenge group members by turning the question around. Say: Tell the truth. **Do you ever want to be lusted after? This isn't an easy question. Where do we draw the lines between having a positive self-image and a need for others to like us? When we're picking clothes, getting ready in the morning, and going through our regular grooming activities, what do we have in mind? Do we want to look attractive? Do we want to look "hot"? Do we even know?** It could be that some of your kids have less of a need to avoid lusting after others and more of a need to keep from trying to become an *object* of lust. Peter's words in I Peter 3:3-4 are addressed to wives, but should apply to all of us in today's culture.

DATE USED:

Approx. Time

STEP 1: *The Great Cover-Up* _____
❑ Extra Action
❑ Large Group
❑ Mostly Guys
❑ Short Meeting Time
Things needed:

STEP 2: *The Fine Line of Lust* _____
❑ Large Group
❑ Heard It All Before
❑ Mostly Guys
❑ Extra Fun
❑ Media
❑ Short Meeting Time
❑ Urban
Things needed:

STEP 3: *What's Love Got to Do with It?* _____
❑ Small Group
❑ Heard It All Before
❑ Little Bible Background
❑ Fellowship & Worship
❑ Mostly Girls
❑ Combined Junior High/High School
❑ Extra Challenge
Things needed:

STEP 4: *Lustbusters* _____
❑ Extra Action
❑ Mostly Girls
❑ Urban
❑ Combined Junior High/High School
Things needed:

STEP 5: *You Can Do It* _____
❑ Small Group
❑ Little Bible Background
❑ Fellowship & Worship
❑ Extra Fun
❑ Media
❑ Extra Challenge
Things needed:

Are Mountain-Moving Prayers Possible?

YOUR GOALS FOR THIS SESSION:

Choose one or more

☐ To help kids gain new insights into prayer.

☐ To help kids understand why some prayers may seem to go unanswered.

☐ To help kids persist in prayer for some unresolved issues.

☐ Other:_____
_____

Your Bible Base:

Matthew 17:14-20
Luke 11:5-13
James 4:3
1 John 5:14-15

Word Pictures

(Needed: Copies of Repro Resource 2, pencils)

Before the session you'll need to make several copies of "Fractured Answers" (Repro Resource 2). Cut most of the sheets in half lengthwise and discard the right side. But be sure to keep several whole sheets for a charade activity.

Have group members form teams of four. Explain that the teams will be competing in a charade activity. Ask each team to choose one member to act out the charade and another to record the team's answers.

Give team members copies of the left side of Repro Resource 2. Then gather the "actors" from each team together and give them full copies of Repro Resource 2. Explain that they are to act out each phrase ("wet behind the ears," "rub my nose in it," etc.) for their teammates. They may not say anything to their teammates or even mouth words, but must act out the meaning of the words. As a last resort, they may act out words that sound like the words in the phrase. (The "sounds like" signal is pulling on the ear.)

Send the "actors" back to their teams to begin. The first team to guess its actor's clues and complete the four clichés wins.

Afterward, ask: **What do all these phrases that were acted out have in common—"wet behind the ears," "rub my nose in it," "the straw that broke the camel's back," and "risen to new heights"?** (They're all clichés, metaphors, and figurative ways of saying things.)

Explain: **Today's tough passage is tough not only because it talks about how to do the impossible, but because it's also written in figurative language.**

Have group members turn in their Bibles to Matthew 17:20. Ask a volunteer to read it aloud.

Then say: **Jesus wasn't saying that Christians are supposed to go up to mountains and say, "Hey, take a swim." What do you think He was saying?** (Through prayer, Christians can accomplish great things.)

In New Testament times, people used figurative language or metaphors to describe their great teachers who could explain difficulties. They called these teachers "uprooters"

of mountains, much the way today we call people who get things done "movers and shakers."

Ask: **How much faith did Jesus say you needed to be a spiritual "mover and shaker"?** (Not much—"faith as small a mustard seed," which is very small.)

How does this fact make you feel? Some group members may feel empowered that such a small faith can produce so much. Others may feel ashamed that they don't have even that much faith. Still others may be bewildered because their small faith does not seem to produce these dramatic results.

S.O.S. Prayer Requests

(Needed: Copies of Repro Resource 3, pencils)

Explain: **This verse about moving mountains with a small amount of faith makes some people wonder why their small faith doesn't seem to do much good. Let's look at some of the prayers you may have prayed that may or may not have been answered.**

Distribute copies of "Everyday Teen Prayers" (Repro Resource 3) and pencils. Read aloud the instructions. Then give an example of a substitution for the first prayer (e.g., "that the car keys I locked in the car would miraculously appear in my pocket") to give group members an idea of what you're looking for.

Give group members a few minutes to work. When they're finished, ask volunteers to share some of their responses.

Then say: **This list mentions a few serious matters such as gangs and getting along with parents. What are some other serious items that you've prayed for? Have they been answered?** If possible, try to remember group members' responses. You can refer to them later in the session.

STEP
3

Clues to Unanswered Prayer

(Needed: Bibles, chalkboard and chalk or newsprint and marker)

Say: **When our prayers aren't answered the way we want them answered, it's easy to feel disappointed with God. It's also easy to feel disappointed in our own faith—that it's so small we can't move a mountain, or even a molehill! That's how the disciples felt when Jesus told them about the power of prayer.**

Have someone read aloud Matthew 17:14-20. Then explain the background for this incident: **The disciples had failed to cast out a demon because they lacked faith. Jesus tried to inspire them, to give them hope. With just a little faith, He said, they could do great things!**

Write the following question on the board: "Why do some prayers seem to go unanswered?"

Have group members form three teams (perhaps the same teams you used for the charades game in Step 1). Assign each team one of the following Scripture passages: James 4:3; 1 John 5:14-15; Luke 11:5-13. Instruct the teams to look up their assigned passages to find clues to the question on the board.

Give the teams a few minutes to work. When they're finished, have each one share its clue. Write the clues on the board as teams share them. Use the following suggestions to supplement the teams' responses.

- Clue #1: Some requests are made with wrong motives (James 4:3).
- Clue #2: Some requests don't follow God's will (1 John 5:14-15).
- Clue #3: Sometimes God wants to teach us something by making us wait—but that doesn't mean we shouldn't keep asking with boldness (Luke 11:5-13).

Use the following information to guide your discussion of the three assigned Scripture passages.

For James 4:3: **Some prayers are unwise. We pray with wrong motives, focusing on our own pleasure and disregarding what others need. This may explain why the disciples' faith was not strong enough to cast out the demon** (Matt. 17:16). **Perhaps their motives were impure and they were "showing off" God's power.**

What kinds of prayers probably aren't answered because they're asked with the wrong motives? (Prayers for luxuries and riches so that we will feel better about ourselves, so that we can impress others, or so that we won't have to work hard, etc.)

Point out that this doesn't mean God doesn't want people to enjoy themselves, but self-indulgence makes a person self-centered. Self-centeredness taints our relationships and takes our focus off God's purpose in our lives.

For I John 5:14-15: **This is similar to the problem of having mixed motives. God is eager to give us what we want, but He wants us to seek His will.**

How can we know what God's will is? (The simplest way to define His will is by the clear commands of Scripture.)

Point out that the two greatest commandments are to love God and to love others (Matt. 22:37-40). As Jesus said, these two commands sum up all the law and the prophets.

What kinds of prayers probably aren't answered because they violate these two commandments? (Requests that would harm others, requests that would lead to sexual impurity or other sin, requests that are selfish, etc.)

For Luke 11:5-13: **This passage may provide the best answer to our question; but it, too, is difficult. Jesus is not saying that God is like the grouchy neighbor who doesn't want to be bothered, though sometimes it may seem like it. Jesus tells the disciples to ask, to seek, and even to knock if they have to in order to get what they want. In other words, keep praying. Don't give up. You will get what you ask for, and even more, if you keep on praying.**

What kinds of things might God be able to teach us by making us wait for the answer to a sincere prayer? (He can teach us patience and faith. He can help us learn about ourselves— what's really important to us that we're not willing to give up on. He can teach us about Himself. He might not give us what we thought we wanted, but He could give us a better relationship with Himself.)

What kinds of prayers do we often have to wait to see answered? (Prayers for someone's salvation, prayers for relationships, prayers for personal growth, prayers for understanding for why something has happened, prayers for health concerns, etc.)

Ask: **Is it possible that we don't see our prayers answered because we give up too soon?** Get a few responses.

If you have time, offer one other explanation for prayers that seem to go unanswered. Explain: **God will not violate a person's free will on behalf of another person. In other words, we can't change others or force them to do certain things just by praying. People can choose whether or not to accept Christ,** or to like you or not like you. God will not allow us to use prayer and faith as "weapons" to control others.

What kinds of prayers seem to go unanswered because people exercise their free will against God's will? (Prayers that nations will not attack each other in war, prayers for safety—people endanger their own lives and others by being careless, prayers that family members will make peace with each other, etc.)

Explain: **Even though God will not violate another person's free will, He does influence people. And we must remember that He is ultimately in control. Despite what anybody else does or doesn't do, God will accomplish His purposes. Our prayers are a part of that process—otherwise He wouldn't have commanded us to pray.**

STEP
4

Practice Prayers

(Needed: Chalkboard and chalk or newsprint and marker, a hand-held weight, copies of Repro Resource 3)

Hold up a hand-held weight. Ask: **Which comes first—the ability to lift a weight or the muscles to do it? I could say that I can't lift weights because I don't have enough muscles. I could also say that I don't have muscles because I don't lift weights. The truth is that the two build each other. As you lift weights, your muscles gain strength. As your muscles gain strength, you can lift more weights. Prayer and faith are the same way. Prayer builds faith and faith builds prayer. You keep practicing and working out, and they both grow.**

Let's look again at some of the requests on the "Everyday Teen Prayers" handout. The clues on the board help us see that we need to examine our motives, make sure that what we're asking for is in accordance with God's will, be persistent in our prayers, and remember that other people have free wills of their own.

Focus group members' attention on some of the following requests from Repro Resource 3 or on some of the requests group members mentioned at the end of Step 2.

Ask: **What would a prayer of faith sound like for this request?**

OPTIONS

HEARD IT ALL BEFORE

FELLOWSHIP & WORSHIP

MOSTLY GIRLS

MOSTLY GUYS

MEDIA

EXTRA CHALLENGE

- *Request #3: That I'll make the final cut for the basketball team.* ("Lord, I need Your guidance. Will it help me or hurt me to be a part of the basketball team? Is this an ego trip? Do I want this because it could help me get a scholarship to college or because I just plain enjoy it? It would help me stay fit, but how will I react if I don't make it? Lord, I want Your will in this.")

- *Request #4: That a certain person of the opposite sex would notice me.* ("Show me, God, if this person would be a good influence on me. If so, how could I serve this person instead of hoping he or she will make me look good to others or feel good about myself? Help this person follow Your will too. If this person would not be good for me, please help me give up my feelings for him or her.")

- *Request #7: That a hot car would appear in my driveway tomorrow for me.* ("Lord, You know how much I want a car. If I had a nice car, I would want to use it to serve You. But I know that it would also be an ego trip to impress others. Help me be content with what I have and trust You to meet all my needs.")

- *Request #9: That a friend who's been ignoring me will want to be friends again.* ("Show me, Lord, if I've offended my friend. Do I have any attitudes that hurt other people? If my friend is going through troubles, help me figure out how to be his or her friend without being a pest. If this friend keeps ignoring me, help me to get over the hurt and find other friends.")

- *Request #10: That I would get along better with my parents.* ("God, help me to try to be more respectful to my parents even when we disagree. Help me explain my position calmly and not resent them or get mad at them. Help them to give me a break, to see that I want to try to get along with them.")

The Pause That Refreshes

Close the session with a time of prayer. Say: **Think of something you've prayed for that seems to have gone unanswered. Or maybe you haven't formally prayed for it, but you've wished for it.** Give group members a minute or two to think. **Consider the reasons on the board why prayers don't seem to be answered and pray again about this issue.**

Allow a few minutes of quiet time for prayer. Then close by praying aloud, asking God to help you and your group members bring your requests to Him, remaining open to His will and His answers to prayer.

Fractured Answers

1

What's wrong with that new cook? Can't he fry burgers?

REPLY: No, he's …

1

wet behind the ears.

2

You sure did a bad job!

REPLY: Don't …

2

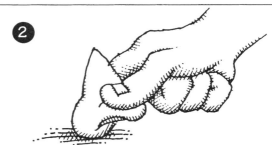

rub my nose in it!

3

I'm sorry I dropped your mirror and spilled your styling gel. Now I've broken your hair dryer too.

REPLY: That's the …

3

straw that broke the camel's back.

4

I knew she liked to study, but I can't believe she's going to be valedictorian.

REPLY: Yes, she's …

4

risen to new heights.

Everyday Teen Prayers

Check the prayers below that you've prayed. Below the ones you don't check, write the closest thing to it that you've prayed.

_____ 1. That my lost contact lens would miraculously reappear in the soap dish after gurgling down the drain.
Similar prayer: _____
_____

_____ 2. That I would instantly understand everything I didn't learn in Algebra I so I can understand Algebra II.
Similar prayer:_____
_____

_____ 3. That I'll make the final cut for the basketball team.
Similar prayer: _____
_____

_____ 4. That a certain person of the opposite sex would notice me.
Similar prayer: _____
_____

_____ 5. That a zit would disappear overnight.
Similar prayer: _____
_____

_____ 6. That a younger brother or sister would disappear overnight.
Similar prayer: _____
_____

_____ 7. That a hot car would appear in my driveway tomorrow for me.
Similar prayer: _____
_____

_____ 8. That I would be safe from gang activity.
Similar prayer: _____
_____

_____ 9. That a friend who's been ignoring me will want to be friends again.
Similar prayer:_____
_____

_____ 10. That I would get along better with my parents.
Similar prayer: _____
_____

EXTRA ACTION

STEP 1

To begin the session, have group members form two or three teams for a relay. At one end of a large room or open area, pile up a large stack of assorted junk. Some things should be small and others large—but not so large that they couldn't be picked up by all group members. (All you need to do is clean out a closet and pile up the items you take out.) Teams should line up, single file, parallel to each other, across the length of the room. At your signal, the teams should try to move the stack of stuff from one end of the room to the other by picking up one item at a time and passing it, fire-brigade style, to the other end. Each team should maintain a stack separate from the others' at the other side of the room. After several minutes, stop and check to see who has the largest pile and/or the most items. Refer to this exercise when you get to the verse about moving mountains, and explain that there's an easier way.

STEP 2

Begin this step by dividing members into teams. Have each team write and perform a skit. The theme of the skit should be "You never listen to me!" The teams may do anything they want for that theme. Some skits may deal with parents, friends, brothers and sisters, teachers, and so forth. Although the skits will probably contain a lot of humor, you should also be able to detect students' *feelings* when they sense they aren't being heard. This information will be valuable as you approach the topic of unanswered prayer. If they feel bad when they feel ignored by someone they love, how do they feel when they think God is ignoring them?

SMALL GROUP

STEP 1

To help emphasize the "faith the size of a mustard seed" concept, bring a variety of fruits and vegetables (and possibly flowers). Have each group member take a different fruit or vegetable, dig out a few of the seeds, and show the size difference among the seeds. In some cases the difference won't be phenomenal (in a blackberry, for instance). In other cases, there will be major size differences. (Try to have on hand some sunflower seeds, acorns, or pecans and discuss the potential of such seeds.) Explain that it would be easy enough to eat or disregard the seeds. But if they are planted, with a bit of faith and a long period of patient waiting, they will produce large, delicious fruit. Apply this concept not only to prayer, but to your group as well. Emphasize that being small in size (or numbers) is not necessarily good or bad in itself. More important is what you do as a small group and the attitudes you have as you wait for growth.

STEP 3

Instead of breaking into even smaller groups to study the Bible passages, go through them together. Just be sure everyone stays involved and is not allowed to sit back while other people answer all of the questions. One way to keep everyone in the discussion is to use group members' names when you refer to various prayers. If it's Denny's prayer that a hot car appear in his driveway or Belinda's desire that a certain guy would notice her, the session will take on a more personal appeal. And just hearing their names being used will usually pull most people out of their daydreams and back into reality.

LARGE GROUP

STEP 1

To introduce the topic of prayer, say: **True or false—Large groups don't need to be quite as devoted to prayer as small groups. After all, if we need a mountain moved, we can usually shovel it away ourselves or hold a fund-raiser to get it done.** Most kids will say that the answer is false. But challenge them to prove it. Can they think of a time when one person's small prayer was more powerful than the actions of another large group? (They might recall Moses at the Red Sea as God took the Israelites safely through while the Egyptians drowned [Exod. 14:13-31]; Elijah and the priests of Baal [I Kings 18:25-40]; etc.) Explain that perhaps the main obstacle to effective prayer is trying to handle things on our own. Sometimes in a large group, that tendency is even stronger than in other groups. Challenge group members to think in terms of their one-on-one relationship with God during the rest of the session.

STEP 3

Think of a simple trick that anyone can do if he or she knows the "secret"; but choose one that most of your group members won't know. One simple trick is the "magnetic" Bic pen. Hold a Bic pen in one hand and the pointed cap in the other. Slowly bring them closer together. As soon as they get close, the cap "magically" leaps onto the pen with considerable force. (With a bit of saliva on the thumb and forefinger holding the cap, and a squeeze, the cap will shoot out of your hand and onto the pen.) Pass the "magic" pen around and see how many people have the same "power" you have. Point out that it can be embarrassing to be in front of a large group and fail to figure out some simple thing that someone else can do easily. Tie this into how the disciples might have felt when they publicly failed to cast out the demon that Jesus removed at once. Explain that kids can avoid that powerless feeling if they begin to establish a direct link to God through prayer.

STEP 3

To help your kids understand why God may not answer prayer as we wish He would (even though they may assume they know), preface the discussion with a skit. Group members should act as a group of kids who have come to a Christian conference to spend the weekend, hear some speakers and musicians, and get to know each other. They've just arrived, and this is the first time they've seen each other. Hand out slips of paper to assign different roles for kids to play. One person's paper should say, "You desperately want to make friends with these people. Your goal is to spend quality time with every person while you're here." All of the other papers should say things like "You've been up all night for the past three days, studying for exams, and you're desperately tired." "You're in a coma." "You were forced to come here. You don't like Christians or anything they stand for." Begin the roleplay and watch as one person tries to communicate with the others. Afterward, explain that sometimes there are perfectly good reasons why other people don't respond to us in the way we expect. The same is true of prayer. We may expect a certain answer from God, but He may have a good reason not to respond as we anticipated.

STEP 4

Demonstrate the need for commitment not only to individual growth, but to the group as well. Have one of the largest kids in the group sit in a chair. Then ask the smallest person to pick him up—chair and all. After he or she attempts this, add another small person. Let the two struggle. Then add a third, and so on. Show that as you keep adding people, the job becomes less of a hassle—and maybe even more fun. Emphasize that, while individual spiritual growth (and prayer) is very important, we can draw a lot of support from other people as well. We need to pray for them and help them pray for us by sharing our needs, hopes, and dreams.

STEP 1

It's likely that group members who have only a little Bible background may find it particularly hard to comprehend the figurative language of being able to "move mountains" with prayer. However, in this case, you can help them by referring them to a phrase they may be more familiar with: "making mountains out of molehills." Discuss the meaning of the familiar expression. Then explain that Jesus was trying to show us the other side of the expression. We do tend to make mountains out of molehills in many areas of our lives. But with prayer, we can make mountains *into* molehills. Worry exaggerates our problems. Prayer reduces them down to a manageable size— because we trust God to do the managing instead of ourselves. Be sensitive throughout this session for phrases that may seem quite natural in Christian circles—but that may seem strange or incomprehensible for some of your group members.

STEP 3

When you get to the "clues" as to why God may not answer prayers, slow down and take your time with the section. It's more important that your group members understand these concepts than that you get finished with the session. On one hand, you're telling them that sometimes God has good reasons for not answering us as we wish He would. On the other hand, you're telling them to pray persistently and with all of the faith they can muster. You're right in both cases, but a person new to Christian teaching may not see the logic in repeated praying and steadfast faith if God has good reasons not to answer. Provide a lot of time to encourage questions during this portion of the session.

STEP 4

Have your group members do a bit of self-evaluation when they get to this step. Since "prayer builds faith, and faith builds prayer," it is important to continue to develop both. Ask: **In your own life, which would you say is stronger— your faith or your prayer life?** Give kids time to think about it and respond. Then put the strong-faith people in one group and the strong-prayer people in another. Let those who can't decide go to the group with fewer people. Ask each group to compose a list of guidelines that would help the other group. (The prayer people should do a "Tips for More Effective Praying" list to give the faith people, and the faith people should do a "Tips for Building Stronger Faith" list for the prayer people.) Lists should include hints that members can attest to from personal experience as well as other things they know to be true from Scripture or previous teaching. During the next week, make copies of both lists to hand out to everyone as you challenge group members to "build up their muscles" in both of these areas.

STEP 5

One of the worst things you can do is talk about prayer all the way through this session and then quickly close in prayer as you normally do—without any practical application of what you've been talking about. Encourage everyone to take part in the closing, even if he or she says just a sentence prayer. If nothing else, kids should be able to express thanks for something they learned during the session. In that case, part of the prayer might focus on how we can benefit when God answers prayer; another part might focus on how we can benefit when God *doesn't* answer prayer as we expect. In either case, we can always count on God's faithfulness to us, and should take plenty of time to express our thanks to Him.

STEP 2

After your group members respond to "Everyday Teen Prayers" (Repro Resource 3), ask them to think of questions they've had about prayer in the last few years. Have them try to remember how they understood prayer or felt about praying when they were young children. See if they can recite any prayers that they learned as children, like "Now I lay me down to sleep . . ." Then ask: **What is different about your concept of prayer now? What are your questions about prayer now?**

STEP 4

Ask your group members to form teams of four to discuss the following questions: **"Is my faith in my ability to pray or in God and His power? What difference would it make either way?"** Give the teams a few minutes to discuss their responses; then have them share what they discussed.

STEP 3

As you discuss God's responses to our requests, be particularly sensitive to the fact that many people—perhaps guys more than girls—tend to see their heavenly Father in much the same way that they see their human fathers. Guys who've been pushing for more privileges, or who may be going through a rebellious stage, could at this point in their lives have a strained relationship with their fathers. They may be told no quite often when they ask for things. As a result, they may come to expect the same tension any time they ask God for something. Ask: **How do your parents usually respond when you ask them for something out of the ordinary? What's the most unusual request you've made of them lately? What's the most unusual request you've made of God lately? Do you make assumptions about God based on the responses of your parents? If so, in what ways?** If you don't deal openly with these issues, your guys may interpret many of the comments in this session as a spiritual version of "Because I said so, that's why!" Do what you can to make a distinction between an all-knowing, all-loving God and our human, fallible, imperfect parents.

STEP 4

Say: **Be completely honest here. What would you be most proud of—a very strong and muscular body, or a very strong and productive prayer life? Why?** Let guys respond. Then ask: **Does prayer sometimes seem a bit "feminine" or "wimpy" to you? Do you usually pray for everything you need, or mostly for the things you know you can't get on your own? Do you really believe Jesus when He says that strength comes from prayer?** Try to detect any underlying attitudes that prayer is a "last resort" or that "real men don't pray." Emphasize that prayer is the only constant source of real strength—for any person in any situation.

STEP 3

Sometime during this step you might find it effective to play "Gossip." Have group members sit in a circle. Whisper a message into the ear of one person. (The message should be written, word for word, on a piece of paper.) The message should then be whispered, person to person, around the room. A person may not repeat the message after he or she has said it once. Each person must pass along exactly what he or she thinks he or she hears. When the message gets to the last person, have him or her say it aloud. Then compare it to what was written on the paper. Most of the time the message will be considerably different, and you can backtrack to see where it got distorted. This exercise can point out that sometimes a message (or perhaps an answer to prayer) can start out clear, but become distorted by other noise or circumstances so that we misunderstand what is being said.

STEP 5

Wrap up the session with all of your group members (except for the smallest guy) sitting in a circle on the floor, close enough together for all of their feet to touch in the center as they extend their legs. The smallest guy should stand in the center of the circle with the others' feet pushed up tight against him. The center person should then hold his hands to his side, make his body stiff, and topple in the direction of his choice. The other group members should be close enough to reach out and keep him from falling, passing him on to others in the group. With some practice, a group can get a person spinning around the circle pretty fast. Point out that as your center person learns to trust the others, the experience can be thrilling. So it is with God. As we learn to trust Him more completely when we come to Him in prayer, our lives take on a new vitality.

STEP 3

In conjunction with the Bible study teams, have group members suppose they are reporters for a first-century tabloid, *The Jerusalem Tattler.* Ask them to create attention-grabbing headlines for the passages they are studying (Jas. 4:3; I John 5:14-15; and Luke 11:5-13). You can use the passage you already covered (Matt. 17:14-20) to practice with. Some examples might include:

• "Lose Tons in Just Days with New, Mountain-Moving Prayer Diet"

• "Amazing Mustard Seed Miracle Cure for Demon Possession"

• "Country Preacher's Astounding Claim: Nothing Is Impossible!"

Point out that many tabloid stories miss the point and don't quite print the truth. So in each case, the headlines can be a bit exaggerated (after all, they need to sell papers), but teams should also be able to cite all of the facts as well.

STEP 4

Follow up on the "muscle development" theme in this step. Put together a workout video that would help others tone up flabby spiritual muscles. Work together as a group on the project. Some group members will need to determine what exercises need to be done and how often they should be repeated for proper strength. Others will need to actually demonstrate the exercises on camera. Still others should be responsible for the taping, lighting, and other technical aspects of the video (assuming you have access to a video camera). You might also want to think about appropriate "celebrities" (prominent pray-ers in your church or community) who might endorse or participate in the video. Have some fun with this, and the kids will remember the point of the exercise far longer than a traditional lecture or discussion.

STEP 2

Give a brief introduction and start the session with Repro Resource 3. When students finish, let volunteers share some of their responses. As you move into Step 3, you can save a lot of time by summarizing the Bible content rather than dividing into teams to discuss it and report back. Consequently, you should still have plenty of time to do Steps 4 and 5, focusing on improving and practicing prayer habits.

STEP 3

Another effective session shortcut is to simply do Steps 3 and 5. With this option, you might also want to open the session with Repro Resource 3. By the time your students work through the handout, divide into groups, discuss the Bible content, and report back, you should have just enough time to discuss the application material at the end of Step 3 and in Step 5.

STEP 3

Try using skits to communicate that prayer is personal conversation with God and that it requires our listening. Ask for volunteers to perform the following three skits:

• *Skit 1*—A kid has a question that only God can answer. While the kid ponders the question, a phone rings. On the other end of the line is God, calling to answer the kid's question. The tension of the skit lies in the fact that the kid can't decide whether to answer the phone or not. The point is that when God calls us with answers, the decision to respond to Him is often left up to the individual.

• *Skit 2*—A kid has a crisis at 4 a.m. and is trying to call someone for help. He or she calls friends, his or her pastor, etc., but everyone is too sleepy to offer immediate help. Finally, the person calls God, who is wide awake and more than willing to help. The point is that we can call God at any time.

• *Skit 3*—A kid is facing an issue in which he or she needs advice from God. The kid calls God several times for advice; but each time God starts to respond, the kid hangs up, thinking he or she has just come up with a solution on his or her own. The point is that it's no good to call God (pray) if we're not willing to listen or take the time to hear the answer God gives.

STEP 5

Have your teens include their own city in their prayers. Before praying, discuss some of the "mountains" that need to be moved in the city—problems that seem impossible to overcome. Your list will probably include things like crime, drugs, violence, racism, broken families, gangs, and AIDS. This list should help your group members pray more specifically.

STEP 1

Consider the maturity level of your group members before you even begin this session. Many junior highers may need a basic session on "What is prayer?" "How do you pray?" and "What's the big deal about praying?" before they're ready to try to move mountains. Ask: **If you knew a person you really liked who could protect you from bullies, give you neat stuff that you couldn't afford on your own, offer good advice to help you make hard decisions, and was willing to be your friend, would you want to develop the relationship? Why? How much time every day do you think you would spend with this person?** Explain that God more than fulfills these criteria for us, and that prayer is one of the major ways we spend time with Him. After you help your junior highers focus more on the importance of getting started with regular, personal prayer, then move on to Repro Resource 3 and the rest of the session.

STEP 3

Instead of dealing with the mountain-moving power of prayer, save that concept for later. Ask: **Does God answer every single one of your prayers?** Let kids respond. **Why do you think some prayers go unanswered?** Have group members examine the Bible texts (Jas. 4:3; 1 John 5:14-15; and Luke 11:5-13) together rather than in teams. You should guide the discussion and answer any questions kids might have. Then *close* with the mountain-moving concept, which should be an encouragement to younger and smaller members. After showing the importance of prayer, and the power that comes with more faithful praying, challenge your students to get more involved with regularly scheduled periods of prayer.

STEP 4

As you discuss the faith-prayer cycle and how the two are related, have someone read aloud Mark's version of the story of the man whose son had an evil spirit (Mark 9:14-29). Discuss the passage as a group, focusing on Jesus' words to the boy's father and the father's response. See if anyone else feels the same way as the father (who replied, "I do believe; help me overcome my unbelief!"). Ask: **What does it mean to believe, but to experience unbelief at the same time?** (Perhaps some people believe God is *capable* of doing anything, but not particularly interested in doing it for *them*.) Tie in this response to the need for strengthening our faith "muscles" and becoming stronger as we keep "working out."

STEP 5

In some cases, we may overlook the importance of prayer simply because we take so much answered prayer for granted. Maybe we only notice the times that God *doesn't* answer as we had hoped. If so, consider beginning a prayer journal for your group. At each meeting, ask for prayer requests and write them down, with the date. As prayers are answered, record those dates as well (and continue praying for the yet unanswered requests). Also keep up with notes of thanksgiving, which should be included in your prayers as well. Before long, your group members should be able to look back and see an intensely active God who plays a regular role in providing for their needs, helping them through hard times, and allowing them to experience truly abundant lives.

DATE USED:

Approx. Time

STEP 1: *Word Pictures* _____
- ❑ Extra Action
- ❑ Small Group
- ❑ Large Group
- ❑ Little Bible Background
- ❑ Combined Junior High/High School

Things needed:

STEP 2: *S.O.S. Prayer Requests* _____
- ❑ Extra Action
- ❑ Mostly Girls
- ❑ Short Meeting Time

Things needed:

STEP 3: *Clues to Unanswered Prayer* _____
- ❑ Small Group
- ❑ Large Group
- ❑ Heard It All Before
- ❑ Little Bible Background
- ❑ Mostly Guys
- ❑ Extra Fun
- ❑ Media
- ❑ Short Meeting Time
- ❑ Urban
- ❑ Combined Junior High/High School

Things needed:

STEP 4: *Practice Prayers* _____
- ❑ Heard It All Before
- ❑ Fellowship & Worship
- ❑ Mostly Girls
- ❑ Mostly Guys
- ❑ Media
- ❑ Extra Challenge

Things needed:

STEP 5: *The Pause That Refreshes* _____
- ❑ Fellowship & Worship
- ❑ Extra Fun
- ❑ Urban
- ❑ Extra Challenge

Things needed:

SESSION 3

What, Me Worry?

YOUR GOALS FOR THIS SESSION:

Choose one or more

☐ To help kids discover what God says about seeking His kingdom instead of worrying about the future.

☐ To help kids understand that there is a balance between proper planning and worry.

☐ To help kids choose not to worry about things over which they have no control.

☐ Other:_____
_____

Your Bible Base:

Proverbs 6:6-11
Matthew 6:25-34

The Blindfold Conspiracy

(Needed: Chalkboard and chalk or newsprint and marker, blindfolds)

Ask three or four volunteers to write a list of their five favorite music groups (or some other list of five or more things) on the board while they are blindfolded. Explain that the winner is the person whose list has the straightest left margin. If the margins are equally straight, the first one finished wins.

Blindfold the volunteers. Quietly whisper to one of them that you're going to remove his or her blindfold. Motion to the rest of the group not to say anything as you do so.

Say: **Ready, set, go!** Have the volunteers write their lists. When they're finished, have them all remove their blindfolds. Judge the columns. The contestant who wasn't blindfolded probably will have the straightest left column. Declare him or her the winner.

Afterward, explain to the rest of the contestants what you did. Then ask: **Why was it easier for the person who wasn't blindfolded to win?** (He or she could see what he or she was doing.)

What advantage was there in being able to see the board? (It gives the writer more control.)

Explain that today's "tough teaching" is about worry: "Do not worry about tomorrow, for tomorrow will worry about itself" (Matt. 6:34). Read the verse aloud.

Then say: **This brings up a lot of questions: How can I not worry when the world is in such a mess? Am I supposed to expect the things I need to drop out of the sky? If I don't plan for the future, won't I end up starving or homeless?**

No matter how hard the blindfolded people tried, they really couldn't make a straight list because they couldn't see the whole picture. In the same way, none of us can see the whole picture of our lives. We don't know what's going to happen tomorrow. But we have an advantage over other "blindfolded people." We know someone who can see the whole picture. God has no blindfold on.

Why Worry Shouldn't Win

(Needed: Bibles, pencils, copies of Repro Resource 4)

Have group members turn in their Bibles to Matthew 6:25-34. Distribute copies of "The Super-Duper, In-Depth Quiz for Astute Kids" (Repro Resource 4) and pencils. Instruct group members to complete the multiple-choice quiz, using Matthew 6:25-34 as a guide.

Give group members a few minutes to work. When they're finished, go through the answers one at a time. Use the following information to supplement group members' responses.

(1) b. Verse 25 says not to worry about your life (what you eat and drink) or your body (what you will wear).

(2) b. See verses 31 and 32.

(3) c. Verse 28 says the lilies do not labor or spin, but God still takes care of them—and we are more valuable than they are.

(4) b and c. Verse 34 teaches us to face our problems one day at a time. We should do what we can do about today and not worry about every little detail of the future. Verse 33 offers another reason not to worry about tomorrow: God provides the necessities.

(5) b. Verse 33 talks about seeking God's kingdom and righteousness, and trusting God to provide "all these things" (the necessities of life). Helping to supply basic necessities for others is commanded, and enjoying one's self is encouraged in other Bible passages, but they aren't mentioned here. (See I John 3:17 and Eccl. 3:1-8.)

Ask: **What does it mean to seek God's kingdom?** (To do His will, to acknowledge Him as Master and Lord.)

What does it mean to "seek ... [God's] righteousness"? Get a few responses. Then explain: **To seek God's righteousness means to desire to do the right thing, for the right reason. God is the only one who is truly righteous, but He commands us to be righteous as well** (Lev. 19:2). **Therefore we must seek His power to help us live righteously.**

(6) c. In verse 27, Jesus asks (tongue in cheek) if worrying does any good. Can it add even one measly hour to our lives? Yet some people like to worry. They figure maybe bad things won't happen if they worry and suffer enough.

Say: **The command not to worry about tomorrow may sound to some as though Jesus was telling people not to plan for the future at all.** But the Bible never contradicts itself,

O P T I O N S

SMALL GROUP

LARGE GROUP

HEARD IT ALL BEFORE

LITTLE BIBLE BACKGROUND

FELLOWSHIP & WORSHIP

MOSTLY GUYS

EXTRA FUN

SHORT MEETING TIME

EXTRA CHALLENGE

and other **passages tell us about the value of planning ahead. Proverbs 6:6-11 is one of those passages.**

Have someone read aloud Proverbs 6:6-11. Then say: **It's obvious that the ant wasn't lazy, but there's more than that. What can you learn about life through the ant?** (The ant planned ahead. During summer and fall, it harvested and stashed its food to eat during the winter when food would be scarce. The ant was resourceful. Also, the ant didn't need a boss. It did the job without being told to—it had initiative.)

What do you see as the difference between these two passages? Allow group members to come up with their own conclusions. Then go on to the next activity.

STEP
3

Extreme Thinking

(Needed: Chalkboard and chalk or newsprint and marker)

Draw a horizontal line from one end of the board to the other. Write "Worriers" on one end and "Sluggards" on the other. Draw a center point and some midpoints so that the line looks like a continuum. Point to the word "Worriers" and describe them. Be as extreme and sarcastic as you can.

Perhaps something like the following: **Worriers are sure that someone will figure out the combination to their lockers, break in, and steal their candy bar stash. When their VCRs break down, they don't call a repairman, they call a suicide hot line.**

Point to the word "Sluggards" and describe them similarly: **Sluggards think that their dirty clothes zoom through a secret passage from under their beds to the washing machine, wash themselves, and then zoom back into their drawers. They think that the answers to their homework will miraculously appear if they leave their homework in their locker overnight.**

These are extremes, of course, but tell us where on this continuum you would place yourself. Are you more of a worrier or more of a sluggard? Allow all of your group members to tell you where they fit on the continuum. Make a mark on the board to represent each person. Ask for examples of times group members

have either gone too far toward the worry side or too far toward the sluggard side of the continuum.

Say: **God does not want us to worry about tomorrow, but that's not an excuse to be lazy and make no plans either. What He does want us to do is trust Him.**

Write the word "Trust" in the middle of your continuum between "Worriers" and "Sluggards." Then say: **What Jesus was really trying to get at is "What is your ultimate goal in life?" We don't need to be obsessed or worried about the necessities of life. God knows we need those things. One of the things that should make a disciple of Jesus Christ different from a non-Christian** (the "pagans" in the Matthew passage) **is that our goal in life should not be our own financial security or status. We can trust that God will take care of us. We should not be foolish like the sluggard, but we don't have to be obsessed about material things either.**

STEP 4

Getting Concrete

Briefly discuss how the Matthew 6 and Proverbs 6 passages could apply to various things in your group members' lives such as getting good grades, buying a car, deciding on a career, deciding whether or whom to marry, going shopping, etc.

Ask: **Where does normal, constructive planning leave off and obsession begin? On the other hand, when does trusting God for our needs leave off and being a sluggard begin?** These are tough issues. Your group members will probably come up with different answers.

To get this discussion going with concrete examples, start with a for-instance such as what to do with your summer. Ask: **What should be the first step in figuring out what you're going to do with your summer?**

There are probably three general kinds of things group members might think of doing with their summers. One is fun and recreation. They might plan some kind of trip or anticipate spending as much time as possible at the beach, in the mountains, or doing some kind of recreation. Another obvious thing is to find a job to help save money for college, a car, etc. A third option would be to spend the summer, or

OPTIONS

LARGE GROUP

HEARD IT ALL BEFORE

MOSTLY GUYS

URBAN

JR.HIGH HIGH SCHOOL COMBINED

part of it, in some kind of mission or service project. Many kids may think about doing all three.

It is hoped they will see that the first thing they should do with this kind of a decision is to seek God's kingdom. In other words, to pray and ask God what *He* wants them to do with their summer.

Make sure you point out that God is not against us having fun, so thinking about recreation is not necessarily selfish—unless that's our first, and perhaps only, priority.

God is also not against making money. Getting a job may be the most responsible thing we could do. But it could also be a selfish goal.

Participating in some kind of service, going to camp, or taking advantage of some other opportunity for spiritual enrichment or mission is a good idea for most people at some time in their lives. It's something to consider, but it isn't necessarily the obvious answer to the prayer.

Say: **Suppose you've prayed about it, and you're sure that because of your plans to go to college, you need a job for all or most of the summer. Give an example of someone being a sluggard about getting a summer job.** (Sitting around expecting someone to call you about a job; not checking the want ads; not asking around about what jobs are available; not going out looking and filling out applications; not presenting yourself well in interviews—being late, being sloppily dressed, or acting unconcerned.)

Give an example of someone being obsessive about getting a job to make money over the summer. (Calling 50 times and bugging people for whom you've filled out an application; taking the first offer you get, even though it might not be a good place to work, just because you're scared you won't get another offer; only accepting the highest paying job, or trying to work two or three jobs in order to make as much money as possible; lying on your applications so that you can work more hours or get a job you're not really qualified for; etc.)

Give an example of someone trusting God to meet his or her need for a good summer job. (Filling out applications at as many places as possible; being prepared for interviews by being well-dressed, on time, and polite; weighing the pros and cons of the hours, pay, and environment at various places before you accept a job offer; continuing to seek God's help; etc.)

Afterward, say: **Notice that your motivation is the key. Once that's straight, you do what you can and leave the rest to God. Sometimes that means waiting, and that can be hard.**

STEP 5

Walking Away from Worry

(Needed: Small pieces of paper, pencils, wastebasket)

End the session with a time of reflection and prayer. Distribute a small piece of paper and a pencil to each group member.

Say: **Think about some things in your life that you've been worrying about.** (Responses might include things like whether or not to go to college, getting into the colleges of their choice, buying a car, having the right clothes, not having a girlfriend or boyfriend, etc.)

Are these things you've sought God's opinion on? Remember, prayer is more than just asking for things. It's also a time to consider how God is working in our lives and what He may be leading us to do. If this is something you need to take action on, write down something you will do about it as God leads.

Have group members fold their papers in half and write the action they need to take on one side.

Then say: **Remember the lists we made at the beginning of the session? It was impossible for those who were blindfolded to make a straight list. They had no control because they couldn't see the whole picture. Think of one or two problems over which you have no control. Write those problems on the other side of your paper. If there's something you do when you start worrying about them that you need to stop, write that as well.**

Instruct group members not to look at each other's papers. After allowing them a few minutes to write, ask them to tear their papers in half, with one side being the action they need to take and other side the things they need to let go of.

Lead the group in prayer, asking God to help group members let go of all the things over which they have no control, and to trust that God will tend to those things and help them stop worrying about them. Also pray that God will help them have the proper balance between trust and good planning.

Ask group members to crumple up the halves of their papers on which they wrote the things they have no control over and throw them into the wastebasket before they leave.

THE SUPER-DUPER
In-Depth Quiz for Astute Kids

Using Matthew 6:25-34 as a guide, answer the following questions. Can more than one answer be correct? It's your call.

1. Jesus said not to worry specifically about …
   a. finding shelter.
   b. what you eat, drink, or wear.
   c. dressing as well as Solomon dressed.
   d. the birds in the air overhead.

2. The pagans "run" after …
   a. other pagans.
   b. food, drink, and clothing.
   c. false ideas.
   d. the birds in the air.

3. The lilies of the field …
   a. do not grow.
   b. do not worry.
   c. do not work.
   d. do not like the birds of the air.

4. You shouldn't worry about tomorrow because …
   a. you can't change what's going to happen anyway.
   b. today gives you enough to worry about.
   c. God will provide the necessities.
   d. there will still be birds in the air, after all.

5. Because God supplies what you need, you should …
   a. try to provide basic necessities for others.
   b. concern yourself with seeking God's kingdom and righteousness.
   c. concern yourself with supplying the luxuries.
   d. kick back and enjoy yourself.

6. Jesus challenged people to question whether worry would …
   a. lead to heart attacks.
   b. give you clothes as cool as Solomon's were.
   c. add an hour on the end of your life.
   d. shoo away the birds of the air.

NOTES

STEP 1

To make the same point as the chalkboard activity while getting more people actively involved, make some "jigsaw puzzles" before the session. The pieces of each puzzle should be identical, which can be accomplished by cutting several sheets of different colored construction paper into small pieces at the same time, then separating the pieces by color. However, one puzzle should be cut from a picture out of a magazine (the same size as the construction paper). Provide an "identical" puzzle for each team or individual in your group. More than likely, the person or team trying to piece together the picture will finish before the students working with the solid colors. You can then make the point that when we are able to see the big picture, we tend to be more successful than when we can't.

STEP 5

Rather than merely throwing away the lists of worries over which group members have no control, let group members destroy those worries in a more symbolic way. Each list should be put into a balloon. The balloon should then be blown up (with the list inside), tied at the end, and attached to the person's ankle with a length of string (about twelve to eighteen inches long). Then say (tongue in cheek): **OK, the goal here is to see how long you can hang on to your worries. But the other helpful people in our group are going to try to help you get rid of them.** Give a signal and let group members try to step on and pop the other balloons while keeping their own out of reach. People can continue to play even after their own balloons have popped, so it doesn't usually take long for all of the balloons to become memories. *Then* you can throw away the lists along with the popped balloons.

STEP 2

Before you do anything else in this step, let group members brainstorm the things they are currently worried about. Then ask them to agree on "weights" for each worry, ranging from one pound to one hundred pounds. (If they can't reach an agreement, take an average.) One of the advantages of a small group is that it becomes easier to direct your teaching toward group members' specific needs. So the better you can determine those needs, the more effective you can be in supplying examples and valuable help during the rest of the session.

STEP 3

It won't take the members of a small group long to find their individual places on the continuum, so let everyone have some experience in being both Sluggards and Worriers. Establish a signal that you can give that will clue the group to switch from one extreme to the other. Begin as a group of Sluggards as you ask questions and generate group discussion. (**Do you think the Bulls will win the championship this year? How do you like school? What's the best thing that's happened to you this week? What's the worst?**) As soon as group members begin to get into a rhythm, sound the signal and have them immediately switch to Worriers. When they've had some practice, sound the signal more and more often. Then you can put up the continuum and see where the kids think they belong.

STEP 2

Begin this step by having group members, one person at a time, share personal worries. Challenge them to share worries that they think no one else in the room will have. (You might first rattle off a list of common worries: grades, dating relationships, getting into college, not being liked by others, and so forth.) In a large group, it's good to let members maintain their individuality from time to time. In addition, this is an excellent way to get to know each other better. For example, you might discover that one person is anxiously awaiting word on a scholarship, that someone has a seriously ill relative, that someone is hoping to get into medical school, and so forth. Keep going around until group members cannot think of anything else. But once kids get started in thinking of specific concerns, they usually get better at it.

STEP 4

When you get to the point in the discussion in which students consider what they might want to do over the summer, divide into teams and let your group members make the points made by the author. Form three teams: (1) summer fun and recreation; (2) saving money for college, a car, etc.; and (3) participating in a mission or service project. Each team should explore the possibilities of its assigned activity from three perspectives— (1) a Sluggard; (2) a Worrier; and (3) someone who trusts God for wisdom and help. In other words, each team will report on three courses of action for its assigned area of concern. The teams should discover that attitudes can make significant differences in the results of any decision. They should also arrive, by their own logic and common sense, at a good balance between worry and inaction.

STEP 2

Instead of using Repro Resource 4, create a list of worries and let kids rate them in significance using a scale of 1 (least) to 10 (most). Kids can vote simply by holding up the number of fingers they feel is appropriate. Here are some worries you might use:

• **A mom sees her two year old tottering on the edge of a cliff.**
• **Your mom might fix Spam omelets for breakfast tomorrow.**
• **It looks like you're going to make a D in English this term.**
• **Your parents are fighting a lot, and it sounds serious.**

Afterward, read aloud Matthew 6:25-34. Then ask: How in the world could Jesus tell us not to worry? Don't people have every right to show concern over most of the things we listed? See if anyone makes a distinction between worry and concern. Eventually kids should discover that concern for others is a basic element of Christian love. What Jesus refers to, however, is worry about things we can't control.

STEP 4

Try to deal with Steps 3 and 4 together. Begin by comparing the Matthew 6 and Proverbs 6 passages. Before putting up the continuum or getting into the text material, try to generate some challenging questions that will spark debate among your group members. For instance, you might ask: **If Jesus commanded us not to worry in one place, how can we possibly be expected to model our lives after the ant, who works like crazy all of the time? If it's the pagans who "run after" things they want, isn't that what we will appear to be if we become ant-like workers trying to provide for our own needs?** See if group members can make appropriate distinctions between worry and apathy, genuine work and being "driven" to make money due to a lack of faith in God's provision, etc.

STEP 2

Using Repro Resource 2 is a good way to get new people involved with Scripture. For those who don't know the Bible very well, you might want to follow up with an explanation of the context of the Sermon on the Mount, from which this passage comes. Point out that Jesus was making some bold challenges as to how people related to each other and to God. He was not satisfied with "status quo," and was instead providing a much higher level of expectation (and satisfaction with life). Encourage questions about the Bible text. If kids don't ask anything, *you* should. To make sure they understand what is being said, ask: **Is it realistic for people to not worry about anything? What's so wrong with being concerned for food, shelter, clothing, and the other basics in life? Why would Jesus say something like this—doesn't He care about us?** Make sure kids understand that the only way we can do as Jesus instructs is to strengthen our relationship with Him, which is always beneficial to us.

STEP 3

Begin this step with a review of Jesus' statement in Matthew 6:27. Ask: **If you knew you had only one more hour to live, how would you spend it? Do you think you would enjoy that hour?** Some might attempt a lot of thrilling (death-defying) activities, but more than likely, it would be impossible for us to enjoy anything if we knew we were about to die. The only worthwhile activities would seem to be anything that would bring us closer to God. Explain that Jesus was making essentially the same point. We can spend our lives doing any variety of activities, but anything that takes us away from God usually involves a great deal of worry. And how much can we truly enjoy anything we worry about? So it is more beneficial to include God in all of our needs—physical and emotional, as well as spiritual—and use our energies in getting to know Him better rather than worrying.

STEP 2

Have someone read aloud Matthew 6:25-34 as if the words were being spoken by Jesus on the mountainside. All other group members should listen as if they were hearing the words for the first time. After the reading, ask: **What questions would you have? What was said here that might make you feel good? Did anything that was said make you feel a bit of confusion or hesitation?** Encourage group members to be completely honest about their feelings. Then spend some time dealing with any possible misunderstandings or negative feelings. Finally, have group members share their current worries. Explain that the rest of the session will deal with helping each person keep a proper perspective on his or her worries. But to make it more effective, group members should become vulnerable to each other about the things they are feeling and/or worrying about.

STEP 5

It's easy to say, "Don't worry. Trust God." Most kids will truly believe that is the correct thing to do. However, we all experience pressures that cause us to get off track from time to time. So at the end of the session, work together as a group to write a prayer to be used whenever personal worries become stronger than they should. It need not be long or complicated, but it should be complete. Ask: **When we begin to get worried, what things do we need to confess to God? What requests do we need to make of Him? What steps do we need to take?** When your group completes a prayer that everyone is satisfied with, arrange to have copies made and distributed at the next meeting.

STEP 1

After completing the blindfold activity and reading Matthew 6:34, ask group members to decide how they would feel if they *could* know everything about the future. Ask: **What difference would this make? Do you think you would worry less? Why or why not?**

STEP 3

Have your group members form two teams for a debate. Ask the teams to prepare their responses to the following statement, assigning a yes response to one team and a no to the other: "Spending a lot of time planning what to wear and how to look attractive is inappropriate worry." After the teams have had some planning time, allow them to present their arguments.

STEP 2

To begin this step, ask: **What are your weaknesses?** Guys may be slow to respond at first. (After all, they're *guys*.) But go on to explain that even Superman was susceptible to Kryptonite. Indiana Jones had a terrible fear of snakes. Samson was rendered powerless by a haircut. Explain that there is no shame in admitting our weaknesses. In fact, there is more danger in denying that we are affected by certain things. After guys begin to open up a bit, turn the discussion toward worry. It might be that these potential weaknesses are sources of worry for your group of guys. Ask: **To what degree do you worry about these things? How can you tell when you begin to worry about something?** After group members respond, keep their specific questions and comments in mind as you move ahead with the session.

STEP 4

At an appropriate spot during this step, ask: **What are some "manly" things that guys do to keep from showing that they're worried about something? What macho things do they do to cope with worry?** Some guys may admit to withdrawing from friends and/or family members and dealing with the problem in silence. Some may get angry or violent (even to the point of hitting something) as a response. Some may go jogging or work out, counting on the sweat and fatigue to lessen the concerns they feel. Sometimes, if guys are worried that they can't do something, they will take a stupid dare to prove that they can. Explain that as they get older, men who mishandle worry frequently have workaholic tendencies as well as higher probabilities of ulcers, heart attacks, and other health problems. Challenge your group of guys to learn *now* to deal with worry in productive ways, rather than expecting to do something about it later.

STEP 2

Play a game of "You Think *You're* Worried?" Have kids sit in a circle. The first person says, "You think *you're* worried? *I'm* worried about _____." The second person repeats the phrase and the first person's worry, and then adds a worry of his or her own. The third person must repeat the first two worries and add a new one. (You get the idea.) Truthful answers may show through in spots, but encourage kids to have fun with this exercise. So by the time the sixth person has a turn, he or she might say, "You think you're worried? I'm worried about going to school in my pajamas one day, dying from eating bad liver, having to work at Burger Buddy my whole life, discovering that my future wife grows fangs during full moons, forgetting the quadratic equation after I graduate, and beginning to wear pants like my dad when I get to be his age." Whenever someone is unable to remember all of the previous comments, he or she is out and the game continues. Play until one person remains.

STEP 3

Rather than merely discuss the differences between sluggards and worriers, roleplay a world that consists of only these two personality types. Divide into two groups. Designate one group as cheerleaders for the Sluggard High School Slugs. Designate the other group as cheerleaders for Worry High School Warts. Explain that an imaginary game is taking place. Have the cheerleaders create some cheers appropriate for its school. In addition, you can play the role of stadium announcer, and the cheerleading groups can react to your announcements. For example, you might announce at intervals:
- **Please rise to sing the national anthem.**
- **It looks like a player is hurt.**
- **That's the end of the first half. Worry High is ahead 36-0.**
- **A fight has broken out on the field.**

STEP 3

As you discuss Sluggards and Worriers, ask group members to think of TV and movie characters who fit these descriptions. When they think of someone, kids should stand and do an impromptu impersonation while others guess who it is. If you wish, you might also be ready to show some of your favorite scenes of classic worriers (Woody Allen, Barney Fife, etc.) or sluggards (Fred Sanford, Al Bundy, Homer Simpson, etc.). But count on kids to come up with the characters who are most relevant to them. Use their characters as examples as you continue the session.

STEP 5

Conclude your session by playing the Bobby McFerrin song, "Don't Worry, Be Happy" (from the album *Simple Pleasures*, © 1988, EMI-Manhattan Records). The song consists of simple rhyming couplets followed by the phrase, "Don't worry, be happy." It is a simple matter to create additional verses to incorporate the things group members have learned. Play the song to provide the meter and rhythm as students work on their own verses. You may want to have them work in teams so your more creative people can help others. When everyone has come up with one or two verses, perform your version of the song by going from person to person (or team to team) to hear group members sing what they've written. Everyone should join in on the "Don't worry, be happy" part each time. Afterward, discuss how the message of this song is similar to or different from Jesus' teaching on worry.

STEP 1

Open the session by having everyone create his or her own "Top 10 List" of things he or she worries about. Explain that according to statistics, less than 10 percent of the things we worry about ever come to pass. So in most cases, group members need be concerned about only one of the things on their lists. Then spend time reading and discussing Matthew 6:25-34 to see what Jesus recommends for handling the remaining items on their lists. Use portions of Step 2 where applicable. And since the kids have already made their lists, the exercise in Step 5 (determining which things they need to take action on and which ones to let go of) is good to use to conclude the meeting.

STEP 2

Open the session with Step 2 (beginning with Repro Resource 4), and cover the material thoroughly. Ask kids to provide their own specific examples as they go along. (When the topic is worry, kids should have no trouble coming up with examples.) Encourage questions and comments along the way, and personalize the session as much as possible. Then, if time permits, move on to Step 5. If not, summarize the key points of your discussion and close in prayer.

STEP 3

On the board, draw two gauge-looking devices (that look like speedometers). Label one of them "Worry Meter"; label the other "Sluggard Meter." Draw three zones of intensity on each meter: "Low," "Medium," and "High." On the "Worry Meter" these zones will represent the amount of *trust* in God group members will need to reduce worry. On the "Sluggard Meter," the zones will represent the amount of *self-motivation* group members will need to reduce their sluggardly ways. Have each group member ponder where he or she believes he or she is on each meter. Then distribute paper and pencils. Instruct each group member to write a plan for increasing trust and self-motivation in each of the following six areas:
(1) personal life
(2) family life
(3) relationships with others
(4) prayer (faith) life
(5) at school
(6) in the city

STEP 4

Have your group members discuss what they'd say to the following people:
• a woman who's afraid to leave her home for fear of being mugged or raped.
• a person who's having sex with a lot of different partners and isn't at all worried about AIDS.
• a person on welfare who has the ability to work, but not the interest.

You could also have kids roleplay conversations with these people or write an advice column directed to them.

STEP 1

For some reason, junior highers seem to have a particular affinity for *Mad* magazine. Find a recent issue or two that features Alfred E. Newman prominently on the cover. (It shouldn't be hard, since most of them do.) Hold up the issue(s) and ask: **How much do you know about this guy?** Let students respond. Then say (tongue in cheek): **Mr. Newman is also a model of a mature Christian. He demonstrates one essential quality that Jesus taught us to exhibit.** Encourage group members to speculate about what you might be talking about. If no one figures it out, remind them that Alfred E. Newman's motto is, "What, me worry?" Explain that the topic of today's session is how to keep from needless worry. Later, when you get to the definition of a sluggard, you can again hold up the covers and clarify that even though Alfred E. Newman manages to avoid worry, perhaps his method is not the best one.

STEP 4

If you have a lot of junior highers, you'll probably want to change the "How might you spend your summer?" anecdote in this step. Most junior highers don't yet devote a lot of time to worrying about college, cars, summer jobs, and so forth. Perhaps, instead, you could let them envision the summer between junior high and high school as they consider specifics of Worriers vs. Sluggards. What might they be worrying about? (Losing old friends; not being accepted; too much change and challenge; etc.) How might their sluggard tendencies take over? (Keeping to themselves rather than making the most of the time with their current friends; refusing to read books or otherwise start preparing for a more disciplined schedule; etc.) Make sure to keep the discussion at an applicable level for your younger students.

STEP 2

After you discuss Jesus' teaching about worry, challenge kids to come up with specific examples. Ask each person to try to think of a Bible character and circumstance in which the person's faith defeated worry. (If your kids aren't up to this challenge, form teams and let each team brainstorm ideas.) You might want to award some kind of "extra credit" for kids who can also provide the proper Scripture reference for the stories they think of. If you wish, you can compile their answers, make copies for everyone, and hand them out at a future meeting.

STEP 5

Ask: **When we stop worrying, does that mean bad things will stop happening to us? If not, what might we assume Jesus is trying to tell us when He says not to worry so much?** As students think about the life of Jesus, they may discover that He never seemed to worry. Yet His life ended in the greatest possible degree of unfairness, suffering, and pain. Perhaps Jesus wants us to discover that constant worrying is worse than occasional suffering. The sooner we learn to expect a certain amount of injustice, persecution, and discomfort, the better off we can be. We're going to have our share of those things whether or not we worry about them. So if we can learn to stop worrying, even while anticipating occasional periods of unpleasantness, we'll be better off. You might discuss Paul's notation of this discovery. "I have learned to be content whatever the circumstances. I know what it is to be in need, and I know what it is to have plenty. I have learned the secret of being content in any and every situation, whether well fed or hungry, whether living in plenty or in want. I can do everything through Him who gives me strength" (Phil. 4:11-13). Follow with a prayer that God will provide the strength for your group members to remain faithful to Him and worry-free, no matter what their circumstances.

DATE USED:

Approx. Time

STEP 1: *The Blindfold Conspiracy* _____
- ❏ Extra Action
- ❏ Mostly Girls
- ❏ Short Meeting Time
- ❏ Combined Junior High/High School
Things needed:

STEP 2: *Why Worry Shouldn't Win* _____
- ❏ Small Group
- ❏ Large Group
- ❏ Heard It All Before
- ❏ Little Bible Background
- ❏ Fellowship & Worship
- ❏ Mostly Guys
- ❏ Extra Fun
- ❏ Short Meeting Time
- ❏ Extra Challenge
Things needed:

STEP 3: *Extreme Thinking* _____
- ❏ Small Group
- ❏ Little Bible Background
- ❏ Mostly Girls
- ❏ Extra Fun
- ❏ Media
- ❏ Urban
Things needed:

STEP 4: *Getting Concrete* _____
- ❏ Large Group
- ❏ Heard It All Before
- ❏ Mostly Guys
- ❏ Urban
- ❏ Combined Junior High/High School
Things needed:

STEP 5: *Walking Away from Worry* _____
- ❏ Extra Action
- ❏ Fellowship & Worship
- ❏ Media
- ❏ Extra Challenge
Things needed:

SESSION 4

Why Bother with Annoying People?

YOUR GOALS FOR THIS SESSION:
Choose one or more

☐ To help kids discover what it means to love enemies in the biblical sense.

☐ To help kids understand that they can work through anger and resentment toward enemies without putting their enemies down or being unkind to them.

☐ To help kids choose to pray for enemies in specific ways.

☐ Other:_____

Your Bible Base:

Matthew 5:43-45
1 Corinthians 13:4-7
2 Corinthians 11:20
Ephesians 4:26

People You Love to Hate

(Needed: Paper, pencils, prizes)

Distribute paper and pencils. Instruct group members to write the numbers 1-5 on their papers. Emphasize that there should be no talking during the following activity.

Then ask: **What are your five biggest pet peeves—the five things that irritate you most? List them from one to five on your paper.**

Wait for your group members to finish their lists. Then, when you say **Go,** group members should go around the room and try to find other people who share the same pet peeves. When a person finds someone who has a peeve he or she listed, the two should initial each other's papers next to that item. (The wording does not have to be exact, obviously, but the peeves should be similar. You'll be the judge in case of close calls.) The first person to get all five peeves initialed (or the most peeves initialed after a certain amount of time) is the winner.

Award a prize to the winner. You may also want to award a prize to the two people whose lists were most similar and to the person whose pet peeves were unique (the person with the least number of signatures).

Ask: **How do you feel about people who exhibit these pet peeves or who do things that irritate you?** Get responses from several group members. If no one mentions it, suggest that people who irritate us regularly can become our enemies. That's the topic of this session—dealing with enemies.

Combat Styles

(Needed: Scrap paper, pencils, copies of Repro Resource 5)

Ask: **What is an enemy?** (Someone who doesn't want to be friendly with you; someone you feel suspicious of or competitive with; someone whose values are so different from yours that he or she threatens you; someone who is difficult to deal with or who has hurt you; etc.)

Explain: **By these definitions, an enemy could be a teacher, coach, or parent, as well as people at school who bug you or are out to get you. There are times when even brothers and sisters or friends can become our enemies.**

Distribute pieces of scrap paper. Instruct group members to write down the names of people they would define as enemies. Emphasize that no one else will see what they write down.

Say: **You don't have to answer this question out loud, but look at the names you wrote down. How do you usually deal with these people?** Give group members a moment to consider the question.

Distribute copies of "If You Were on the Yellow Brick Road" (Repro Resource 5). Give group members a minute or two to choose their answers. Then ask each person to tell the group which character he or she selected and why.

Afterward, say: **These are four ways that people commonly respond to an enemy. They are what we consider normal behavior. That's why one of the toughest passages in the Bible is Matthew 5:43-45.** Ask a volunteer to read the passage aloud.

Then ask: **How does Jesus say Christians should treat their enemies?** (We should love them and pray for them.)

Point out (or allow group members to point out) that it's not natural for us to love our enemies or pray for them. Then, before you go on, ask group members if there's anything unusual that stands out to them in this passage. They might notice, for instance, that Jesus says by loving our enemies we are being like God Himself. That's what makes this teaching so radical. You will come back to this idea later in the session.

Love in Enemy Territory

(Needed: Copies of Repro Resource 6, Bibles, pencils)

OPTIONS

Distribute copies of "Love Is . . ." (Repro Resource 6). Say: **Part of what makes it difficult to love our enemies is that we aren't sure what "love" is and isn't. Let's look at I Corinthians 13:4-7 and see how it helps us define love.** Ask a volunteer read the passage aloud. Then, as a group, go over the instructions for Repro Resource 6.

Have group members work in pairs in completing the worksheet. When they're finished, have each pair share its responses. Use the following answers to supplement group members' responses.

(1) Yes. Love does not boast, it is not proud (I Cor. 13:4).

(2) No. "Always trusts" (13:7) doesn't mean we have to trust our enemies to keep our secrets. It means that we trust them enough that we aren't always suspicious of them.

(3) No. It would be phony to pretend to enjoy being with them. But we can be polite and kind (13:4-5).

(4) Yes. Love "is kind" (13:4) and "rejoices with the truth" (13:6), but "is not rude" (13:5). Mudslinging, or telling others how terrible someone is, is "delight[ing] in evil" (13:6). It can be tough to speak the truth, and it can be tough to speak with love, but we are commanded to do both (Eph. 4:15).

(5) Yes. "Love does not delight in evil" (I Corinthians 13:6). We may see that they've gotten what they deserve, but we shouldn't see it as personal revenge.

(6) Yes. "Love is patient" (13:4), "[love] always hopes," and "always perseveres" (13:7) means that we're willing to give people the benefit of the doubt. "Keeps no record of wrongs" (13:5) means we should be willing to forgive and start again.

(7) Yes. If we keep no record of wrongs, we aren't concerned about getting even. Being "kind" (13:4) is the opposite of getting even.

(8) No. While we don't need to be defensive, we can stand up for ourselves. Justice is a concern for Christians; therefore, we "[speak] the truth in love" (Eph. 4:15).

(9) Yes. Love is kind, it does not boast, it is not rude or self-seeking (I Cor. 13:4-5). Putting someone down is usually a form of lifting yourself up.

(10) No. Love does not mean we condone wrongdoing. "Love does not delight in evil but rejoices with the truth" (13:6).

Have someone read aloud 2 Corinthians 11:20. Explain that in this passage, Paul is rebuking the Corinthians for following abusive, authoritarian false teachers instead of the true apostle (himself), who came to them humbly and never demanded anything from them. In this passage it is clear that Paul does not advocate Christians letting themselves be abused or exploited—at least not by people who claimed to be preachers and teachers.

Ask: **So what is the difference? How do we truly love our enemies without becoming victims of abuse or exploitation?** Get several responses.

Then have group members consider the example Jesus gave. Ask: **Did Jesus allow Himself to be taken advantage of on the cross?** (Some group members may say yes. After all, Jesus let Himself be whipped, beaten, scorned, and crucified—and He never defended Himself. He never even opened His mouth. Other group members may say no. After all, in reality, Jesus was in charge every step of the way. His persecution was a master plan to pay for the sins of the world. He chose not to defend Himself or to stop even His own murder, though the Bible says He could have called 72,000 angels to deliver Him if had chosen to [Matt. 26:53].)

STEP
4

What Love Looks Like

Ask two volunteers to participate in a couple of spontaneous roleplays. One of the volunteers will be play a kid who's attempting to love his or her enemies. The other volunteer will play his or her enemy.

Have the two actors sit next to each other in front of the group. Explain that the actors will perform each roleplay twice. In the first roleplay, your actors will demonstrate what happens when the first doesn't do well in "loving" his or her enemy. In the second roleplay, the actors will demonstrate what happens when the first person does well in loving his or her enemy.

The situation in the first roleplay is that the enemy is making fun of the other person's shoes. The situation in the second roleplay is that the enemy is bragging about having just received a new car from his or her parents. Allow each roleplay to run about 45-60 seconds.

After each roleplay has been performed twice, ask the rest of your group members to evaluate the first person's performance in loving his

OPTIONS

or her enemy. Did he or she do a good job? What else could he or she have done?

Afterward, give your actors a round of applause. Then say: **Sometimes it's easier to "love" an enemy when you're face-to-face with him or her than it is to love him or her when you're with others. For instance, have you ever been in a group in which someone started gossiping or talking badly about someone you didn't like?** (Probably most of your group members have.)

What's the temptation in a situation like that? (To join in the gossiping.)

What *should* we do in a situation like that? (Say nothing at all, change the topic of conversation, defend the person being talked about, etc.)

What if you feel really angry at your enemy? Should you pretend that you aren't? Get responses from several group members. Then have someone read aloud Ephesians 4:26.

Explain: **The sin isn't anger—it's holding a grudge or seeking revenge. What are some practical things you can do to avoid sinning in your anger?** Use the following suggestions to supplement group members' responses.

• The ideal solution is to talk with the person one-on-one about the problem. However, that's not always possible.

• If you're really upset and talking to the person is impossible or doesn't help, journaling is an excellent tool for venting your feelings. Write down your feelings and ask God to help you deal with them.

• It can also be helpful to find someone else to talk to about your feelings. But be careful that you don't just rag on your enemy or get the other person to side with you against your enemy. Choose someone who will understand how you feel and be supportive of you, but who will also challenge you as well. So much the better if this person can act as mediator between you and your enemy.

STEP 5

Prayer Conquers All

Wrap up your session on loving our enemies with the following comments: **When Jesus told us to love our enemies, He knew a tremendous secret: You can't hate someone if you really pray for that person. You can still hate what the person does, but you can't hate him or her. Let's list some things we could pray for our enemies.** Use the following ideas to supplement group members' responses.

- Pray for reconciliation with the person if it's a broken friendship or family relationship.
- Pray that the person would come to know Christ or that his or her relationship with Christ would grow.
- Pray for the person's physical, emotional, or spiritual health. (Sometimes illness or chronic pain can make a person grouchy and affect his or her behavior.)
- Pray for Christ to form His character in his or her life *and* in yours.
- Pray that God would help the person work through insecure feelings. (Teachers facing retirement can be fearful and grouchy; parents who don't know how to handle kids can overreact; kids who hate themselves hate everyone else too; etc.)

Close the session by praying for your group members' enemies. Include some of the preceding issues in your prayer.

After the session, make yourself available to talk privately to group members who are dealing with serious situations. For instance, when someone we love—such as a parent—is abusive, it's very hard to follow the advice given in this session. Be available to pray with these kids and walk with them through their difficult situations.

If You Were on the Yellow Brick Road

In dealing with your enemies, which of the following characters from *The Wizard of Oz* do you act most like?

Scarecrow

"Usually I can't outwit my enemies. I don't have the brains to come up with terrible things to say to them when they tease me—but I wish I did. I usually just keep my anger bottled up inside me."

Tin Man

"I don't really have a heart for my enemies, but I pretend I do. I usually try to be nice to my enemies so they won't get mad at me."

Cowardly Lion

"I don't have the courage to face my enemies. If I see one in the convenience store after school, I'll go somewhere else."

Wicked Witch of the West

"I'm mean to my enemies. I treat them badly and they hate me. In fact, some of them are scared of me."

NOTES

♥ ♥
♥ 𝓛ove Is… ♥

Read each of the following statements. If the statement describes something that's involved in loving enemies, write "Yes" in the blank. Then write the phrase from I Corinthians 13:4-7 or Ephesians 4:26 that the statement illustrates. (The first one is done for you this way.) If the statement does *not* describe something that's involved in loving enemies, write "No" in the blank.

Loving my enemies means I should …

(1) avoid bragging about myself and competing with them.

Yes. Love does not boast, it is not proud (I Corinthians 13:4).

(2) try to be best friends with them and tell them all my secrets.

_____

(3) pretend that I enjoy being with them.

_____

(4) speak the truth in a kind but matter-of-fact way, without gossiping or being a mudslinger.

_____

(5) not be glad when bad things happen to them.

_____

(6) be ready to forgive them.

_____

(7) not try to get even with them.

_____

(8) let them take advantage of me.

_____

(9) avoid putting them down (in words and tone of voice).

_____

(10) pretend that I like their wrong behavior or that I approve of it.

_____

NOTES

STEP 1

Rather than having each person write out his or her pet peeves, start out with kids in teams. Instruct each team to discuss the pet peeves of each of its individual members, compile a list, agree on an order of irritation (from most irritating to least irritating), and be ready to act out the situations it has listed. Then have each team perform the top item on its list. (Performances need not be long or complicated. Most pet peeves can be demonstrated in just a few seconds.) When teams finish acting out their situations, have them explain exactly what pet peeve they were trying to communicate. See how many other teams listed the same (or a very similar) pet peeve. Teams need not duplicate something that has already been acted out. They should instead go on to the next item on their lists.

STEP 3

Using the behaviors listed on Repro Resource 6, create conflict situations between two people and deal with them as court cases. For example, the behavior for #2 could become "The Case of the Secretive, So-called Friend," in which Joe Smith accuses Jane Jones of not being a true friend because she won't pass along information she knows about some third party. (Tailor the specifics to fit your own group.) Appoint a judge, prosecutor, defender, and defendant in each case. The other students become jury members. (Jury members don't have to just sit there. They can ask questions "for clarification" of the prosecutor, defender, or judge.) You'll probably need to choose which of the "cases" you want to act out. Students can then take home the handout to deal with the others on their own.

STEP 1

In a small group, trying to match pet peeves from a five-item list is not likely to be as effective or feasible as in a large group. So instead have kids form pairs and come up with as many pet peeves as they can think of. They should brainstorm for quantity, rather than quality at first. As pairs report on what they've come up with, record all of their responses in a master list on the board. Afterward, let each person "vote" for his or her top five choices as you tally the votes on the side. Then you can easily see the vote total and determine which are the most annoying pet peeves for your group as a whole.

STEP 4

The roleplays in this step call for a few volunteers, but in a small group try to get everyone involved. The roleplays set up conflict situations between individuals, but they can be just as effective between two groups of friends who don't get along with each other. In fact, peer influence may be a major reason why some of your group members don't settle disagreements with their "enemies" more quickly. So add some "supporting players" to the roleplays as written and have all group members take part. Later, discuss not only the feelings of the people directly involved in the conflict, but the attitudes and actions of their friends as well.

STEP 3

Make two copies of Repro Resource 6 for each person. The first time through, ask group members to ignore the instructions. Have kids fill out the sheet based on their actual actions and attitudes—not according to what the correct biblical answers would be. As stated, #1 on the sheet reads, "Loving my enemies means I should avoid bragging about myself and competing with them." But revise it to read, "*If* loving my enemies means I avoid bragging about myself and competing with them . . ." Students should then finish the statement with either "I love my enemies" or "I guess I don't love my enemies." The advantage of doing this in a large group is that when kids complete their sheets, you can review their answers, figure the percentage of people who answered each way, and determine approximately how loving your group is from a statistical standpoint. You will also be able to see which specific areas are strongest and weakest in your group. Then you can hand out the second copy of Repro Resource 6, have group members do the assignment as written, and discover what kinds of goals they should set for themselves.

STEP 4

Rather than having just a couple of people involved in the roleplays as written, divide into teams and have each team create a conflict skit based on the personal experiences of one of its members. Some skits may reflect good conflict resolution on the part of the people involved. Others probably won't. In either case, skits shouldn't deviate too much from what actually happened. After each team performs its skit, the other group members should comment on how the conflict was handled. What actions do they agree with? What things might they have done differently? (These real-life conflict situations can also be used as specific examples when you deal with conflict resolution later in the session.)

STEP 3

As important as I Corinthians 13 is to our understanding of what real love should be, this is a section of Scripture that probably triggers the "heard it all before" reflex quicker than almost any other. You still need to have kids deal with it, but you may not want to use Repro Resource 6 if they think they already know it. Instead, have them read the chapter and create a profile of the world's *least* loving person. Rather than letting them get by with "He's quick to become angry, not patient, not kind," challenge them to come up with specific actions that would reflect such characteristics. Use the example of Paul Bunyan or Pecos Bill, and explain that this person should become another legend of folklore based on his or her unloving behavior. After they've written a paragraph or two, have group members share their profiles. Then point out that no one could possibly be as bad as the characters who have been described. Thankfully, everyone has some good qualities, and we should focus on those traits as we try to love our enemies.

STEP 4

Create a dispute between two groups of people that might require a negotiator to help settle it. (Most kids probably won't relate well to negotiating peace treaties, labor contracts, or other "adult" situations. Some of them might be better acquainted with gang treaties or perhaps marriage/ divorce counseling.) Let a person who may assume he or she knows it all already be the negotiator. Everyone else should take a side and try to hold firm to his or her position. See how well the negotiator does with a lot of intense feeling on both sides of the dispute. It's one thing to discuss the importance of reconciliation; it's something else to know how to practice it effectively. After the roleplay, point out that we may not be able to influence the actions and attitudes of other people, but we are certainly responsible for our own. We can learn to "negotiate" conflicts that may involve some of our own selfish behaviors.

STEP 2

Begin this step by having group members complete some sentences. Start with **"I hate . . ."**; move on to **"I hate it when . . ."**; and conclude with **"I hate people who . . ."** See how long it takes for personal conflicts to be mentioned. The first two sentences might focus on detested foods, classes, or situations. But they might also include barriers between the speaker and certain types of people. If not, those are likely to come out in response to the third sentence. Discuss how comfortably most of us are able to speak of "hate"—perhaps for no good reason. Then continue with Step 2, emphasizing Jesus' command to love our enemies. Ask: **Is this possible? Is it feasible? Is it really important not to hate anyone? Why?** If you raise more questions than answers at this point, that's fine. Many of the questions will be answered during the rest of the session.

STEP 3

If your group is new to the basic teachings of the Bible, I Corinthians 13 is an excellent place to let them linger for a while. When you get to Repro Resource 6, make sure not to rush them. Give them plenty of time to come up with their answers. Also take your time as you discuss the handout and add comments as noted in the session text. Encourage questions about any of the statements on the Repro Resource. While the Bible text is clear and easy to understand, the applications may seem unnatural and confusing. (If so, explain that the applications aren't natural—they're *supernatural*. Only God can provide the degree of love described in this passage. We fall far short when we rely on our own efforts.) If this is a new passage to your group members, encourage them to reread it every night during the next week. Each reading is likely to initiate new insights into God's love and how we should apply it toward each other.

STEP 2

Ask each group member to share briefly about one personal experience with an enemy. (But emphasize that kids shouldn't mention any names.) After each group member shares, briefly discuss how the person became an enemy and how the group member feels about that person today. Has anyone's Christian faith made a difference in the relationship? Be prepared to share a story of your own, preferably one in which there was reconciliation with the enemy.

STEP 5

This session concludes with a natural worship activity—detailed prayer for those people we might consider our enemies. Yet the tendency for some group members may be to pray (and truly mean it), but then leave the session and not give the matter any more thought. Remind group members that a genuine love for God is proven by our actions toward each other (1 John 4:19-21). Consequently, their worship will not be complete by simply praying and leaving. Therefore, also ask each person to think of one "action step" that would initiate reconciliation with one of his or her "enemies." This step might include sending an anonymous card or gift, offering to do something together, making an apology for a past action, etc. Then include in your closing prayer a request for God to provide the courage for each person to take his or her predetermined step sometime during the following week, and for His help in achieving reconciliation in each person's relationship.

MOSTLY **GIRLS**

MOSTLY **GUYS**

EXTRA **FUN**

STEP 4

In addition to the roleplay situations described in the session, ask your group members to think of two or three other situations that might arise with an enemy. Using these situations, have your volunteers present each one twice. The first presentation should detail a poor attempt at "loving" the enemy; the second should detail a more successful attempt. As you talk about the situations, discuss the role competition plays in creating a difficult relationship. Ask: **Can people become enemies because of natural competition? What are we usually competitive about? When can understanding our own competitive natures help us with those we don't get along with?**

STEP 5

After listing the ideas about praying for our enemies, talk about the times in which we aren't willing to pray for them. Ask: **What do you do when you can't pray for the person who has hurt you? Are you willing to let that person come between you and God because you don't want to talk to God about him or her? Even if it isn't easy to pray, can you admit to yourself that God loves that person as much as He loves you? How does acknowledging that God loves that person affect your thinking?**

STEP 2

Most guys won't need a lot of help understanding how enemy relationships get formed. Many of them are likely to have been in fights—or intense ongoing arguments—with other guys. For some of them, conflict may be a fine art. To see how good your group is at starting conflicts, randomly select two volunteers. The first person should try to initiate a fight with the second one. The second person should react as he would normally. Other observers should note the techniques of how conflicts get started (name-calling, cruel teasing, physical abuse, etc.). They should also decide whether the second person was justified in his response, and suggest actions he might have taken instead. Afterward, point out that Jesus wasn't just talking to women when He said we should love our enemies.

STEP 4

With a group of guys, you may want to spend more time discussing how to handle anger. The advice given in the session (talk one-on-one, write in a journal, or talk to someone else) is good, but guys may need more options. Begin by having them make a list of things they've tried that haven't worked well—things *not* to do when you get angry. (Guys may have stories of hitting trees, kicking immovable objects, etc.) While some reactions may be comical, don't miss the serious problem of being unable to control anger. Guys who are physically bigger and stronger than other people need outlets for anger that don't involve violence. Brainstorm what some of those outlets might be. (You might suggest going for a long run to work off energy, playing a sport in which you can take out your anger on a ball, or finding a place in which you can be alone until your anger subsides.) Everyone should come up with at least three options that he feels would work for him. Challenge group members to remember these options the next time they get angry.

STEP 1

Open with a group-participation skit titled, "A World without Conflict." The setting should be someplace where young people tend to congregate, such as a mall or school cafeteria. As kids meet and interact, explain that they are to remain happy and sweet—no matter what is said or done to them. Then add that, of course, there may be *some* people in the crowd who will take advantage of this situation and say exactly what they think of others. Have kids mill around (in character) and converse. Some of them are certain to "test the waters" and see if they can provoke conflict. Watch to see how others handle such attempts. Do they smile through gritted teeth? Do they break down and react negatively? Do they come right back with equally nasty comments without shifting out of their pleasant demeanor? Afterward, discuss the activity. Point out that a world without conflict seems phony and unrealistic. We live in the "real" world—one filled with conflict, misunderstanding, and personality clashes. We are certain to form enemies as we interact with other people, so we need to know what to do in such cases.

STEP 5

Close the session by playing "Hug Tag." You'll need an odd number of people to play. Everyone should have a partner, except for one person who is "It." Explain that everyone should hug his or her partner until you give a signal. Then kids should let go and wander around the room. When you give a second signal, they must again find a partner—but not the one they had previously. When two people are hugging, they are safe. In the meantime, as soon as you give the second signal, "It" will be trying to find a partner, which will leave someone else partnerless. That person then becomes "It." After a while, shift from hug partners to hug trios or quartets. Afterward, point out that hugging to bond together is a lot more fun than holding grudges and making enemies.

STEP 2

After discussing the conflict-management styles of the *Wizard of Oz* characters, say: **You know, someone has done a "Christian version" of Mother Goose as well as other classic works of literature. But no one has done The *Wizard of Oz* yet. Maybe we should.** Show one of your favorite scenes from the film on video and then ask volunteers to reenact the scene as it might be done in a Christian version. Depending on what your group members think about products such as the "Christian Mother Goose," you may get a serious treatment of the scene or a whimsical parody. But either way, group members will probably come up with some significant observations and applications that apply to Christian behavior as we relate to people who are different than we are—the people we may classify as enemies.

STEP 5

To close the session and to help group members see where some of their conflict-management skills may have originated, show some classic cartoons. Try to choose some that emphasize an ongoing adversarial relationship between the characters (Elmer Fudd and Bugs Bunny, Sylvester and Tweety Bird, or even a few Itchy and Scratchy segments from *The Simpsons* [which are hard-hitting parodies of the violent nature of some cartoon shows]). Ask volunteers to tell what their favorite cartoons were as children, and what they learned about conflict from those shows. If possible, you might want to conclude with a Road Runner cartoon. Explain that he is an excellent model. By ignoring and/or outsmarting Wile E. Coyote, rather than trying to retaliate, Road Runner's perpetual enemy almost always does himself in. We can learn much from that example.

STEP 1

Open the session with a word-association game. Have each person in turn provide a different synonym for the word *enemy*. Whenever one person is unable to come up with a new word, he or she is out. Play until no one else can think of any new words. This activity should draw out several pet peeves as well as inconsequential offenses and more serious observations about people your group members don't particularly like. With all of these synonyms in mind (and perhaps written on the board as well), have someone read Matthew 5:43-45. Follow with a condensed summary of Steps 4 and 5, focusing on the Bible passages, Repro Resource 6, and relevant applications as you have time.

STEP 2

The essence of this session can be summed up with three words: "Love your enemies." Of course, you could meet for hours discussing various specific considerations of what this means. But since you don't have hours, simply have someone read Matthew 5:43-45. Then, for the rest of the session, ask questions to help group members understand what Jesus was saying. Begin with *who* your kids consider as enemies and *what* those people did that still causes friction in the relationships. (Group members need not answer these aloud, but should have specific people and offenses in mind.) Move on to *why* and *how* we should love our enemies. Draw relevant material from the session—especially the need to pray for enemies. In discussion, each group member should refer to "the people I've thought about," rather than using actual names. Finally, save enough time to help group members think about *when* and *where* they plan to initiate the reconciliation process.

STEP 3

Explain to your group members that God loves the city and wants to redeem it. Then share and discuss two essential Scripture verses concerning God's love:
• I Corinthians 13:8—Love (agape) never fails (falters, becomes invalid, or comes to an end).
• I John 4:18—There is no fear (phobia) in love.

Then explain that agape (God's love) is not a mushy, bleeding-heart love, but a confrontational, tough, rugged, unaffected-by-anything love. In short, real agape is fearless because God is all-powerful. Next, have your group members come up with a list of "Ten Things People in the City Fear Most." Then ask how your group members can use love (tough, fearless agape) as a practical force to confront each item on the list. Finally, choose one or two ideas that your group will actually use in confronting in love as social action.

STEP 4

To present anger and sin on a social level, ask: **What things about the city make you angry?** List group members' responses on the board as they are named. Then say: **It's good that you're angry; after all, anger is an indication of injustice. But what I want to know is what you're going to do with your anger.** List these responses in two columns: "Anger That Curses" and "Anger That Blesses." Afterward, challenge each teen to begin to transfer his or her just anger into some form of action that can bless the person or situation with which he or she is angry.

STEP 2

Some young teens are just beginning to hold serious grudges. Some haven't formed real enemies yet. Be sensitive to this as you discuss the information in this step. Instead of going through Repro Resource 5 as written, list on the board some of the main characters from *The Wizard of Oz*—Dorothy, the Wicked Witch, Scarecrow, Tin Man, Cowardly Lion, the Wizard, etc. Then ask: **When it comes to conflict situations, which of these characters do you act most like, and why?** Some kids may say they're like the Scarecrow, not thinking before they speak. Others may say they run away from conflict like the Cowardly Lion. Still others may say they're mean like the Wicked Witch of the West.

STEP 4

If your kids don't enjoy roleplays, try another approach. Bring in a large supply of modeling clay. Give some to each person. As you describe the following situations, group members should shape their clay in a way that describes how they feel.
• **A kid at school makes fun of the way you look as you're undressing in the locker room. This person continues to make fun of you every day.**
• **You tell a secret to a friend, who promises not to tell anyone. The next day, your "secret" is all around school.**
• **There's a really weird kid at school that no one likes. He knows he's obnoxious and uses that to his advantage. He goes out of his way to embarrass you in front of your friends. You don't treat him as badly as some kids do, so he's starting to hang around you more. He sits with you at lunch every day. He calls you at home. He's starting to tell people that you're his best friend.**

Afterward, have group members mold their clay into a symbol for loving enemies. Then talk about each case again, describing what it would mean to love that person.

STEP 2

Briefly review the parable of the Good Samaritan (Luke 10:30-37). Discuss the difference between an enemy and a neighbor. Have kids paraphrase the parable in a modern setting, using these characters: a person with AIDS, a professing homosexual, a gang member, someone who is pro-abortion, a drug addict, a person in prison, a guy who gets a girl pregnant and claims no responsibility. Ask: **How, specifically, can a Christian show love to these people as the Samaritan showed love to someone who was supposed to be his enemy?**

STEP 4

Read aloud the following poem:
O Lord,
Remember not only the men and women of goodwill,
But also those of ill will.
But do not remember the suffering they have inflicted on us,
Remember the fruits we brought thanks to this suffering,
Our comradeship, our loyalty, our humility,
The courage, the generosity,
The greatness of heart which has grown out of all this.
And when they come to judgment Let all the fruits that we have borne Be their forgiveness.
AMEN AMEN AMEN
(From *Lord of the Journey* by Roger Pooley and Philip Seddon, eds. [London: Collins, 1986].)

Have kids guess the circumstances surrounding the writing of these words. Then explain that they were found on a piece of wrapping paper next to the body of a dead child when Allied troops liberated the Ravensbruck concentration camp from the Nazis in 1945. Over 92,000 people died there. Discuss the kind of love for enemies expressed in the poem and whether it's humanly possible to show this kind of love. Point out that such love is supernatural. Only God can bring it about.

DATE USED:

Approx. Time

STEP 1: *People You Love to Hate* _____
❏ Extra Action
❏ Small Group
❏ Extra Fun
❏ Short Meeting Time
Things needed:

STEP 2: *Combat Styles* _____
❏ Little Bible Background
❏ Fellowship & Worship
❏ Mostly Guys
❏ Media
❏ Short Meeting Time
❏ Combined Junior High/High School
❏ Extra Challenge
Things needed:

STEP 3: *Love in Enemy Territory* _____
❏ Extra Action
❏ Large Group
❏ Heard It All Before
❏ Little Bible Background
❏ Urban
Things needed:

STEP 4: *What Love Looks Like* _____
❏ Small Group
❏ Large Group
❏ Heard It All Before
❏ Mostly Girls
❏ Mostly Guys
❏ Urban
❏ Combined Junior High/High School
❏ Extra Challenge
Things needed:

STEP 5: *Prayer Conquers All* _____
❏ Fellowship & Worship
❏ Mostly Girls
❏ Extra Fun
❏ Media
Things needed:

Why Should I Give Money Away?

YOUR GOALS FOR THIS SESSION:
Choose one or more

☐ To help kids examine what the Bible says about money and possessions.

☐ To help kids understand the dangers of greed and the importance of giving.

☐ To help kids choose ways they will share their resources.

☐ Other:_____

Your Bible Base:

Mark 10:17-27
2 Thessalonians 3:10-11
1 Timothy 6:10
1 John 3:17

Found Money

(Needed: Play money, a real dollar bill, envelopes)

Before the session, you'll need to place several pieces of play money in envelopes and hide the envelopes around the room in places that will be difficult to find. You'll also need to hide a real dollar bill in one envelope. When group members arrive, explain to them what you've done and give them a few minutes to find the money.

After the money is found, congratulate the person who found the real dollar bill. Then ask the rest of the group members how they feel toward the person who found the real dollar. Note any feelings of jealousy or greed.

Ask: **Did you feel that way toward _____** (the one who found the real money) **before you arrived?** (Probably not.)

How many of you came to the meeting expecting to get a dollar bill? (Probably no one did.)

If you weren't expecting to get any money today, then why are you upset with _____? (They were presented with the opportunity to find money with little effort on their own, and they're sorry they missed it.)

Explain: **Today we're going to talk about money, greed, and giving, and how they're all related.**

Teen Talk

(Needed: Copies of Repro Resource 7, pencils)

Distribute copies of "The Teen on the Street" (Repro Resource 7) and pencils. Say: **Here are some comments that typical high school kids might make about giving.**

Ask six volunteers to read aloud the six parts on the sheet. Encourage the volunteers to use accents or strange voices. (To

make your volunteers more comfortable, you might want to demonstrate a strange voice for them. You could hold your nose while you talk,
use a high or low voice, or speak with an accent.)

Explain: **As these parts are read, put a check mark by the
comments that resemble any thoughts you've ever had
about giving.**

Afterward, take a poll to see which of the attitudes is most common
among your group members. You'll want to make a note of group
members' responses on your sheet because these characters will be
mentioned in subsequent steps, and you'll want to know which attitudes
to spend more time on.

Hooked on Money

(Needed: Bibles, chalkboard and chalk or newsprint and marker)

Have your group members turn in their Bibles to Mark 10:17-28.
Ask for three volunteers to read the speaking parts of these characters:
- Jesus (vss. 18-19, 21, 23- 25, 27)
- wealthy man (vss. 17, 20)
- disciples (vss. 26, 28).

Write the references on the board so the readers can find them
more easily. A narrator (you or one of your group members) should
read all the words between the speaking parts.

Afterward, say: **Today's tough teaching is the command
Jesus gave the wealthy man: "Go, sell everything you have
and give to the poor, and you will have treasure in heaven."
Many Christians wonder what Jesus meant by this.**

**What do you think He meant? Was He commanding all
Christians to give everything away, or just this wealthy man?**
If no one mentions its, point out that this is the only situation recorded
in the Bible in which Jesus made this command. However, verses 28-31
show that the disciples voluntarily did so and were commended for it
and promised blessing because of it.

**Why do you think Jesus asked the wealthy man to give
away everything?** (Riches were very important to the man—perhaps
even more important than Jesus.)

**Jesus told the man he would have "treasure in heaven"
if he gave everything to the poor. Is giving to the poor a**

OPTIONS

"price" we can pay to be saved? If not, how do you explain Jesus' words? (No. Jesus paid the only price necessary for our salvation on the cross. Salvation is a gift of God, not the result of our works [Eph. 2:8-9]. However, Jesus does talk about "counting the cost." Becoming a Christian does cost us something; it costs us ourselves. Jesus said that anyone who is not willing to "take his cross and follow me is not worthy of me. Whoever finds his life will lose it, and whoever loses his life for my sake will find it" [Matt. 10:38-39]. Jesus identified the cross for the rich young ruler—it was giving up his possessions.)

It's interesting that when Jesus said it's hard for the rich to enter the kingdom of heaven, His disciples were shocked. "Who then can be saved?" they asked. Point out that in those days, being rich was considered a sign of God's blessing. So Jesus is saying the exact opposite of what the disciples would have expected.

What do you think Jesus meant when He said, "With man this [a rich man being saved] is impossible, but not with God; all things are possible with God"? (Jesus' words indicate that salvation is impossible for anyone by human means because it is a gift of God's grace. Perhaps it's harder for rich people because they're used to depending upon themselves. If they think their wealth means that they've pleased God, they might not think that they're sinners in need of God's grace.)

Do you think it's a sin to be rich? (No. For example, Joseph of Arimathea, who owned the tomb in which Jesus was buried, was a rich man [Matt. 27:57-59]. But according to Mark 10:23, it is difficult for a rich man to enter the kingdom of heaven.)

Have someone read aloud I Timothy 6:10. Then ask: **If being rich isn't a sin, what's wrong with money?** (Nothing's wrong with money per se, but the love of money is at the root of all kinds of evil. The problem is greed.)

How is greed at the root of all kinds of evil in the world? Have you seen examples of this? (Greed is behind all kinds of corruption in society. Some people will do anything to get or stay rich. They will exploit others, lie, cheat, steal, or even kill.)

Explain that this kind of greed can happen to anyone, even us. Say: **To love money is to become hooked on it. We begin to think we need all the things it buys. Then, before we know it, we don't own our possessions—they own us.**

How can our possessions own us? (We spend a lot of time buying, repairing, and taking care of our possessions. We discard them before they're worn out to buy bigger and better versions of them. We work so hard to make enough money to buy them that we neglect ourselves, our relationship with God, and our relationships with other people.)

Teen Talk Revisited

(Needed: Bibles, Repro Resource 7)

Refer back to Repro Resource 7. Have group members look again at the characters' comments. Ask: **Is being hooked on money limited to those who have it?** (No, Waldo the Worker is a good example of someone who could get hooked on money because his family doesn't have it. If you don't have it, it's easy to think having money would solve a lot of problems.)

If Waldo the Worker continues his present level of fascination with money, how do you think it will affect the following areas of his life:

- **His family?** (Waldo may choose not to have a family. But if he does have a family, he probably wouldn't spend any more time with them than he does his teenage friends.)
- **His friends?** (Any friends he has will probably be from his job because that's all he'll have time for. He could become a lonely person who has only his "toys" [possessions] for company.)
- **His choice of job or his purpose in life?** (He certainly won't have time to focus on what God's purpose in his life could be. He will only think about how much money he can make, not about whether he's doing something necessary and worthwhile.)
- **His spiritual life?** (If he has any interest in spiritual things, it will be smothered by his obsession with making money. God will definitely take second place.)

Do you think Waldo's focus on money would go away if he inherited a million dollars? Why or why not? (Acquiring money doesn't usually decrease the desire for it. For instance, when your grandparents give you money at Christmas, it's wonderful at first. But then, it's not enough to do all the things you'd like to do with it and you wish you had more. If you have a serious case of loving money, it's agonizing because you'll always want more.)

Look at some of the other teens' comments on this sheet. Do any of them agree with Scripture?

Have someone read aloud 2 Thessalonians 3:10-11. Point out that in the early church, people took care of one another. There was no government welfare or social security system. The church fulfilled that function. Each member who could work was expected to care for his family's own needs as well as contribute to the community, so that those who could not work would be taken care of. A lazy person would then become a drain on the community. Paul says lazy people should not be given a handout because that would only reinforce their dependence on the community.

Say: **Lorenzo the Logician's comment seems compatible with this verse. But what's wrong with his attitude?** (For one thing, he's assuming that all poor people are lazy, which is not true. And he does not seem compassionate at all.)

Have someone read aloud I John 3:17. Then say: **Lorenzo the Logician needs to read this. Francesca the Fanatic's comments seem to be a blunt version of this. What's wrong with her attitude?** (Francesca cannot blame all the poverty and hunger in the world on Christians. Jesus even said, "The poor you will always have with you" [Matt. 26:11]).

What is I John 3:17 talking about? (This verse is talking about the needs a Christian sees, but does not respond to. It's talking about being insensitive to the needs that are all around you.)

Christians shouldn't be blamed for all the suffering in the world, but sometimes we don't see things because we don't want to see them. What are some of the obstacles that keep Christians from seeing the needs around us?

Write group members' responses on the board as you discuss them. Use the following suggestions to supplement their responses.

(1) We may not be *aware* of the poverty around us because we are so caught up in our own worlds.

(2) We may not *want* to know because we don't want to cut down on the ways we're currently spending money.

(3) We may not know *how* to help, so we'd rather not know about needs that we don't think we can do anything about—it's too depressing.

What's wrong with Penelope the Problem Solver's approach? (While it may seem compassionate and biblical, it's totally unrealistic. She wants to fix everything for people instead of doing what she can to help them help themselves. Her approach is smothering.)

Point out that Jesus met specific needs of needy people, but He left their dignity intact. He healed their blindness, but they had to remake their lives. If you just throw money at people, you haven't helped them for the long term. There's an old saying—if you give a man a fish, you feed him for one day. But if you teach a man how to fish, you feed him for a lifetime.

Look at Talulah the Too-Young-to-Be-a-Giver's comment about teens being too young to give. Does her reason for not giving make sense? (If you wait until you're an adult to start giving, it will actually be more difficult for you because you'll have no "practice." Anyhow, the Bible doesn't differentiate between "teen commands" and "adult commands.")

Why is Owen the Ower's argument not valid? (Teen expenses may be high, but adult expenses are even higher. If you start using Owen's excuse now, you'll probably use it for the rest of your life.)

The Biggest Obstacle of All

(Needed: Copies of Repro Resource 8, pencils)

Refer to the list of obstacles you wrote on the board earlier. Point to Obstacle #1 ("We may not be *aware* of the poverty around us because we are so caught up in our own worlds").

Say: **We may not be aware of poverty and starvation because we avoid it. We avoid it because it's so unpleasant. When a program about starving kids comes on TV, we probably switch the channel.**

Distribute copies of "How Rich Am I?" (Repro Resource 8) and pencils. Give your group members a few minutes to complete the sheet.

Then say: **If your score is 30 or above, you're "rich" by global standards. Most of the world's population do not have any of these things. People in North America earn more money in one year than many people outside North America will earn in a lifetime.**

When Jesus told the wealthy man to sell everything he had and give the money to the poor, He was not saying that this is the ultimate solution to poverty. What did He mean? (Jesus knew that the man's possessions were more important to him than anything else. Jesus was testing the man to be sure he was really serious about obeying what Jesus said.)

Point to Obstacle #2 ("We may not *want* to know because we don't want to cut down on the ways we're currently spending money").

Say: **How sad that this so often is our attitude. But I John 3:17 reminds us that we cannot claim to be God's children if we do not have compassion on those in need. Giving to the poor is a mark of a person who has the love of God in him or her. So what can we do?**

Point to Obstacle #3 ("We may not know *how* to help, so we'd rather not know about needs that we don't think we can do anything about—it's too depressing").

Say: **Let's not shut our eyes and ears to the needs around us because we don't know how to help. What are some things we can do to meet real needs?**

Conduct a brief brainstorming session to come up with practical suggestions for meeting real needs. You might want to concentrate on three areas: awareness, prayer, and involvement.

Don't underrate awareness. It's the first step. Some people cut themselves off geographically from certain areas or neighborhoods. Find out what's going on in your community. Are there homeless? If so, is there anybody trying to do something about it? You could appoint several kids to form a task force to find out what's going on in your community—both in terms of need and in terms of what kinds of efforts are already in place to meet those needs. They can keep the rest of the group updated for prayer and, ultimately, for involvement.

Kids can get involved in anything from volunteering at a homeless shelter or a soup kitchen to starting an after-school program of recreation and tutoring to keep kids off the streets. Your group could also sponsor a child overseas through a relief organization, or participate in a summer service project locally or cross-culturally. As you brainstorm, try to steer group members away from *only* giving money. There's nothing wrong with giving money, but personal involvement is far better.

Have someone reread I John 3:17. Then say: **God doesn't command us to give to the poor so we'll feel guilty and grouchy. He does it because it teaches us to be like Him— giving, while expecting nothing in return.**

Close the session in prayer, asking God to show your group members how much He loves the poor and how He wants us to reflect that love.

The ► Teen on the Street

Francesca the Fanatic

"How can Christians say they love others, and then let them starve? Tell me that!"

Waldo the Worker

"I have to admit it—I work hard because I like to have money. My family doesn't have much, but I like to buy nice clothes and stereo equipment. So while other kids play sports or hang out with friends, I work to make money. How can I be hurting anyone?"

Talulah the Too-Young-to-Be-a-Giver

"I think it's crazy to ask teenagers to give money to the church or to help the poor. We have plenty of time to do that later."

Lorenzo the Logician

"I don't understand why I should give money to help people who sit around and won't work."

Penelope the Problem Solver

"When I see people begging on the street, I'm totally messed up. I just wish I could take them home with me, buy them a house, and fix their lives."

Owen the Ower

"People all around the world have problems, but so do I. Why do I have to help the world? Storing up treasures in heaven is fine, but my car insurance is sky high here on earth!"

How Rich Am I?

Give yourself five points for each item that's true for you.

_____ The main meal at your house consists of more than rice and beans.

_____ Your parents/guardians pay for your health care needs.

_____ A school is available for you to attend, free of charge.

_____ Your grandparents have access to social security and/or pension plans.

_____ No one at your house goes to bed severely hungry.

_____ Your family is able to buy or charge something—a TV, a refrigerator—when they need it or within a few months after they need it.

_____ Your family lives in an apartment or house bigger than a tool shed.

_____ Your family owns a car.

_____ Your family owns two cars.

_____ Your family owns one car for every person in the family who drives.

_____ Your apartment or house has two bathrooms.

_____ Your apartment or house has three bathrooms.

_____ Your house has indoor plumbing.

_____ You have a telephone in your house.

_____ TOTAL

NOTES

STEP 2

When you "take a poll" to see which of the attitudes on Repro Resource 7 are most common among your group members, ham it up a bit. Let your six volunteers who represent the characters stand in front of the room. One at a time, have them repeat their comments. After each one, use "applause meter" techniques (clapping, cheers, whistling, etc.) to have students indicate their agreement with each statement. They may applaud for more than one person, but should vary the degree of enthusiasm (volume) depending on which comments they *most* agree with. After each of the six people has been evaluated, you might want to eliminate the ones who received little support and try again with only the top two or three.

STEP 5

To wrap up this session on giving, you might want to let your group members practice among themselves before trying to apply what they've learned on a larger scale. Challenge them to give a gift to everyone else in the group. The gifts may be things they have in their pockets or purses, things they find on the grounds (such as dandelions—stealing should be discouraged), or things they make from available materials. They may give actual gifts or symbolic ones (a rock to symbolize strength, etc.). They may give gifts of service, represented by handmade coupons. This may not be a simple activity, but it can be a lot of fun. And it's also a good exercise to help kids start seeing that they can be creative in their approach to giving.

STEP 3

With a small group, by the time you include three or four people in an activity, you may as well include everyone. So in addition to the people already involved in the speaking parts for the story of the rich young ruler, add a reporter and let everyone else become observers who witness the event. After the actual reading, the reporter should "recap" what was said (as is done after political speeches) and then try to get crowd response by interviewing the witnesses. He or she might also want to interview the rich guy to discover his feelings, his future plans, and so forth. The disciples could be questioned to shed light on why Jesus appeared so demanding in this situation. As a result of these interviews, the students will probably cover many of the questions that are included in the session after the reading. And even if they don't, you could "prompt" the reporter and deal with much of the information in the context of the skit rather than a traditional question-and-answer follow-up.

STEP 5

As you discuss how to apply what you've learned, you may need to put more effort into a "pep talk" for a small group. In many cases, a group with only a few people may also have few resources, a low budget, and limited opportunities to do the things they want to do—much less shell out a lot of cash for others. Group members may already have a strong awareness of need, and perhaps be active in prayer, yet may be too discouraged to be actively involved in addressing the problems. Gear applications specifically for your small group—nothing grandiose or unrealistic. Perhaps kids could start by committing to help their own church. While kids may not have a lot of extra money, they usually have free time on their hands that could be "given" to the church to mow yards, paint, repair, clean, and so forth. After they see that they can make a difference there, perhaps they will be more willing to think bigger.

STEP 2

Introduce the topic of giving by asking several volunteers to create worthy "causes" and make speeches to get others to give to those causes. (Volunteers may use real organizations or create ones of their own that they think would cause other people to give—even if they are "scams" to put money in their own pockets.) The rest of the group will represent the elite people of society, gathered to hear the "pitches" of all the worthwhile organizations seeking funds. Each person has $1,000 to spend—if he or she can be persuaded to part with it. Give your volunteers a few minutes to prepare. As each person makes his or her pitch, write his or her name and "cause" across the top of the board. When all of the pitches have been given, have each person determine how to spend his or her money. Group members may give it all to one person, split it among two or more, or keep it if he or she didn't think any of the causes were worthwhile. This exercise may reveal some truths about the world of fundraising. Does most of the money go to the best cause or to the person who was most entertaining? Was it difficult to get people to part with their money? Was it hard for anyone to ask for donations?

STEP 4

You might consider dealing with your "Teen on the Street" concept in a talk-show setting. Your six characters can be a panel on the stage, you can be the host, and the rest of your group can be the audience. After each person makes his or her initial statement, have panel members remain in character as audience members ask questions and make comments. Most of the information in Step 4 can be covered in this format, and may get your kids more involved. (With six people to keep up with, however, you might want to provide large nameplates to put in front of your volunteers for easy identification.)

STEP 1

After you do the money hunt, but before you announce the topic of the session, give everyone an imaginary $100 and ask how he or she would spend it. Group members may break the money down however they want to—spending it all in one shot or breaking it down into a lot of little purchases—but they should be as specific as possible. As everyone explains how he or she would spend the money, listen for any emphasis on giving, tithing, charities, and so forth. (Some of your kids may figure out where you're headed and say what you want to hear. If so, you could ask other group members to confirm if what your "giving" people have said sounds correct.) If few people give consideration to allotting a portion of their "windfalls" to the church or to needy people, you should have their attention as you go into the rest of the session.

STEP 3

As you discuss of the rich young ruler (a story many of your group members may be familiar with), reward correct answers with quarters or dimes. Don't explain. Just keep asking questions and see if the interest level increases. If so, later you can point out that the actions of group members confirm the teaching of the Bible text. Whenever a choice must be made between spiritual commitment and desire for material possessions, spiritual things too often become secondary. You might want to add one more question: **Based on what you learned from the story of the rich young ruler, how many of you are willing to give what you received from answering questions to the church, wait for treasures in heaven, and follow me through the rest of this session?** Anyone who chooses to return his or her money to the church should be congratulated, and then challenged to maintain that same giving attitude when more than dimes or quarters are involved.

STEP 3

If this is one of the first times many of your group members hear the story of the rich young man and Jesus, it may not make sense in light of all they have heard about Jesus so far. But before you even begin to explain, let kids express their opinions in a debate. Divide into two teams to debate this topic: "Jesus had no right to ask the young guy to give up *everything* before he could follow Him." It may be tempting to jump in and try to clarify certain points, but simply make note of such things as kids debate among themselves. Later, depending on how the debate goes, you may need to spend a while explaining that this is one of the harder Bible stories to fully understand. After you go through the rest of Step 3, check to see if everyone seems to understand. If not, take more time for questions before moving on.

STEP 5

The entire concept of giving might be new to some of your group members. So rather than closing by providing various alternatives for giving more faithfully, you might instead want to explain the importance of giving. For example, many kids new to Christianity may not have any idea where the money comes from to run a church. Emphasize that the pastor's salary, the building, the hymn books, the electricity, and everything else is paid for from the giving of congregation members. In addition, the church may be supporting missionaries in various parts of the world or providing ministries to help the people in the community. Sometimes we tend to deal with the topic of giving as merely a personal discipline and obligation. But if kids see *where* the money goes, giving can become an exciting incentive. So don't rush into the "how you can give" section before you deal with what can result from regular giving.

STEP 3

After discussing the story of the rich young man, have kids do "personal possessions inventories." Ask each person to create a list of top 10 possessions, in order of personal value. Then ask each person to draw a line at the point in which he or she would have difficulty parting with an item if requested to do so as part of his or her commitment to Jesus. Explain that the young man in the Bible story apparently wasn't a bad guy; but money was tops on his list, and he just wasn't able to let go of it to follow Jesus. If kids confess to owning things they aren't quite ready to give up, don't put a lot of pressure on them at this point. Perhaps they will never be expected to give up what they've listed, but they *will* be expected to put their relationship with Jesus above any piece of personal property. If they are having trouble doing so, they should pray about the matter, asking God to become so close to them that they will desire a relationship with Him above anything else they might be offered.

STEP 5

The session provides a number of possible actions that can be taken to get involved with the needs of other people. But you might want to take a different approach. Yes, your kids can give money. Yes, personal involvement is even better. Yet the best possibility for ongoing results is to help group members discover what their skills are and get them involved in some area where they feel comfortable and competent. Ask each person to list his or her strengths, interests, talents, and abilities. Then, as a group, try to figure out good ways to "give" those skills away for the good of others. For example, people with good singing voices can get involved in nursing-home ministries. Those with mechanical skills can help repair church lawn mowers or vehicles. Those who enjoy little kids might be able to teach or assist with nurseries or Sunday school classes. Try to show ways in which almost any talent can be "given" to others.

STEP 2

As you distribute copies of "The Teen on the Street" (Repro Resource 7), ask your group members to make the following changes before the parts are read: Change Waldo to Wanda, Lorenzo to Lorena, and Owen to Owena. While the volunteers are preparing to read, give them the opportunity to add a few sentences to what their characters say.

STEP 3

Have your volunteers read the speaking parts of the people in Mark 10:17-28. Then ask three other volunteers to read the same passage. Have one person read the part of Jesus; have another read the part of a wealthy businesswoman rather than the wealthy man; and have the third the part of one of the women who followed Jesus, instead of the disciples. After the story is read with these changes, ask: **If the people involved were women, would this change your response to this story? Why or why not?**

STEP 3

Don't overlook the opportunities involved with having a Bible text centered on a young *man.* Your guys may not relate to being rich, but they still have youth and masculinity in common with the character. Point out that Jesus loved this guy (Matthew 10:21). Then ask: **Why did Jesus let this young man walk away? Couldn't He have tried to convince him a little harder?** Explain that Jesus always gives us choices as to whether or not we follow Him. **But what if we don't make the right decisions concerning our relationships with Him on our own? Based on other people you've seen who put money before anything else, what can happen?** The whole Yuppie movement has shown that wealth in itself is not fulfilling. Guys can acquire the best cars, homes, and clothes that money can buy, and still feel intense dissatisfaction. Nothing can fill a person's inner, spiritual hunger except Jesus.

STEP 5

Theoretically, most people will agree that giving is important; yet, in real life, many of us find other uses for our money. To help your guys think through their actual commitment to giving, provide them with a number of activities to consider. Have them suppose they've agreed to give a portion of anything they make to the church during the next year. However, during the year, a number of opportunities come along. They won't have enough money to do the activity *and* give anything to the church. Which activities might persuade them to skip their regular giving for a while? Choose activities you know your group members would especially enjoy, which might include:
• a spring break beach trip
• a white-water-rafting trip
• a ski weekend in the Rockies
• buying leather school jackets
• a date at the coolest (most expensive) place in town.

STEP 1

At one end of the room, place a big pile of loose change with plenty of quarters, dimes, nickels, and pennies. At the other end, form relay teams. Explain that you will announce an amount of money and a number of coins. Teams should provide the exact amount using the number of coins you specify. The rules are as follows:
• The change must come from the pile across the room.
• Only one person at a time can go to the pile of change. That person must return to the team before the next person can go.
• Team members can only transport one coin at a time.
• Any extra change must be returned to the pile (one coin at a time) before you will accept the total.

You might ask for the following:
• **Change for a dollar, using four coins.** (Four quarters.)
• **Change for a dollar, using six coins.** (Three quarters, two dimes, one nickel.)
• **Change for a dollar, using 17 coins.** (Two quarters, three dimes, two nickels, ten pennies.)

Teams may have difficulty organizing to get the exact number of coins needed. Listen for any arguments or accusations. You can refer back to such comments and show that if we're ready to fight over coins, then larger amounts of money might lead to *real* conflict if we're not careful.

STEP 2

Have your group members play a drawing game using Pictionary rules (no talking, no words or symbols, etc.). Divide into teams. Have a player from each team come look at a word you will show him or her. The person should then return to the team and, at your signal, draw something that will help team members guess the word. The first team to do so gets a point. Use words connected with the session's topic: *money, greed, giving, possessions, selfishness, sharing, riches.*

STEP 3

The movie *Indecent Proposal* got a lot of publicity for the ethical question it raised: Would it be worth a million dollars to a young couple for the wife to spend one night with a stranger? If any group members have seen this movie, ask them to report on it. Then ask: **What do you think is the minimum dollar amount most people would ask for to commit each of the following sins:**
• **adultery?**
• **premarital sex?**
• **murder?**
• **shoplifting?**
• **lust?**

Indecent Proposal also dealt with the guilt and second-guessing involved after the decision had been made. Ask group members to consider whether they think the rich young man ever regretted *his* decision. If so, have them write a plot synopsis for *Rich Young Ruler 2: The Sequel* to describe what they think might have happened to this guy after he turned down Jesus' invitation to follow Him.

STEP 4

Have group members form a couple of "camera crews." Give each crew a camcorder. Instruct the crews to do actual teen-on-the-street interviews. (This could be done prior to discussing the content of Step 4 or as a follow-up activity sometime after the session.) First, crews should create a list of questions they could ask to get to the heart of other people's attitudes toward money. Then they should go to some public place, explain what they're doing, and get people's permission to ask a few questions and record the answers. (You might want to provide some adult supervision for this exercise, but the adults should remain in the background as the kids do the interviewing and taping.) Then return to watch the tapes and see how *real* teens feel about money, possessions, giving, and so forth.

STEP 1

Repro Resource 7 is used quite heavily in the session as written, so one option to shorten the meeting is to work around it. You can begin with Step 1, eliminate Step 2, and move to Step 3 without any break in continuity. Also eliminate Step 4 and pick up again in Step 5 where you hand out copies of Repro Resource 8. Skip the references to Obstacles #1, #2, and #3 (which were listed in Step 4), but otherwise follow the text of Step 5 as you wrap up the session.

STEP 2

Another option is to focus almost entirely on Repro Resource 7. In this case, you can deal primarily with Steps 2 and 4. However, almost all of the Bible content is in Step 3, so you should summarize the most important points as you move from Step 2 to Step 4. Also, Step 4 ends somewhat abruptly, so close with some of the best suggestions for practical application at the end of Step 5.

STEP 2

With an urban group, you might want to supplement the statements on Repro Resource 7 with the following typical urban excuses for not giving:
Rashan the Poverty Stricken—"My family is poor and on welfare; we hardly know where our next month's rent is coming from. What I have I cannot give."
Lae-Li the Minority—"Because I am a minority in a racist country that doesn't want me, I can give only to those who are of my cultural group."
Julio the Neglected—"I have some money; but no one ever gave me anything when I was in need, so why should I give to others?"
Feather the Old Soul—"This city has existed for nearly two hundred years, and poverty hasn't gone anywhere except up. No amount of money can make a change. I'd rather hold onto my funds."

Refer back to each of these characters in Step 4.

STEP 3

Have your group members consider how a conversation might have gone between Jesus and each of the following people:
• a prostitute
• a gang leader
• a drug dealer
• an alcoholic
• an abusive parent
• a superstar athlete
• a straight-A student.

Ask: **How might the conversation have been similar to or different from the one between Jesus and the rich young man?**

STEP 2

A group with a lot of young teens might not find Repro Resource 7 as effective as older groups. Junior highers may not yet have strong opinions (if they've formed opinions at all) about social concerns, giving, and so forth. Many still expect their parents to take care of such things. Yet they also frequently have an intense craving for more and better possessions—the best athletic shoes, bicycles, clothes, and so forth. Your time may be better spent helping them identify and express their attitudes and helping them see the "big picture" concerning the use of their monetary resources. Show them the importance of starting now to set aside a portion of what they have for the church and/or the support of those who are less fortunate. Help them see that if they don't begin now, it will never become any easier.

STEP 5

As you discuss practical applications of what has been discussed, you'll probably need to get more specific with junior highers. The session text has some good ideas, but young teens usually want to see for themselves what needs to be done. As you deal with awareness, prayer, and involvement, take kids through each stage. For awareness, walk around the church grounds and see where improvements could be made if more money were available. Or drive around the sections of town where your group members don't usually go and look at the needs of the poorer people in the community. For prayer, challenge the kids to begin to pray for others on a regular basis (which may be quite different from the usual "personal request" prayers of many young people). And finally, when you get to involvement, try to come up with some suggestions (to begin with) that are short-term, and that your students can do on their own. Explain that you will expect accountability, providing an opportunity in the future for each person to describe the results of any actions he or she chooses to take.

STEP 3

To help your group members get a better perspective on the story of the rich young man, have them read the parables of the hidden treasure and the pearl (Matt. 13:44-46). Ask: **How do these parables relate to the story of Jesus and the young man?** (The men in the parables who discovered the treasure and the pearl were able to recognize the value of what they had found. They knew it was a "real deal" to trade everything they had to acquire their new-found treasure. But the rich young man in real life failed to see that following Jesus was a far better treasure than the pile of money he had at home.) Also have group members discuss some things they can do to ensure they don't make the same mistake the young man made.

STEP 5

Sometimes we are unable to give our time or resources to others because we are unaware of their needs. People may not like to admit that they are "needy" in any way. So without referring to *needs*, have each student make a list of "Things I Wish I Had" and "Things I Could Use Help With." Explain that these should be serious concerns—not fantasy cars or dream vacations. When they finish, collect the sheets and make a master list. (If you wish, you can keep the names, but make the master list anonymous.) Then in the weeks to come, students should see if they can help with the concerns of other group members in some way—by sharing possessions, helping with difficult homework assignments, or whatever. It may be difficult for your group members to get serious about helping others if they are ignoring each others' needs.

DATE USED:

Approx. Time

STEP 1: *Found Money* _____
- ❑ Heard It All Before
- ❑ Extra Fun
- ❑ Short Meeting Time

Things needed:

STEP 2: *Teen Talk* _____
- ❑ Extra Action
- ❑ Large Group
- ❑ Mostly Girls
- ❑ Extra Fun
- ❑ Short Meeting Time
- ❑ Urban
- ❑ Combined Junior High/High School

Things needed:

STEP 3: *Hooked on Money* _____
- ❑ Small Group
- ❑ Heard It All Before
- ❑ Little Bible Background
- ❑ Fellowship & Worship
- ❑ Mostly Girls
- ❑ Mostly Guys
- ❑ Media
- ❑ Urban
- ❑ Extra Challenge

Things needed:

STEP 4: *Teen Talk Revisited* _____
- ❑ Large Group
- ❑ Media

Things needed:

STEP 5: *The Biggest Obstacle of All* _____
- ❑ Extra Action
- ❑ Small Group
- ❑ Little Bible Background
- ❑ Fellowship & Worship
- ❑ Mostly Guys
- ❑ Combined Junior High/High School
- ❑ Extra Challenge

Things needed:

NOTES

Unit Three: What Do You Think?

Tackling Controversial Issues

by Paul Borthwick

"You just don't understand!"

The 15 year old blurted his frustration toward me because I had made a few jokes about some of the issues he was wrestling with.

When I tried to justify my response, he retorted, "You simply don't understand! In the world you grew up in, abortion was rarely public and seldom discussed. Euthanasia and genetic engineering were unheard of, and the idea of choosing your sexual preference was unacceptable."

He is a child of the nineties; I am a product of the sixties. He was right. I didn't understand the myriad of choices and the wide-ranging moral opinions facing his generation. His response made me feel old, but it also reminded me of the new challenges facing today's teenagers.

The challenges are even greater for young people who desire to follow Jesus. Many young Christians are weak in their understanding of what the Bible teaches. When asked what the biblical perspective is on moral or ethical issues, they have no idea where to turn. And those who are biblically literate live in a world that dictates a set of values that directly contradict biblical teaching.

A Wise Approach

The goal in the weeks ahead is to discover what high schoolers *really* think about some of today's toughest issues. Our approach to these issues will determine whether we receive honest responses from our group members or the answers they think we want to hear. If we can create an environment in which kids feel that honesty will be accepted, they will be more likely to be open to hearing the biblical perspective.

Keep in mind the following principles:

• *Approach the topics with grace.* The controversial issues covered in this book can bring out a spirit of condemnation in people, especially in those who have not really struggled with the issues personally. Several of the issues—especially euthanasia and homosexuality—might also provoke crude humor that can oppose a spirit of grace.

Our responsibility as leaders is to set a tone of grace in the meetings in which these topics will be discussed. Presenting the topics in a spirit of grace will make for better interaction and sharing.

Grace means allowing for disagreements and differences of opinion. Group members will be more inclined to share their opinions when they know that diversity is tolerated. We need grace ourselves to allow group members to share opinions that disagree with the teaching of the Bible. If we want to change their opinions to be more biblically based, group members need to know that we understand and accept where they are now.

Grace also involves creating an atmosphere that communicates forgiveness. Group members will share more openly if they know that God's grace will be adequate to forgive them—either for wrong opinions or for actually violating biblical standards.

• *Approach the topics with sensitivity.* In one youth group meeting, we ended the session with a 15-minute question-and-answer session. A group member asked me about the biblical perspective on abortion. I proceeded to give a detailed explanation on how abortion is sin, murder, and against the will of God.

What I did not understand was that a young woman in that youth group had just had an abortion. I learned this after the meeting. I wish I'd known it before I responded so harshly and matter-of-factly. I wish I'd been sensitive enough to speak with a gentler spirit and a tone of forgiveness.

In all of the sessions ahead, be sensitive to the emotional volatility of the topics. In a youth group of almost any size, there may be high schoolers who've had abortions, who've thought about euthanasia for their terminally ill grandparents, who have a sibling or another family member who's chosen a homosexual lifestyle, whose parents are divorced, or whose mother or father work in the defense industry. As a result, it will be difficult for these group members to maintain objectivity in the discussion. If we present the topics with sensitivity to the potential of personal involvement in these issues, we will be more successful in drawing group members out.

• *Approach the topics discreetly.* Some of the topics ahead may be morally repulsive to us. Others might be "clear-cut" issues (from a Christian perspective) in our minds with little room for discussion. However, keep in mind that discussions about war and peace, for example, may be based on political ideologies rather than biblical values.

Whatever our personal opinions or convictions, it is important that we not reveal our ideas too soon—either by reacting negatively to some of the "far-out" opinions of group members or by filling the quiet moments of the meeting by speaking out on our own views to relieve the awkward silence. We must guard against the tendency to present our own opinion or what we perceive as the biblical opinion before group members say anything.

For maximum growth, we need to allow kids to think through these tough issues on their own. Remember, our goal is to teach them how to think, not to dictate to them what we think.

What Are We After?

Keep in mind the following aims:

• *We want to understand group members' perspectives.* If someone is lost and looking for directions, the first question we ask is "Where are you now?" We need to understand where our kids are and what they think before we direct them to where we think they should go.

Young people today are lost in the myriad of opinions taught to them in an increasingly godless and secularized society. They need direction, but first we must understand their present opinions. Before we can influence group members' views concerning the controversial issues in this book, we need to draw them and their ideas out.

There are several methods we can use to do this. For instance, we might consider using an anonymous survey with open-ended questions concerning the issues at hand. This could be administered the first week of the series or before the series begins. Questions might include multiple choice queries about the topics or agree/disagree statements like "War is always wrong" or "Adultery is acceptable grounds for divorce." The survey might also include an opportunity to respond to recent news events (a story about euthanasia, a gay rights protest, etc.).

We might also consider making use of the research of others that expresses popular beliefs on the topics covered in this book. Resources like *Youthworker Update* (1224 Greenfield Drive, El Cajon, CA 92021) or *USA Today* provide statistics that can be accumulated and shared with the group to reveal prevalent views on these tough topics.

WHAT DO YOU THINK ?

We might also consider taking a "devil's advocate" approach at the start of the meeting, outlining the various reasons for an unbiblical or anti-Christian position on the issue under consideration. The way in which group members respond will reveal whether they support that approach or oppose it because of Christian convictions.

• *We want to teach group members to explore the Bible.* Our goal is not simply to allow group members to wander aimlessly in their own opinions as they consider these tough topics. Our goal is to help them start to explore the Bible for answers regarding the issues at hand.

The basic message we should convey is that no matter what *my* opinion or *your* opinion or *our culture's* opinion is, what matters is *God's* opinion. Thus, in each session we will turn our attention away from our own opinions and search the Scriptures to see what God has to say. Even if group members disagree with what the Bible teaches, they will at least be able to compare their opinions against scriptural teachings.

• *We want to help group members develop personal convictions.* I asked a small group of high school freshmen, "How many of you have developed your own convictions regarding the issue of abortion?" Only Jennifer raised her hand. I asked the others why they hadn't.

They replied, "Well, Jennifer has a friend who got pregnant, so she's had to think about the issue. When we have to, then we'll decide."

I used that moment to teach the kids about the difference between subjective opinions (often dictated by the emotion of the situation) and convictions. I explained that they should be developing their biblical convictions now, so that they know what they believe about tough topics like abortion before they're in the "heat of the moment."

The goal of this book is to help group members develop their own solid, biblical convictions regarding issues like abortion, euthanasia, and homosexuality. We want to equip them to face the challenging issues of our time with strong biblical foundations. As a result of this study, group members should feel free to express their ideas; they should understand that God is big enough to face all of their questions; and they should realize that the Bible helps us sort through tough questions.

Paul Borthwick is minister of missions at Grace Chapel in Lexington, Massachusetts. A former youth pastor and frequent speaker to youth workers, he is author of several books.

The images on these two pages are designed to help you promote this course within your church and community. Feel free to photocopy anything here and adapt it to fit your publicity needs. The stuff on this page could be used as a flier that you send or hand out to kids—or as a bulletin insert. The stuff on the next page could be used to add visual interest to newsletters, calendars, bulletin boards, or other promotions. Be creative and have fun!

Who's Right?

We live in a world of controversy. What are your opinions about issues like abortion, gay rights, euthanasia, divorce, and war?
More importantly, how do your opinions compare with what the Bible says?
We're going to explore these controversial issues—
and what the Bible says about them—
in a new course called *What Do You Think?* Won't you join us?

Who:

When:

Where:

Questions? Call:

Unit Three: What Do You Think?

What do you think?

(Write your own message in the thought balloons.)

Breaking up is hard...on everyone.

What's going on here?

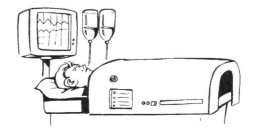

Pro-Choice or Pro-Life? (Abortion)

YOUR GOALS FOR THIS SESSION:

Choose one or more

☐ To help group members think about their personal views on abortion in light of biblical support for when life begins.

☐ To help group members understand some of the complexities involved in the abortion debate.

☐ To help group members respond with compassion, love, and empathy to those people facing the question of abortion, and to love their "enemies" in the abortion debate.

☐ Other:_____
_____

Your Bible Base:

Exodus 20:13
Psalm 139:13-16
Jeremiah 1:4-5
Matthew 5:13-16, 43-48
Luke 1:39-44

NOTE TO LEADERS: In this unit we've chosen to deal with some very controversial topics. We applaud your willingness to deal with subjects like these at church. It's not an easy task. We recognize that churches don't always agree on some of these issues and that you might find yourself disagreeing with us. Our purpose is not to tell young people what to think or to settle these controversial issues once and for all in one short session. Rather, we want to help you help your group members develop skills to wrestle with these and other issues and arrive at a biblical world view.

Stunts 'R' Us

(Needed: Index cards prepared according to instructions, container, materials for the various stunts)

Open the session with a decision-making activity for the whole group. Ask for several volunteers to come to the front of the room. Explain that the volunteers will be performing various stunts. One at a time, each volunteer will draw two index cards (which you've prepared beforehand) from a container. Each card will have the name of a stunt written on it. The volunteer will read the names of the two stunts to the group. The rest of the group members will then decide (by a majority vote) which stunt the volunteer must perform.

Once the group has decided on a stunt, the group member will return the name of the other stunt to the container. You will then read the explanation of the stunt the group chose. The volunteer will have 90 seconds to complete the stunt. (In preparing the index cards, make sure you write only the *names* [which are fairly vague and nondescriptive] of the stunts, instead of writing out the entire explanations.)

The following is a list of stunts you might want to use. You might also supplement this list with some ideas of your own.

Birthday Humdinger—Pinch your nose closed and hum a verse of "Happy Birthday to You." If you can't do it, whistle it without laughing.

Sit on It—Blow up a balloon and pop it by sitting on it.

Life at MacDonald's—Sing to the rest of the group "Old MacDonald Had a Farm," using at least four different animals in the verses.

Here Comes Santa Claus—Create a shaving cream beard, mustache, and eyebrows on your face and wear them for the next five minutes.

Schnozzball—Using just your nose, roll a football to the other side of the room and back.

Chocolate Surprise—Without using your hands, remove and eat a banana from a bowl filled with chocolate sauce.

The Chewy Challenge—Without using your hands, remove and chew a piece of unwrapped bubble gum from a bowl filled with flour.

Stuck on You—Tape a piece of paper to your back.

Afterward, ask those group members who didn't have to perform a stunt: **Were you uncomfortable deciding which stunt the volunteers had to do? Why or why not?** Probably many group members will say they weren't uncomfortable. After all, their decisions didn't affect *them* at all.

If you had it to do over again, would you make a different choice for any of the volunteers? Get a few responses.

Ask your volunteers: **Did the group make a good decision for you? Do you think it's fair that the rest of the group got to choose which stunt you had to perform? Why or why not?** Get a few responses.

Ask the entire group: **What are some other examples in our society today of people making choices for others?** (Parents decide where their kids will live, what school they will go to, etc. Managers decide what projects their employees will work on. Teachers decide what homework students will work on.) See if anyone brings up the abortion issue.

STEP 2

Where Do You Stand?

(Needed: Newspapers, copies of Repro Resource 1, pencils)

Suggest: **Some people say the abortion issue is a matter of people trying to make decisions for others. They say that the pro-life movement wants to take away from pregnant women the choice of what to do with their own bodies. Do you agree with this statement? Is the pro-life movement trying to take away a pregnant woman's right to choose? Do pro-choice advocates limit anyone's choices? What are the main arguments on both sides of the abortion debate?** Use questions like these to get the discussion going. Don't ask kids to share their personal views unless they want to. Encourage discussion, but not a fight!

OPTIONS

EXTRA ACTION

SMALL GROUP

LARGE GROUP

HEARD IT ALL BEFORE

URBAN

JR. HIGH HIGH SCHOOL COMBINED

EXTRA CHALLENGE

Before you delve too deeply into the issue of abortion, update your group members on any recent developments in the pro-choice versus pro-life conflict. Give your group members an overview of where the issue stands in your community. Are there any "hot spots"—clinics, hospitals, doctor's homes—in your area that have been targeted by pro-life forces? Have there been any pro-choice rallies in your area? Bring in several local and/or national newspapers and summarize any relevant articles concerning the abortion issue. Ask your group members to share any information they've heard or read on the right-to-life/freedom-of-choice debate.

If you can't find any quotes, read this: **Here's something that was printed in the paper about abortion. The headline calls it "The Evil of the Age." The article begins by saying, "Thousands of human beings are murdered before they have seen the light of this world." Where do you think this piece appeared? What view of abortion do you think the author holds?** Let kids guess. Then tell them it was a feature story in the *New York Times*—on August 23, 1871! Ask whether they think a story like that would appear in a major paper like the *New York Times* today. Have kids suggest reasons why abortion is more "acceptable" today than it was a long time ago.

Once you've got kids talking about abortion, distribute copies of "Where Do You Stand?" (Repro Resource 1) and pencils. Give group members a few minutes to complete the sheet, keeping it completely anonymous. Collect the sheets and quickly tally up the responses.

Go through the statements one at a time and see where the group as a whole stands. Let kids comment as you go along. Do *not* force anyone to share who doesn't want to. If you think the discussion might get too controversial, simply report the findings and move on.

[NOTE: Don't make the mistake of assuming that all of your group members are committed to the pro-life agenda. Some may believe that abortion is wrong, but may not feel motivated to act on their beliefs. Others may be embarrassed by the actions of certain pro-life demonstrators and may not want to be associated with them. Still others may be committed to a pro-choice agenda. Try to create an atmosphere of openness and mutual respect. That's not to say that you shouldn't encourage debate between group members who hold opposing views; but you should *not* allow those debates to turn into personal attacks.]

As you go over Repro Resource 1 with your group members, use the following questions to supplement your discussion.

If you took a poll among people in this church, what percentage of them would you say is pro-life?

What percentage of the kids at your school would you say is pro-life?

What percentage of the teachers and staff at your school would you say is pro-life?

If all you knew about the abortion issue was what you saw on TV and what you read in magazines, what would you think of pro-life activists? (Many TV shows and teen magazines portray pro-life activists as narrow-minded fundamentalists out to take away women's freedom of choice.) What would you think of pro-choice activists? (Many are portrayed by secular media as politically correct patriots trying to protect constitutional freedoms. Some Christian media may depict pro-choice people as immoral liberals out to destroy the fabric of society.)

Life Begins at …?

(Needed: Bibles, chalkboard and chalk or newsprint and marker, paper, pencils)

Ask: **What is the central question of the abortion issue?** Group members' responses to this extremely open-ended question should tell you a lot about their perspectives. Some may say the central question is "Do people have the right to tell a pregnant woman what she can and can't do with her body?" Others may say it's "What other options are there for a pregnant woman who doesn't want to have a baby?"

If no one mentions it, suggest that the central question of the issue is "When does life begin?" Write the question on the board.

Say: **If we believe that the fetus is a living person, then abortion is murder. So not only must we consider the rights of the pregnant woman, we must also consider the rights of the unborn baby.**

Explain that there are various theories as to when life begins. Some people say life begins at conception. Others believe it begins approximately three months after conception, when various physical developments occur. Others believe life begins when the unborn baby is capable of living outside the womb. Still others believe life begins at birth. List the various theories on the board as you name them. Instruct group members to write down their opinion as to when life begins on a sheet of paper. Save a tree by using the back of one of the Repro Resources.

Have volunteers read Psalm 139:13-16; Jeremiah 1:4-5; and Luke 1:39-44. Then ask: **What do these verses tell us about the unborn?** (God knows us and has plans for our lives even before

OPTIONS

EXTRA ACTION

HEARD IT ALL BEFORE

LITTLE BIBLE BACKGROUND

MEDIA

we're born. John the Baptist leaped for joy while still in his mother's womb, suggesting he was "alive.")

Of the different theories on the board concerning when life begins, which one does the Bible seem to support? (Because God recognizes and interacts with us even before we're "formed . . . in the womb" [Jer. 1:5], it would seem that the Bible most closely allies with the theory that life begins at conception.)

So what do you think is the Bible's position on abortion? After a couple of volunteers have offered their opinions, ask someone to read Exodus 20:13. Point out that if, according to Scripture, life begins at conception, then abortion is murder.

Have group members look again at the responses they wrote on the back of Repro Resource 1. Ask: **If your answer is different from the Bible's, what does that mean? Do you need to reconsider your position? Is it really a big deal if you believe that life begins later than the Bible indicates?** Give group members a minute or two to consider these questions. See if anyone can give a reason for why it is a big deal. Be prepared to give your own reasons.

Caught in the Middle

(Needed: Copies of Repro Resource 2, pencils, chalkboard and chalk or newsprint and marker)

Say: **While pro-life and pro-choice advocates wage their battles over the issue of abortion, there are many people caught in the crossfire—specifically the people who are actually considering abortion.**

Distribute copies of "The People Behind the Issue" (Repro Resource 2). Explain: **Here are six case studies of people who are considering abortion. The approach of some pro-life advocates might be to lecture these people for even thinking about abortion—or carry "Abortion Is Murder" signs in front of abortion clinics. Let's not use that approach. Instead, let's try to empathize with these people—to understand how they might be feeling and what they might be thinking.**

Have group members form pairs to work on the sheet. Instruct the pairs to read each case study and then write down how the people in that case might be feeling, and what might be influencing the decision of whether or not to have an abortion.

Give the pairs a few minutes to work. When everyone is finished, go through the case studies one at a time and have each pair share its responses. Use the following information to supplement group members' responses.

Shari—She is probably feeling bitter disappointment at the prospect of having her dream of becoming a doctor ruined. Since she's worked so hard already, she may consider abortion as another sacrifice she has to make to achieve her goal.

Edwardo and Luisa—They are probably feeling extremely confused, scared, and helpless. Their lack of insurance and the "expert" advice of their doctor are probably weighing heavily in their decision.

Rhonda—She is probably feeling overburdened. Raising three kids in near-poverty conditions is difficult enough; raising four might seem impossible. She is probably considering the fact that her other children might suffer if she has to raise a fourth child on her limited income.

Ben and Li—They are probably feeling very stunned and worried. Having a baby is probably one of the last things a couple in their forties thinks about. The fact that Li could die if she carries the baby to full-term is probably agonizing not only to Ben and Li, but to their three children as well.

Laticia—In addition to the feelings she's dealing with as a result of the rape, Laticia is also probably feeling torn and confused. Her pro-life stance may be causing her to reject the idea of aborting the baby. However, the idea of giving birth to a child who is the offspring of the man who raped her—a child who may have severe medical problems—is probably repulsive to her.

Ken and Allie—They might be feeling guilt or anger about the situation they're in. They probably think they're too young to be parents and that a baby would interfere with their future plans and dreams. Allie might be angry at Ken for wanting her to have an abortion and for what seems like a lack of commitment to her. Ken might be angry at Allie for not wanting to get rid of the baby. Allie might be thinking about alternatives like raising the baby alone or giving the child up for adoption.

Afterward, ask: **Which of these cases do you think is most common?** Point out that the cases of Edwardo and Luisa, Ben and Li, and Laticia are the exceptions. Don't get hung up on discussing what should be done in cases of rape, incest, possible birth defects, or when the mother's life is in danger. The vast majority of unwanted pregnancies are the result of people's deliberate choice to have sex. Most abortions are performed to undo the consequences of that. Nevertheless, all of the cases are difficult, with many factors to weigh.

How do you think each of these people would feel if someone told them, "You must not have an abortion"? Why?

What if Li was your mother or Laticia was your sister? How would you respond to someone yelling at her, "Don't kill your baby!"?

OPTIONS

LARGE GROUP

MOSTLY GIRLS

MOSTLY GUYS

SHORT MEETING TIME

URBAN

JR. HIGH / HIGH SCHOOL COMBINED

EXTRA CHALLENGE

Point out that these complications don't change God's standards of right and wrong. Sometimes no solution seems best. However, these situations should help us think about the way we respond to people in crisis who might be considering abortion. Instead of condemning them, we should attempt to empathize with them and find out what they're feeling and what factors are influencing their decision.

Also point out that at the same time, Christians are called to be salt and light to the world. Read Matthew 5:13-16. Then say: **Suppose you were talking to the people in these cases. What might it mean to be salt and light in situations like these? What might Jesus say to these people?** Briefly review as many of the situations as you have time for.

Have group members remain in their pairs. Say: **Let's say you just found out that a close friend is pregnant and considering an abortion. What would you do?** Give the pairs a few minutes to come up with some strategies—dos and don'ts in talking to the girl about her situation.

After a few minutes, have each pair share its strategy. Pay attention to how much empathy is incorporated in the strategies. See if kids suggest alternatives to abortion like adoption. It's one thing to tell a person not to have an abortion; it's another thing entirely to help provide workable alternatives.

Do What to My Enemies?

(Needed: Bibles, poster board, markers, chalkboard and chalk or newsprint)

Have kids form two teams. Designate the members of one team "pro-life advocates"; designate the members of the other team "pro-choice advocates." Give several sheets of poster board and markers to each team. Instruct each team to create a few posters that members of its assigned group might prepare for an abortion rights rally. For instance, pro-lifers might create signs that say "Mommy, Don't Kill Me!" and "Baby Killers!" Pro-choicers might create signs that say "A Woman's Body Is Her Business!" and "Freedom of Choice—For Everyone!"

When the signs are finished, stage a mini-rally. Have the members of each team chant slogans and wave their signs as though they were really at an abortion rights rally. Kids with dramatic flair might even engage in a mock argument/shouting match with their opponents. The teams should pattern their performances on the real-life rallies they see on the news.

After a few minutes of this, stand and read aloud (while the teams are still shouting and chanting) Matthew 5:43-48. Read it twice, if necessary, to make sure everyone hears you.

Then ask: **If both pro-life activists and pro-choice activists followed the instructions in this passage, what might an abortion rights rally be like?** Give the teams an opportunity to act this out. Some group members might engage in peaceful conversations with their "enemies." Others might tear up any offensive signs they have. Still others might leave the rally to find less confrontational ways to accomplish their goals. If time permits, have group members create new signs that reflect the sentiments of Matthew 5:43-48.

Then ask: **Do you think most pro-life advocates are helping or hurting the cause?** This is a controversial question that could be approached from many angles. Some might think pro-lifers are helping, by reminding people of the sanctity of life and upholding biblical standards. Others might think they are hurting the cause by using hateful tactics and giving "Christians" a bad name. Challenge group members to think of positive things Christians *can* do to move the abortion debate beyond name-calling toward positive dialogue and solutions. Emphasize that in the abortion conflict, it's possible to love someone with a different view without compromising your own beliefs. If our motives are truly based on love, it's likely that we'll earn the right to share our beliefs with those who disagree with us. If our motives are based on hatred or a desire to prove a point, we may end up alienating people, causing them to tune out whatever we say, and helping them become even more set in their beliefs.

Wrap up the session by following another instruction in Matthew 5:43-48—praying for "those who persecute." Write a list on the board of people or groups that might be "enemies" in the abortion debate. Your list might include doctors and clinic workers who perform abortions, outspoken pro-life or pro-choice leaders, women who are thinking about getting an abortion, people who picket abortion clinics, legislators who are for abortion, legislators who are against it, etc. Ask volunteers to choose one person or group from the list to pray for. Then close the session with a group prayer.

OPTIONS

SMALL GROUP

LITTLE BIBLE BACKGROUND

FELLOWSHIP & WORSHIP

MOSTLY GUYS

EXTRA FUN

WHERE DO YOU STAND?

Use the following key to respond to the statements below.

  1 = Yes, definitely.
  2 = Probably, depending on the circumstances.
  3 = I'm not sure.
  4 = Probably not, depending on the circumstances.
  5 = Absolutely not.

_____ 1. I believe abortion is wrong under any circumstance.

_____ 2. Even though abortion is a terrible thing, under some circumstances (rape, incest, etc.), I think it's justifiable.

_____ 3. I believe that a pregnant woman should have the right to terminate her pregnancy (have an abortion) if she so chooses.

_____ 4. I consider myself a pro-life (abortion is wrong) advocate.

_____ 5. I believe that pro-life activists have a right to do whatever it takes to prevent abortions from happening.

_____ 6. I would counsel a friend against having an abortion.

_____ 7. If I found out a friend of mine had an abortion, I would have no problem remaining friends with her.

_____ 8. I would be willing to use some of my money to support a pro-life cause.

_____ 9. I would be willing to work on a campaign to elect pro-life candidates to political office and to petition politicians to make abortion illegal.

_____ 10. I would be willing to debate a pro-choice representative at a school assembly.

_____ 11. I would be willing to march outside of an abortion clinic to protest its practice.

_____ 12. I would be willing to go to jail for protesting abortion.

NOTES

—— The People ——
Behind the Issue

Shari

Shari, a high school senior, discovers that she is pregnant. Shari is an honors student with a full scholarship to a very prominent university. She has worked hard toward her goal of becoming a doctor. Everything is in place for her to enter the pre-med program at the university. However, there is no way she can pursue her dream if she has a baby—at least, not for several years.

Edwardo and Luisa

Edwardo and Luisa are a young couple who have been married for less than two years. Luisa is pregnant, but has had a very troubled pregnancy. After a series of tests, Edwardo and Luisa discover that their baby will be born with severe mental and physical handicaps. They have no health insurance. The initial hospital stay for the baby after birth will cost tens of thousands of dollars. The doctor advises that the best solution is an abortion.

Rhonda

Rhonda is a young, single mother living on welfare. She has three children already and is pregnant with a fourth. With her government aid and food stamps, she can barely afford to provide shelter, food, and clothing for three children, let alone four. One of Rhonda's friends tells her about a local agency that provides free family planning and birth control—including abortions and sterilizations.

Ben and Li

Ben and Li are in their late forties. They've been married for over twenty-five years and have raised three children. To their surprise, they discover that Li is pregnant. The doctor explains that Li's pregnancy poses a severe health risk for both the baby and the mother. In fact, because Li is diabetic, the pregnancy could be life-threatening for her. The pregnancy is in its sixth week.

Laticia

Laticia, a young single woman, was raped almost two months ago. As a result of the rape, she became pregnant. She has no desire to have a child, but she's strongly pro-life in her stance on abortion. To make matters worse, she's just found out that her rapist tested positive for AIDS and is addicted to cocaine. Her doctor warns her that both the disease and the addiction might be passed on to her baby.

Ken and Allie

Ken and Allie are in love. They've been dating since they were freshmen. At the beginning of their senior year of high school, Allie gets pregnant. She wants to keep the baby and marry Ken. Ken, however, wants Allie to have an abortion because he isn't ready for marriage yet.

NOTES

STEP 2

Cut the statements from Repro Resource 1 and tape one to each chair. Make sure the number of statements/chairs matches the number of kids. Instruct kids to sit on statements they feel strongly about—and are prepared to explain their feelings about to the group. Only one person may sit on a chair. If everyone is sitting in two minutes, everyone gets a prize. If anyone is left standing, no one gets a prize. Kids may try to convince each other to sit on certain chairs and help each other prepare explanations. Afterward, discuss the results.

STEP 3

Have kids sit in the fetal position and make appropriate actions while you read the following: **At about six weeks, your heart starts beating. Reflexes like sucking and grasping begin. You can make quick, tiny movements. At two months, most of your major organ systems are developed; your brainwave activity resembles an adult's. At three months, all your major organs are formed. You can kick and frown and curl your toes. At four months you can move around, suck your thumb, and make a face. When a bright light shines on Mom's tummy, you can lift your hands to shield your eyes. You're ticklish. At five months you can react to loud sounds by covering your ears. You get hiccups. Your kicking and punching are hard enough that Mom can feel it. You can cry. You're as sensitive to touch as a one-year-old. This is the earliest point at which you can possibly survive outside the womb. At six months your eyes open and close. You can react to stress with frantic kicking. At seven months you have all the reflexes you'll show at birth—even stepping. By eight months, you could survive fairly easily outside the womb. At about nine months, you're born.**

STEP 2

In a small group, it might be hard to remain anonymous when filling out Repro Resource 1. Instead, assign an identity (a woman considering an abortion, a pastor, a news anchorwoman, a boy who got his girlfriend pregnant, etc.) to each individual. Have group members fill out the sheet as if they were that person. Ask: **What did you assume about your character when answering these questions? Which ones were hardest for your character to answer? Why? Which ones would you have the hardest time answering? Why?**

STEP 5

A mock abortion rights rally probably won't go over real well in a small group. Instead, discuss what group members think of the following bumper stickers: "Stop the Killing!"; "Former Fetus for Life"; "Don't forget the baby!"; "It's my body!"; "If you can't choose, you lose"; "Why do pro-lifers love bombs?" (You might want to write the slogans on the board.) Ask: **What statement is the driver of the car making? What would a strongly pro-life person think of it? How about a pro-choice advocate?** After reading and discussing Matthew 5:43-48, have kids create bumper sticker slogans that echo the words of Jesus.

STEP 2

Tallying the responses on Repro Resource 1 may take too long. Instead, divide kids into two groups. Explain that one group will be pro-life and the other will be pro-choice. Give each group five minutes to make a list of arguments people holding its particular position would give as to why abortion is right or wrong. Each argument should be written on a different piece of paper. After five minutes, have each group share what it came up with. In Step 5, use the argument sheets for a paper wad fight between the two teams. Then call a halt to the fighting by reading the Matthew passage.

STEP 4

Having kids form pairs to discuss the cases and then letting each pair share its responses may take too long in most large groups. To speed things up, read selected cases. (Better yet, ask volunteer actors to "explain" their predicaments to the whole group. For example, someone pretending to be Shari could say, "Hi, I'm Shari. I'm a high school senior. I just found out I'm pregnant. I'm an honors student with a full scholarship to medical school. I want to be a doctor. . . .") Then have the group vote (with a show of hands) on whether each character should or shouldn't have an abortion. Ask: **Is majority rule the best way to decide if an abortion is acceptable? If not, how should we decide?** If you think kids will be swayed by peer pressure or are hesitant to express their opinions publicly, have them vote based on how they think most people in society would vote.

STEP 2

Before you mention the session topic, write the number 1,160,581 on the board. Ask: **What do you suppose this number represents?** Allow several guesses. Then reveal that it's the number of U.S. soldiers killed in the Revolutionary War, Civil War, World War I, World War II, Korean War, and Vietnam War combined. Ask: **How do you think that number compares to the number of abortions performed since Roe vs. Wade passed in 1973?** (Actually, it's less than the number of abortions performed in the U.S. in any single year!) This statistic might help even the most jaded kids to take notice.

STEP 3

Bible passages like Psalm 139 may not convince your kids that life begins at conception. So instead of reading the passages in the session, simply explain that there is disagreement over exactly when an embryo becomes a human being and when it should be protected under the law. Therefore, we have two choices: Allow abortion, and take the chance of killing human beings; or prohibit it, and take the chance of protecting something that is not yet human. Ask: **If you saw a human body next to the road and didn't know if it was alive, would you assume it was dead and keep driving? Or would you stop and try to help, in case the body was alive? To put it another way, would you demolish an old building if you weren't sure whether there were any people living inside? Or would you wait until you could be certain the place was empty?** Note that most people probably would go out of their way to preserve life in such cases—until they were sure that human life wasn't at stake. In the same way, uncertainty over when life begins should lead us to protect the unborn child on the chance that he or she is a human being.

STEP 3

Bring in a pot full of dirt and a few seeds (perhaps for some kind of vegetable). Ask for a few volunteers to assist you by digging into the dirt, planting the seeds, covering them up again, and watering the dirt. Then ask: **In your opinion, when will each seed's life begin? When it pops out of the ground for everyone to see? Perhaps three months after it's been planted? Or is it at the moment when it's been planted in order to grow?** Get several responses. Then say: **What the Bible says about when a person's life begins can be illustrated in much the same way. Is it when the person "pops out" for everyone to see? Is it a few months after the human seed has been planted? The Bible suggests otherwise. The Bible says that God has dealings with us even before we're formed in the womb. This suggests that we're considered living beings as soon as we're planted, much like the seed** (Jer. 1:5).

STEP 5

Kids unfamiliar with the Bible may think it's ludicrous to love their enemies. You could explore the concept further by looking at Luke 6:27-28 and Romans 12:14-21. The Romans passage offers some very practical suggestions for how to love others. Point out the ways Jesus loved His enemies (healing the soldier's ear that Peter cut off, praying for forgiveness for those who were killing Him, etc.). Emphasize that this type of love isn't possible on our own, but it is possible with God's help.

STEP 1

Have kids form pairs. Hand out paper and pencils. Announce that each person will get to decide what his or her partner's typical school day will be like—from classes, to lunch, to social time, to extracurricular activities, to nightlife, etc. Give kids a few minutes to write out a schedule for their partners. Encourage them to be wacky and extreme in the things they come up with. After a few minutes, have them exchange schedules and share some laughs. Explain that this is how many people view the abortion issue—as an infringement by someone trying to make decisions for others. But is there more to it than this? That's what you'll be looking at today.

STEP 5

Portions of Psalm 139 are used quite often in youth materials. But it's rarely used in its entirety. In fact, verses 19-22 may seem to contradict the idea of loving enemies. As a group, read through the entire psalm and then make a list of what it tells us about God. Also make a list of questions the psalm raises—then seek to answer them together.

STEP 1

Ask: **Do you think it's right for some people to be able to make choices for others?** Have your group members list situations in which they think it may be necessary for someone to make a choice for someone else. Then have them list situations in which they think it's not right. Ask: **Do you see any pattern or correlation between the items on these two lists?** It's likely that most of the items on the "OK" list will involve a situation in which a person needs to be protected from hurting himself or her-self—or others around him or her. Items on the "not OK" list may be quite varied.

STEP 4

Say: **It's often easy for us, when we're not directly involved, to tell someone that she shouldn't have an abortion. Women considering an abortion certainly need help now as they're facing a tough situa-tion—but having a baby and raising a child is no picnic either.** Go back to Repro Resource 2 and have the girls list as many specific things they can think of for each situation that they could do for the woman after the baby is born. (Some of the women may need help during the pregnancy itself, so group members should consider those options as well.) Then have them brainstorm specific things they could do in their school or community for women facing unplanned pregnancies. Suggestions might include things like setting up a question-and-answer hotline, collecting donations of infant food and clothing, offering babysitting services, etc.

STEP 4

Your guys may not feel very sensitive or passionate about the subject of abortion. They might find it difficult to relate to what a woman must go through. The case of Ken and Allie can help your guys look at the issue from both a male and female perspective. Ask half of your guys to write down what Allie must be thinking and feeling; ask the other half to write down what Ken must be thinking and feeling. Ask: **Who do you feel most sorry for? Why? What responsibilities, if any, should Ken assume? If Ken were your best friend, what would you tell him? What if Allie wanted to have an abortion and Ken didn't want her to?**

STEP 5

Have guys form two teams. Tape a line on the floor. Have one team stand on one side of the line and the other team stand on the other side of the line. Explain that the object of the game is to see which team can get the most people on its side of the line. At first, guys should simply try to talk others into joining their side. See what kind of reasons they can come up with as to why their side is best. This prob-ably won't do much good. Then let them reach across the line to try to grab people to pull across. To do this, each guy must leave at least one foot on his side of the line. Finally, let them form human chains, with at least one player on his side of the line, connected to others who are ventur-ing into "enemy territory." After a few minutes, call time. See which side has the most people on it. Then ask: **How is this like the abortion debate?** (Verbal arguments rarely convince people to change their position; therefore, people use "more forceful" means.) **But is this the best way?** Proceed with your discus-sion of the Matthew passage.

STEP 1

Have group members sit in a circle. Hand out paper and pencils. Instruct kids to write about their favorite vacation. After about two minutes, say: **Stop.** Kids should stop writing—even if they're in the middle of a sentence—and pass their story to the person on the left. When you say, **Go,** each person should read only the previous sentence before the story stopped, and begin writing from there. After about a minute, say: **Stop.** Continue this process until each story gets all the way around the circle, back to its original writer. Then have each person read his or her own "true" story about his or her favorite vacation. The events may be a bit different from what kids remember, however. Have the group vote on which story turned out the funniest. Then ask group members how it felt to be writing a story about their life, only to have it taken away from them and given to somebody else to dictate. Use this activity to lead in to Step 2.

STEP 5

Have kids form two teams (representing pro-choice and pro-life advocates) for an all-out tug-of-war match. (Try to make the teams as evenly matched as possible.) Have each team grab the rope and start tugging when you say, **Go.** After a winning team is crowned, discuss as a group how this tug-of-war scene is similar to the abortion battle. Have someone read Matthew 5:43-48. Then have the teams try a tug-of-war match again; but this time, each side should show love toward its enemy. Chances are, there won't be much of a fight. Similarly, without the tension of constant fighting, the two sides in the abortion debate might be able to work together to find constructive solutions to the abortion problem.

STEP 1

Before the session, videotape a TV news story or public affairs program about the abortion controversy. Show a portion of the tape to start the meeting. If you can't find such a program, show scenes (after screening them yourself) from the film *A Private Matter*. This made-for-cable movie depicts the story of a woman who, in 1962, provoked national debate when she arranged to abort her unborn child who had been exposed to the drug Thalidomide. Sympathy for the woman helped pave the way for the legalization of abortion. Whether you show the movie or a tape you've recorded, ask: **If this was all you knew about abortion, could you make up your mind about the issue? Why or why not? Were both sides fairly represented? Explain. How do you feel when you see or hear this subject discussed? Why?**

STEP 3

Try one or both of the following options. (1) Before the session, record on audiotape the sound of a beating heart. You could get this from a sound effects record or make the sound yourself by pounding the heels of your hands together in a *lub-dub* pattern. (Experiment a bit to get the best effect.) If possible, record at least two minutes of the heartbeat. Play the tape as you're discussing the question of when life begins or as you're reading the Bible passages. During a pause in the discussion, suddenly reach for the tape player and hit the "Stop" button to show dramatically what happens when abortion occurs after the sixth week or so of a pregnancy. (2) After reading the Psalm 139 passage, play a recording of the contemporary Christian song "Maker of My Heart" by Glad. Ask: **How does this song make you feel? How do you think a supporter of abortion rights might feel about it? Why?**

STEP 1

Try one of the following shorter openers. (1) Bring in a some vanilla ice cream. Announce that you brought in every flavor of ice cream known to man, and that your kids get to choose what kind they want. Then have kids choose the kinds they want from this "great variety." When they see just vanilla, they'll probably be a bit disappointed. Ask: **How does it feel to have your choices limited like this?** (2) To save more time, give unopened boxes of Cracker Jack to three volunteers. Have the rest of the group vote on whether each volunteer must (a) keep the prize, (b) give the prize to someone else, or (c) throw the prize away. After the volunteers obey the will of the group, discuss what happened—adapting the questions at the end of Step 1. You may want to compare the three choices to the choices facing a pregnant teenager. In Step 2, make the transition from Step 1, skip the newspaper discussion, and begin immediately with the statements on Repro Resource 1.

STEP 4

Have kids form groups. Assign just one case study to each group. Skip the case studies involving Edwardo and Luisa, Ben and Li, and Laticia. After a few minutes, have each group share its response. After having pairs work on strategies for talking to a girl who's considering an abortion, read Matthew 5:43-48. Point out that no matter where we stand on abortion, the Bible is clear on how we should treat those who disagree with us. Skip Step 5 and close in prayer.

STEP 2

Say: **You're watching the evening news when you see a report on a disturbance at a local abortion clinic. Apparently, a couple of pro-life advocates bombed the clinic this morning, injuring a doctor and patient who were inside. What would your reaction be to this report?** Ask several volunteers to share and explain their reactions. Lead in to a discussion of the good and bad tactics employed by both sides (pro-choice and pro-life) of the abortion controversy.

STEP 4

After you've discussed Repro Resource 2, ask: **How are your "back door ethics"?** Point out that usually there are plenty of Christians protesting and ministering at the *front* door of an abortion clinic; but rarely will you find Christians at the *back* door of the clinic, waiting to minister to women who've already had an abortion. Instruct group members to go through Repro Resource 2 again, this time assuming that each of the case studies resulted in an abortion. Ask: **How would you minister to the people in each of these case studies after the abortion was performed? Explain.**

STEP 2

Not all group members will have strong opinions about the abortion controversy. This may be especially true of junior highers. Instead of the statements on Repro Resource 1, use the following true-false quiz to introduce the concept of teen sexuality and abortion.

• **Every year, 10 percent of teenage girls in the U.S. become pregnant.** (True.)

• **Twenty percent of today's 14-year-old girls will become pregnant by age 20.** (False. It's about 40 percent.)

• **Twenty-five percent of pregnant teens choose to have abortions.** (False. Forty-five percent do.)

• **Twenty-five percent of pregnant teens choose to give their babies up for adoption.** (False. Fewer than 5 percent do. Thirty-five percent did in 1960.)

• **Thirty percent of abortions performed in the U.S. are among teenagers.** (True.)

STEP 4

Some of the case studies may be hard for younger group members to relate to. To make the feelings involved more concrete, label heavy books or bricks with these feelings: bitterness, disappointment, confusion, fear, helplessness, worry, stress, tiredness, shock, regret, shame, anger, hate, disgust, and hopelessness. After you read each case study aloud, appoint a team to find the books (or bricks) representing the feelings that might apply in that case study. Team members should then pile the objects on a bag of potato chips. See what shape the chips are in when the objects are removed. Afterward, discuss how easy it would be to "break" under the pressure.

STEP 2

Using the first eight questions from Repro Resource 1, have your group members conduct surveys among the following groups to see how they answer the questions:

• Kids at school

• Adults at church

• Other adults (neighbors, teachers, etc.)

Try to get at least 30 completed interviews from each group. Compare your group's responses to the other groups'. To be used most effectively, the surveys should be completed and tallied *before* the session.

STEP 4

After reviewing the case studies, see how your group members would respond to the following statements people might give as to why abortion is justifiable:

• **It reduces the number of unwanted children in the world and helps keep the population level under control.**

• **Poor people—especially in Third World countries—can't afford more children. It's better to abort the child than have it suffer in abject poverty.**

• **It's better to abort the child than have it born into a verbally, physically, sexually, or emotionally abusive household.**

• **I might personally be against abortion, but I have no right telling someone else what to believe, especially if that person isn't a Christian.**

DATE USED:

Approx. Time

STEP 1: *Stunts 'R' Us* _____
- ❏ Fellowship & Worship
- ❏ Mostly Girls
- ❏ Extra Fun
- ❏ Media
- ❏ Short Meeting Time
Things needed:

STEP 2: *Where Do You Stand?* _____
- ❏ Extra Action
- ❏ Small Group
- ❏ Large Group
- ❏ Heard It All Before
- ❏ Urban
- ❏ Combined Jr. High/High School
- ❏ Extra Challenge
Things needed:

STEP 3: *Life Begins at . . . ?* _____
- ❏ Extra Action
- ❏ Heard It All Before
- ❏ Little Bible Background
- ❏ Media
Things needed:

STEP 4: *Caught in the Middle* _____
- ❏ Large Group
- ❏ Mostly Girls
- ❏ Mostly Guys
- ❏ Short Meeting Time
- ❏ Urban
- ❏ Combined Jr. High/High School
- ❏ Extra Challenge
Things needed:

STEP 5: *Do What to My Enemies?* _____
- ❏ Small Group
- ❏ Little Bible Background
- ❏ Fellowship & Worship
- ❏ Mostly Guys
- ❏ Extra Fun
Things needed:

SESSION 2

A Time to Die (Euthanasia/Medically Assisted Suicide)

YOUR GOALS FOR THIS SESSION:

Choose one or more

☐ To help group members identify and explain their personal views on euthanasia and medically assisted suicide.

☐ To help group members understand what the Bible says about death and the purpose of suffering.

☐ To help group members apply biblical principles to difficult situations involving euthanasia and medically assisted suicide.

☐ Other:_____
_____

Your Bible Base:

Genesis 2:7
Exodus 21:12-14
Deuteronomy 30:15-20
Job 1:1—3:36; 14:1-7; 42:1-17
1 Corinthians 15:50-58
Hebrews 9:27

STEP 1

Story Time

(Needed: Earplugs [optional])

O P T I O N S

EXTRA ACTION

LARGE GROUP

FELLOWSHIP & WORSHIP

MOSTLY GUYS

EXTRA FUN

MEDIA

SHORT MEETING TIME

To begin the session, have your group members arrange their chairs in a circle. Explain that the kids will be doing some "progressive story-telling." One person will stand and start telling a story. When he or she sits down, the person on his or her left must stand and continue the story. This process continues around the circle until everyone has had a chance to talk at least once or twice. Here are a few story starters, if your kids aren't feeling especially creative at the moment:

- Fred and Francis Farley woke up early to milk the cows. When they got to the barn, they were surprised to see . . .
- Once upon a time in a kingdom far away there lived a king who liked only the color blue. One day . . .
- It was the day of the big test, and Mrs. Stewart was passing out the exams. Just then, the door opened and . . .

However, there is a twist to this activity. Choose one group member to sit outside the circle—perhaps at the back of the room or even in the hallway outside the room. This person should not be able to hear the story being told. You might even want to give him or her some earplugs to wear. This person will control the direction of the story. When he or she says "Switch," the storyteller must sit down, and the next person must continue the story exactly where it was left off. The person outside the circle will also control the content of the story. If he or she calls out "Romance," the storyteller must introduce elements of romance to it. If the person calls out "Action," the storyteller must introduce elements of action. The person might also call out things like "Comedy," "Horror," and "Sadness." When the person outside the circle calls out "The End," the storyteller must sit down immediately. The next person must then begin a whole new story.

Continue the activity for a few minutes, giving several people the opportunity to "control the destiny" of the stories. Then reassemble the entire group.

If your group isn't very verbal, try having kids write down their stories. Each person in the circle should start a story and then hand it off to the person on the left as directed. Read the finished stories after someone calls out "The End."

Ask: **Do you think any of our stories would have worked well as TV shows? Why or why not?** Some of the stories may have had enough romance, intrigue, and comedy to satisfy a prime-time audience, but chances are the stories were too jumbled to work well— even for network television.

What was the problem with our stories? (The person controlling the destiny of the stories didn't know what was going on.) If no one mentions it, suggest that while some of the stories were a mishmash of different elements, others were simply ended too soon.

Then say: **Today we're going to be talking about whether some lives, like these stories, are ended too soon.**

STEP
2

Go Gentle or Rage?

(Needed: Copies of Repro Resource 3, pencils, chalkboard and chalk or newsprint and marker, newspaper and magazine articles [optional])

Explain: **The poet Dylan Thomas wrote, "Do not go gentle into that good night/Rage, rage against the dying of the light." What do you think he was talking about?** If no one is familiar with the poem, explain that Thomas was writing the poem to his father, who was dying. He was encouraging his father not to give up his battle for life—not to give in to death—but to fight with all of his strength ("rage") against the "dying of the light."

Ask: **If you knew you were dying, would you be more likely to "go gentle into that good night" or to "rage against the dying of the light"? Why?** You will probably pick up some clues about your group members' feelings concerning death from their responses. Some of them may accept the idea of dying passively. Others may be inclined to fight for life as tenaciously as possible. Kids will probably say it depends a lot on the circumstances. Point out that those who are in Christ don't need to fear death, but should also value life and live it to its fullest.

Then ask: **What if you were unable to fight for your own life—perhaps because you were in a coma? Would you want someone to fight for you? If so, how hard?** Get responses from several group members. Again, they'll probably say it depends on the circumstances. Some kids might start mentioning specific criteria ("If I were brain-dead, and a machine was keeping me alive . . .").

Ask the following questions to gauge kids' opinions about life and death: **What if the doctor said there was a 50-50 chance that**

when you came out of the coma you'd be a vegetable? What if the doctor said it was 99 percent certain? What if your brain were still functioning, but you were paralyzed from the neck down?

Write the word *euthanasia* on the board. Ask if anyone in the group knows what the word means. (Contrary to the opinions of any comedians in the group, the word does not refer to young people in Japan and China ["youth in Asia"].)

Webster's Ninth New Collegiate Dictionary defines the word as "the act or practice of killing . . . hopelessly sick or injured individuals . . . for reasons of mercy." In our society today, euthanasia refers to the practice of allowing someone to die without medical intervention when that medical intervention would extend the person's life. It also refers to the practice of allowing a person to commit medically assisted suicide when an illness is terminal and/or the patient would suffer if his or her life were prolonged.

If possible, before the session, collect a few newspaper and magazine articles on euthanasia or medically assisted suicide. You might look for stories of families who are debating whether to "pull the plug" on a loved one who is hooked up to life-support systems, summaries of legislation being considered in these areas, or updates on Jack Kevorkian, the "suicide doctor." Briefly go through the articles. Then give group members a chance to share any information they've heard or seen on the topic.

Ask: **Under what circumstances do you think euthanasia and medically assisted suicide are OK?** As group members identify various criteria, write their suggestions on the board. Explain that you're looking for specific guidelines. For instance, if someone suggests that medically assisted suicide is OK for someone who is terminally ill, ask: **What if the person's illness won't kill him for ten years? Is it still OK? What about five years? What's the time limit?**

After you've got several specific guidelines written on the board, distribute copies of "Decisions to Make" (Repro Resource 3) and pencils. Have group members work in pairs to answer questions on the sheet. These are very difficult cases; kids may have difficulty coming up with answers. That's OK.

As a group, briefly discuss each case. Let kids share what they decided. Then alter the facts of each case to generate further discussion.

What difference would it make if Jack were 88 years old?
What if Marie had parents who loved her very much?
What if Rona were 42 years old?
What if Lionel is a Christian?

You could spend all day discussing these cases. Discuss them only long enough to get kids wondering where they can find solutions to such tough dilemmas.

A Matter of Life and Death

(Needed: Bibles, paper, pencils)

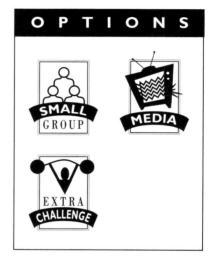

Ask: **Where do you think God stands on the issues of euthanasia and medically assisted suicide? What do you think the Bible says about them?** Encourage kids to offer their opinions. Then explain that, unfortunately, the Bible doesn't mention euthanasia or medically assisted suicide; but, better than that, it gives us principles to help us develop a biblical world view about tough issues like these.

Have group members form teams of three or four. Distribute paper and pencils to each team. Write the following Scripture references on the board: Genesis 2:7; Exodus 21:12-14; Deuteronomy 30:15-20; Job 14:1-17; I Corinthians 15:50-58; and Hebrews 9:27. Instruct the teams to read the assigned passages and then write a brief summary of what the Bible says about life and death, based on the passages. If you're short on time, divide the verses among the teams.

Use the following information to supplement your discussion of the passages.

Genesis 2:7—God is the author of life. Humans are but dust without the breath of God.

Exodus 21:12-14—God opposes deliberately taking someone else's life. Some might argue that these verses may not apply to euthanasia or medically assisted suicide, where the motives are often based on compassion, not anger. Nevertheless, it's clear from Scripture that God opposes murder. The question then becomes "What exactly constitutes murder?"

Deuteronomy 30:15-20—God sets before us options of life and death. In this context, death means living in disobedience to God's commands. Life comes from loving God, listening to Him, and holding fast (sticking with Him no matter what). God wants us to choose life in the sense that we choose to follow His ways. God blesses those who walk in His ways. God wants us to enjoy life to its fullest, and that can only be done when we live for Him.

Job 14:1-17—Our earthly lives are as temporal as flowers in the field. God determines how long we will live. Note that verses 1-12 are very pessimistic—Job had good cause to have such an outlook. In verses 13-17, he gets a bit more optimistic and holds out some hope for future life. His understanding of eternal life was incomplete, but we have a far clearer view.

I Corinthians 15:50-58—The fact that we are "flesh and blood" means that we are perishable, corrupt, weak, and sinful. It is sin that gives death its sting—sin put us under death's power. However, Jesus conquered death—it "has been swallowed up in victory." So for Christians, death no longer has a sting. Through Jesus, Christians don't need to fear death—or artificially prolong life.

Hebrews 9:27—As human beings, it is our inescapable destiny to die.

As a group, use these biblical principles to begin developing some thoughts about euthanasia and medically assisted suicide. Collectively, these verses would seem to suggest that death is a natural part of our earthly existence, not something to be postponed for as long as possible. Therefore, some might say that heroic efforts to preserve life at all costs seems to go against God's intentions.

On the other hand, just as heroic efforts to preserve life may seem to go against God's intentions, so does deliberately ending a life. These passages show us that life is given to us by God; therefore, it seems logical that we shouldn't take steps to end it prematurely.

A biblical view of euthanasia and medically assisted suicide would seem to fall somewhere between these two extremes. Finding that balance is a difficult task.

STEP
4

The Purpose of Suffering

(Needed: A cut-apart copy of Repro Resource 4)

Before the session, you'll need to familiarize yourself with the story of Job. Pay particular attention to Job 1–3; 42. At this point in the session, summarize (in your own words) the story of Job for your group.

Point out that Job was a man who seemed to have everything: a large family, untold wealth, and—most importantly—a close relationship with God. In fact, God held up Job as an example of righteousness during a conversation with Satan. Satan replied that the only reason Job was faithful to God was that God had given Job everything he needed. He then suggested that if everything were taken away from Job, Job would curse God. To prove Satan wrong, God gave Satan permission to afflict Job however he desired—provided that he did not kill Job. So Satan went to work. In one day, all of Job's children were killed, most of his servants were killed, and almost all of his possessions were stolen or destroyed. Later, he developed painful sores all over his body. And to make matters worse, he received very little comfort from his wife and friends during his time of agony. His wife wanted him to "curse God and die." His friends suggested that his suffering was the result of sin on his part.

After you summarize this first part of the story, have kids form three groups. Distribute one section of "The Trials of Job" (Repro Resource 4) to each group. Explain that each group is responsible for coming up with a roleplay based on its assigned situation. One person in each group will play Job; the rest of the group members will play various visitors.

Give the groups a few minutes to prepare. Then have each one perform its roleplay. As the groups perform, pay attention to the various reasons given for whether or not Job should commit suicide. You may want to refer to these arguments later as you relate the account of Job to the issue of medically assisted suicide.

After all of the groups have performed, ask: **How do you think Job's situation turned out? Did he commit suicide or did he suffer for the rest of his life?** After several group members have responded, explain that after Job endured the afflictions heaped on him, God rewarded him for his faithfulness. In fact, He gave Job twice as much as he had before. All of Job's family came to comfort him. He had many more children. And he lived another 140 years.

Ask: **Was there a purpose for Job's suffering? If so, what was it?** (God was demonstrating Job's faithfulness. In the process, He might also have been strengthening Job's faithfulness, showing him that He—God—was the only thing Job needed. The Book of Job doesn't really delve in to *why* God allowed Job to suffer. It deals more with God's sovereignty and the fact that we can't figure Him out.) If no one mentions it, you might also suggest that Job's story serves as an inspiration to people today. It's a comforting book to read when someone is facing trying situations. So in that sense, Job's suffering served a much greater purpose—as a testimony to others of God's goodness.

How did Job feel about his suffering? (At one point, he wished he was dead [3:11].)

What if Job had died in the midst of his suffering? How would this story be different? (Obviously, he wouldn't have received the blessings God gave him after the ordeal. And his story certainly wouldn't be a testimony to us today.)

OPTIONS

HEARD IT ALL BEFORE

LITTLE BIBLE BACKGROUND

MOSTLY GIRLS

SHORT MEETING TIME

URBAN

JR.HIGH HIGH SCHOOL COMBINED

EXTRA CHALLENGE

STEP 5

So What's the Verdict?

(Needed: Copies of Repro Resource 3, pencils)

Armed with the knowledge of what the Bible says about the inevitability of death and the purpose of suffering, briefly review the situations on Repro Resource 3. Based on what they now know, would your kids change their opinions about any of the situations? If so, how—and why? If not, why not?

Summarize the session by developing a list of general principles that could be used to make good decisions in cases like the ones on Repro Resource 3. Here are some possibilities:

- God often uses suffering for positive results.
- Ending life merely to avoid suffering is wrong.
- All people must die sooner or later. Artificial means to prolong life may not always be warranted, especially in cases in which the person has said such efforts aren't necessary.
- Similarly, someone with a terminal illness should be allowed to die naturally if he or she so desires. He or she shouldn't be forced to be hooked up to machines or take medicine that merely prolongs the inevitable.
- Food and water should be provided as long as the patient is alive.
- God values life.
- God is able to use those with severe mental and physical disabilities.

You won't answer all of the questions this subject raises in one short session. Theologians and ethicists have been debating it for years. What you can do is affirm the value of life—and the value of suffering.

As you close the session in prayer, thank God for giving us life and ask Him to help us through times of suffering. Pray for wisdom for those who face tough choices like the ones you've discussed today. You might want to close your prayer time by reading Job's words in Job 42:1-6 or by reading Isaiah 40:28-31.

DECISIONS TO MAKE

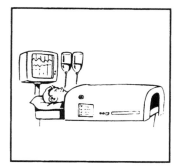

CASE STUDY #1: JACK

Jack is a thirty-eight-year-old business executive with a wife and two teenage children. On his way back from a business meeting, Jack lost control of his car and slammed head-on into a tree. He was barely conscious when the paramedics arrived, and slipped into a coma shortly after being admitted to the hospital. Jack has been in the hospital for two months. During that time, he has shown only the barest signs of life. His every breath is dependent on a respirator. The doctors have said there is virtually no hope for recovery. Before the accident, Jack was a proud, independent man. He often told his wife that he never wanted to be kept alive by a machine. Even so, she's having tremendous difficulty deciding whether or not to have Jack disconnected from the life-support machines. What would you advise her to do? Why?

CASE STUDY #2: BABY MARIE

Baby Marie was left in the parking lot of Mercy Hospital when she was less than two days old. She had been born approximately five weeks premature with many complicated birth defects. The doctors saved her life and put her on a respirator. She may eventually be able to get off the respirator, but her life expectancy does not extend beyond the teenage years. It's almost certain that her entire life will be spent in hospitals and institutions. Because no one has stepped forward to claim her, Marie's hospital bills are the responsibility of the state (and taxpayers). The total bill for her care will easily exceed one million dollars over the course of her lifetime. What do you think should be done for Baby Marie? Why?

CASE STUDY #3: RONA

Rona is a ninety-year-old widow. Two months ago, her husband of seventy years died. Then, three weeks ago, she fell and broke her hip. Childless and unable to care for herself anymore, Rona had to move to a nursing home. To pay for her care she had to sell her house and most of her possessions. Realizing that she has nothing left to live for, Rona wants to die. She wants her doctor to help her kill herself in as painless a manner as possible. What do you think the doctor should do? Why?

CASE STUDY #4: LIONEL

Lionel's cancer had been in remission for two years. Unfortunately, at his last check-up, Lionel's doctor confirmed that the cancer was spreading again—rapidly. That means another long battery of chemotherapy treatments that will not only severely weaken Lionel physically, but bankrupt his family financially. Even with the treatments, Lionel's doctor says there's only a one-in-ten chance that Lionel will live for more than a year. After a lengthy discussion, Lionel and his family decide that he should forego the treatment and allow the cancer to run its course. What do you think of the family's decision? Why?

THE TRIALS OF JOB

ROLEPLAY #1

One person will play Job as he might have been after he lost everything and developed sores all over his body. Other group members will play a doctor, a nurse, a hospital chaplain, and a social worker. These four characters should attempt to persuade Job that it would be medically advisable to commit suicide. If there are more than five people in the group, the others can play medical interns or residents who are on the team to give diagnosis and medical advice. Some of the arguments that might be used by the advocates of suicide could include keeping medical costs low, not being a burden to society, escaping the pain, etc.

ROLEPLAY #2

One person will play Job as he might have been after he lost everything and developed sores all over his body. Other group members will play a pastor, a church elder, a Sunday School teacher, and a church treasurer.

Job is questioning out loud whether or not to continue living. He is asking if a person who fears God could commit suicide, and if that person would go to heaven if he did commit suicide. Everyone from the church group needs to identify his or her role or office at the church, and explain why he or she would be against Job's committing suicide.

ROLEPLAY #3

One person will play Job as he might have been after he lost everything and developed sores all over his body. Job is questioning out loud whether or not to continue living. He is asking if a person who fears God could commit suicide, and if that person would go to heaven if he did commit suicide.

Of the rest of the group, half will play friends of Job who feel that his committing suicide would be the best way out of his misery. The reasons these people give should coincide with the reasons given to support medically assisted suicide.

The other half of the group will play friends of Job who feel that he should be strong and persevere through his losses and illness. These people should offer reasons to convince Job that God has not abandoned him, and that he should be strong and patient.

EXTRA ACTION

STEP I

Before the session, hide several candles, matchbooks, flashlights, and batteries around your meeting place. (Be sure to hide each item individually and away from the other items.) To start the session, announce that you've just learned that in five minutes the power to your meeting place is going to be turned off (and if you're not meeting at night, there's going to be a total solar eclipse too). If you're going to have any light, you'll need to use candles or flashlights—which are hidden somewhere. Have kids form pairs. Each pair is allowed to get *only two* items, and those items must be the *first* two the pair finds. Any pair that happens to find only a candle and a matchbook or only a flashlight and battery will get a prize. Anyone finding any other combination (two candles, or a matchbook and flash-light, for example) loses. Have one or two monitors keep an eye on pairs to make sure they take the first two items they find. After five minutes, award prizes (if anybody won). Tie this contest into the idea of preparing for "the dying of the light" in Step 2.

STEP 2

Designate a light switch in your meeting place as the on/off switch for a life-support system. (You may want to put a sign on it that says "Life Support.") Discuss the cases on Repro Resource 3 one at a time. After each case, have pairs walk past the switch and turn it on or off to indicate their decision. If partners can't agree, they must leave the switch on. In Step 5, do the same as pairs reconsider the cases. But this time tell them that if partners can't agree, the switch will be turned off—which may provide added incentive for reaching a clear decision.

SMALL GROUP

STEP 2

While you don't want to get too "heavy" or morbid on the topic of dying, you may find that discussing suffering and the appropriateness of death causes kids to think about their own mortality. Based on things they've seen or thought about concerning death, have group members write down the method of dying they would welcome the most. Then have them write down the method they would welcome the least. Kids have probably thought about this kind of stuff before. Ask each person in the group to share his or her most and least desired "endings."

STEP 3

Go through the Scripture passages as a group. Divide the board in half, labeling one side "Life" and the other side "Death." After you read each passage, hand a piece of chalk (or a marker) to one person in the group. Instruct him or her to write on the board one thing the passage says about life or death. After doing so, he or she should pass the chalk (or marker) to someone else. It's OK to pass the marker without writing anything, but in order to do so, the person must read the next passage when you're ready for it to be read. In Step 4, don't break into groups to roleplay the three situations. Instead, present Job's case as though you're a judge summarizing it for a jury. Assign roles to various group members (doctor, social worker, pastor, a friend who favors suicide, a friend who doesn't, etc.). Make sure each group member has a role. Tell the group that they have five minutes to decide whether Job should be allowed to commit suicide or not.

LARGE GROUP

STEP I

Instead of using the storytelling activity, have kids form teams. Give each team an electric toaster (the type from which the toast pops up) and bread. If the toasters have a darkness control, make sure each one is set on "Medium." Have each team go to an outlet, plug in the toaster, put bread in it, start the toaster, and pull the plug sometime before the toast pops up. Any team that allows its toast to pop up is disqualified. Award a prize to the team with the darkest toast after one toasting. (You'll probably need a volunteer to monitor each team.) Explain that in this session you'll be talking about whether people should be allowed to "pull the plug" to end someone else's life.

STEP 5

Have kids form groups. Assign each group one of the following hypothetical scientific discoveries. Each group should decide whether its discovery should be approved by the government for widespread use. Here are the discoveries:

• An AIDS test that instantly and painlessly kills the person if the results show that the person has AIDS.

• A cybergenic chamber that allows people to live for hundreds of years in a semi-frozen state with minimal brain and heart activity. Terminally ill patients could then be awakened after a cure has been found for their disease.

• A cancer pill that speeds up the effects of the cancer, so that the patient suffers only one-third as long as usual.

• A complex computer system that calculates a patient's odds of survival, and shuts off all life-support systems if the odds are less than whatever percentage the surviving family members and loved ones determine.

After a few minutes, have each group share its decision.

STEP 2

If kids have heard euthanasia discussed only in relation to the elderly, they may assume the subject has nothing to do with teenagers. Bring up these hypothetical cases based on real life: (1) **Jaleel was a star football player at his high school until a car accident left him paralyzed from the neck down. The doctors say there's no hope that he'll ever move anything below his neck again, much less walk. He can't control his bodily functions, and is totally dependent on others. Jaleel sinks deeper into depression every day. He wants to die, and asks a friend to help him commit suicide.** (2) **Lynette took some tranquilizers before going to a party last year. At the party, she drank some vodka. The pills and alcohol interacted, and she went into a coma that night. She's been in a "vegetative state" since then, connected to a life-support system that breathes for her. Her parents watch her body waste away as people at their church tell them to keep praying for a miracle.** Ask: **What would you do if you were Jaleel's friend? If you were Lynette's parents? Why?**

STEP 4

Using Job as an inspirational example could be difficult with kids who know enough to ask sticky questions. For instance, how could God allow Job's children and servants to be killed just to make a point? How did ruining Job prove "God's goodness"? If you use Job's story at all, avoid trivializing Job's losses or implying that getting new children and servants "replaced" the old ones. As needed, explain that the Book of Job has a lot to say about the supremacy of God, and less to say about why people suffer. And since Repro Resource 4 raises the question of whether suicide victims go to heaven, you may want to prepare to answer it—or rephrase the roleplays to avoid it.

STEP 4

Before looking at the story of Job, say: **There once was a guy named Bob who was really rich. He was a nice guy. He had a nice house in the suburbs, a nagging wife, nice kids, nice cars, even nice pets. One day his best friend, Rod, made a bet with another guy named Stan that Bob would still be a nice guy even if he lost everything he had. So Stan totalled Bob's cars, burned down his house, killed his pets, murdered his children, and didn't touch his wife. One night while Bob slept, Stan snuck into his house and exposed him to AIDS, malaria, mono, the flu, and leprosy. Bob felt pretty lousy.** Ask: **What do you think Bob would say to Rod if he knew about the bet? Bob wanted to die. Do you think he had a right to? How do you think Bob's life might end up?** After a few minutes of discussion, have kids change or add one letter to each name to determine what Bible story this is similar to. Obviously, it's Job (with God and Satan). This unorthodox way of presenting the story won't make the story any easier to understand, but it might help kids relate to it better.

STEP 5

With its focus on death and dying, this session provides a great opportunity to share the good news of Jesus' victory over death and His offer of eternal life. One way to introduce this is by having kids complete the following sentences, privately writing their answers:

• **If I had a terminal illness, I'd . . .**

• **When I think about death, I . . .**

• **After I die, I'll . . .**

Explain that all of us have a terminal illness called *sin.* (See Rom. 6:23.) This illness brings a lot of suffering. And Jesus is the only antidote.

STEP 1

Instead of using the storytelling activity, have group members answer a few questions to introduce the subject. You might have each person roll a die to determine which of the following six questions he or she will answer. The questions are as follows:

1. What's the best age to die?

2. What's the best way to die?

3. Who's the closest person to you who's ever died? How did this person die?

4. How old were you when you first learned about death? How did you learn?

5. What do you know about euthanasia or "mercy killing"?

6. What's the worst type of suffering a person might have to endure?

STEP 5

The topic of this session is sobering. Instead of merely focusing on the ethical issues raised by euthanasia, broaden your discussion to include how Christians should view death itself. One of the key things you'll want to convey is that those who are in Christ don't need to fear death. Have kids create banners or posters using the following verses for inspiration: Isaiah 25:8; 1 Corinthians 15:21, 26, 55; 2 Timothy 1:10; Revelation 21:4.

STEP 2

Add the following information to Repro Resource 3 as you're handing it out to your girls:

• In Case Study #1, you are one of Jack's daughters.

• In Case Study #2, you are a woman who would like to adopt a child. You've read about Baby Marie in the paper and would love to care for her.

• In Case Study #3, you are a nurse in Rona's nursing home who can't believe someone was married for 70 years. Your third marriage is about to fall apart.

• In Case Study #4, you are Lionel's sister. You're the only Christian in your family.

STEP 4

Some of your girls may have trouble relating to the character of Job. To help them get into the story a little more, have them look at it from his wife's point of view. Say: **The Bible says Job's wife wanted him to "curse God and die." Do you think she was justified in her feelings? Why or why not? If you were in her position, what do you think would be your response to these catastrophes? Why?**

STEP 1

Begin the session with a competitive game. Divide kids into unequal teams. Spot the team with the fewest members a large lead before beginning the game. Start the game, with you acting as referee. Let the game go on for a while until the team that started the game way behind starts coming back. Then announce: **The game is over.** The team that was making a comeback may question why you stopped the game when you did. They'll probably say they could have won the game if you hadn't stopped it. Explain: **Since your team had been losing for so long, I didn't want you guys to suffer any longer.** Then introduce the topic of euthanasia. Say: **People wonder if they should "stop the game" for those who are "losing" to disease and sickness, in order to prevent further suffering. But those sick people may be making a "comeback." Who's in the best position to "call the game"?** Encourage a lot of discussion.

STEP 2

Rather than go through the case studies in depth, briefly review them and make a list of the questions they raise. Then have guys debate the following statements:

• **A deer is hit by a car and is severely wounded. The humane thing to do is to put it out of its misery. In the same way, suffering people ought to be helped out of their misery too.**

• **A family's pet dog is getting really old. The family decides to put the dog to sleep. Similarly, elderly people should be allowed to bow out gracefully.**

• **At the animal shelter, a cat delivers a litter of kittens that nobody wants. The animals are killed painlessly. Unwanted humans should be allowed to die painlessly as well.**

STEP 1

It's party time! Have your group decorate the room for a party. Provide food and drink, fun and games, and music. Let the kids enjoy partying for a few minutes. Then abruptly stop the music and yell: **Sorry, the party's over!** If your announcement is ignored, start taking food and drink away from group members. (That should get their attention!) After kids complain, say: **How did you feel about someone simply "cutting you off" and telling you the party's over? How would you feel if this "party" was your life? Would you be in favor of letting someone else other than God determine when your party—or life—is over?** Use this to lead in to your discussion of euthanasia.

STEP 5

A discussion of death, suffering, and euthanasia can get kind of depressing— so you may want to "lighten it up" a bit. Have kids form small groups. Instruct each group to come up with a humorous, original list of the "top four worst ways to suffer before dying." Emphasize that these should not be morbid things, but rather things that would be very displeasing. For example, spending your last few moments smothered in a bin of dirty sweat socks while a New Kids on the Block (or some other talentless group of your choosing) CD plays in the background would be a horrible fate. An even worse form of torture for some kids might be filling out endless reproducible worksheets in a stuffy church classroom while the rest of the world is outside enjoying the most beautiful day your town has ever had. After a few minutes, have each group share its list. Work together to choose the best ones and come up with a top-10 list for the entire group.

STEP 1

Show a few scenes (which you've screened beforehand) from *A Brief History of Time,* the documentary about disabled physicist Stephen Hawking. Despite suffering from Lou Gehrig's disease, being confined to a wheelchair, and being unable to speak and nearly unable to move a muscle, Hawking produced theories and books that have been hailed as brilliant contributions to understanding how the universe was formed. Then say: **It is the year 2050. It's now legal to end the life of a person whose medical care costs more than he or she contributes to society. The case before you is that of the man you've just seen. Do you decide to have him "put to sleep"? Why or why not?** Then say: **Your next case involves a man with the same disability and the same cost of medical care. But instead of doing scientific work and writing books, this man spends his days watching TV. What is your verdict on ending his life? Why?** Then say: **Your third case involves a woman with the same disability and same cost of care. The difference is that she finds no meaning in life and wants to die. What is your verdict? Why?** Point out that issues like these are already being debated today.

STEP 3

Play one or more of the following Christian songs that talk about a biblical view of life and death: "Grave Robber" by Petra, "He Holds the Keys" by Steve Green, or "Good to Be Alive" by Geoff Moore and the Distance. Ask: **How does this song make you feel? How does it reflect what the Bible says about life and death? Would you recommend this song to a person who wanted to end his or her life? Would you recommend it to a person who had to decide whether to take a family member off life support? Why or why not?**

STEP 1

Here's a shorter way to combine Steps 1 and 2. Have kids form two equal groups. Give a piece of candy to each member of Group A. Each member of Group A must secretly decide whether he or she is an "F" or "P." Each member of Group B must secretly decide whether he or she is a "P" or a "T." At your signal, each person in Group A will pair up randomly with someone from Group B. Go from pair to pair, asking the Group A partner to give you his or her candy. An "F" (Fighter) may refuse and keep the candy. A "P" (Passive) cannot. But if a Passive is paired with a "P" (Protector), that Protector can intervene and refuse on the Passive's behalf. If a Passive is paired with a "T" (Taker), the Taker can take the candy and keep it. After seeing who ends up with the candy, repeat the exercise, letting kids again choose their identities and having them pair up with new partners. Chances are you'll have more Fighters and Takers this time. Say: **This is an illustration of what can happen as people face death. Some try to hold on to life; some give in. Others, like the Protectors, try to help the dying hold on to their lives. Still others, like the Takers, encourage them to end their lives. Some Takers even want to decide who should live and who should die.** Use this to lead in to the Step 2 discussion of the Dylan Thomas quote. To save time in Step 2, split up the cases on Repro Resource 3 among teams or individuals instead of having everyone discuss all of the cases.

STEP 4

Skip Step 4. If you want to address the believer's attitude toward suffering and facing death, read and discuss Psalm 23:4-6 and Romans 8:18, 22-23, 36-39. In Step 5, split up the cases on Repro Resource 3 as you did in Step 2.

STEP 2

To make Repro Resource 3 more urban-specific, add the following modifications to the case studies:

• *Case Study #1*—Instead of having Jack simply lose control of his car, have him lose control after being shot by gang members "doin' a driveby."

• *Case Study #2*—Include the fact that Baby Marie was born prematurely because her mother was addicted to crack cocaine. Marie is a "crack baby."

• *Case Study #3*—Instead of having Rona simply fall and break her hip, have her do so while being robbed in broad daylight by a group of young girls.

• *Case Study #4*—Instead of having Lionel battle cancer, have him be HIV-positive. After a second check-up, he is told he's developed AIDS.

STEP 4

Say: **There's an old man who's about 80 years old. He's been living "incognito" for several years because he killed someone. He also has great difficulty speaking. How valuable would you say this man is to society? Explain.** After several group members have offered their opinions, reveal that the man you described is Moses. Explain that Moses was about 40 years old when he killed an Egyptian who was beating a Hebrew. Moses then fled Egypt for 40 years. (See Acts 7:23-30.) When he was about 80 years old, Moses—who had a speaking problem—was called by God to lead the Israelites out of Egypt. See if any of your group members would like to change their response now that they know who the man is. Then discuss how we determine whether or not a person has value.

STEP 2

Some younger group members may have difficulty relating to the people in the case studies. You could approach the subject from a different angle. Have your group discuss the following situations:

• **A new law is about to be voted on that allows "mercy killing." It says that anyone who is suffering should be allowed to die with dignity if he or she so chooses. Do you think this law should pass? Why or why not?**

• **What about a law that says life must be preserved at any cost?**

• **What about a law that says all unproductive members of society—including people with severe birth defects and the elderly—must be eliminated, because they are over-taxing the health care system?**

Let kids speculate on what society would be like if these laws ever passed.

STEP 4

Instead of discussing Job (which may lead to unproductive tangents), divide your group in half. Make sure you have older and younger teens in each group. Have the members of each group put together a list of things they think would have to be considered when dealing with a potential euthanasia situation. Examples might include what the patient wants, how long the patient has been suffering, monetary costs, what the person's immediate family wants, moral convictions, chance for recovery, etc. After about five minutes, have a spokesperson for each group read its list to the other group. Discuss the similarities and differences between the groups' lists. Then ask: **What help does the Bible give in sorting through all of these factors?**

STEP 3

Trying to ascertain the Bible's view on death seems to be enough of a challenge in itself. Have kids form two teams. Instruct one team to look for biblical support *for* euthanasia. Instruct the other team to look for biblical references that could be used to argue *against* euthanasia. With some Bible reference tools and some coaching from you, each group should be able to find appropriate passages on the subject. See which group can come up with the most convincing argument.

STEP 4

Take some time to do a more thorough study of why God allows suffering. Use some of the following passages to get you started: Habakkuk 1:2-4; 3:17-19; Matthew 5:11-12; Romans 5:3-5; 2 Corinthians 1:3-7; Hebrews 10:36; James 1:2-4; I Peter 4:12-16. Create a list of the benefits of suffering. Then make another list of the "costs" of suffering—things a person gives up or loses when he or she is suffering. Ask: **What steps do people take to avoid suffering? If suffering is supposed to be so good for us, why do people go to extremes to avoid it—even to the extreme of wanting to cut life short?**

DATE USED:

Approx. Time

STEP 1: *Story Time* _____
❏ Extra Action
❏ Large Group
❏ Fellowship & Worship
❏ Mostly Guys
❏ Extra Fun
❏ Media
❏ Short Meeting Time
Things needed:

STEP 2: *Go Gentle or Rage?* _____
❏ Extra Action
❏ Small Group
❏ Heard It All Before
❏ Mostly Girls
❏ Mostly Guys
❏ Urban
❏ Combined Jr. High/High School
Things needed:

STEP 3: *A Matter of Life and Death* _____
❏ Small Group
❏ Media
❏ Extra Challenge
Things needed:

STEP 4: *The Purpose of Suffering* _____
❏ Heard It All Before
❏ Little Bible Background
❏ Mostly Girls
❏ Short Meeting Time
❏ Urban
❏ Combined Jr. High/High School
❏ Extra Challenge
Things needed:

STEP 5: *So What's the Verdict?* _____
❏ Large Group
❏ Little Bible Background
❏ Fellowship & Worship
❏ Extra Fun
Things needed:

What God Has Joined Together...
(Divorce)

YOUR GOALS FOR THIS SESSION:
Choose one or more

☐ To help group members identify and explain their personal views on divorce and talk about their own experiences with divorce—whether in their own families or in the families of their friends.

☐ To help group members understand what the Bible says about divorce.

☐ To help group members commit to biblical principles as they look for a spouse, so that they may avoid the prospect of divorce later.

☐ Other:_____

Your Bible Base:

Malachi 2:16
Matthew 5:27-32
Mark 10:2-12
1 Corinthians 7:1-16

STEP 1

Fictional Divorce Court

OPTIONS

EXTRA ACTION

LARGE GROUP

MOSTLY GIRLS

MOSTLY GUYS

EXTRA FUN

MEDIA

SHORT MEETING TIME

JR.HIGH HIGH SCHOOL COMBINED

To begin the session, have group members form teams of four. Make sure each team has at least one girl and one guy on it. Have each team come up with a skit in which a famous fictional couple goes through divorce proceedings in a court of law. Two members of the team will play the couple; the other two will play their attorneys. Once team members have chosen a famous couple to portray, they should come up with some reasons why the couple might be divorcing.

Here are some ideas to get your group members started:

- Homer and Marge Simpson—Homer: "I am no longer attracted to my wife. It's bad enough that she has blue hair—but it's piled three feet high on her head. And I'm tired of making sacrifices for her hair. We can't put ceiling fans in the house. We can't drive a convertible. And we spend 10 percent of our monthly income on hairspray!" Marge: "But we spend 50 percent of our monthly income on food! My husband has a serious eating disorder—and he may have a drinking problem. I don't know how many times he's lost his job at the nuclear power plant. Our son had to get a job doing commercials for Butterfinger candy bars just to keep a roof over our heads."
- Fred and Wilma Flintstone—Fred: "My wife has no concern at all for my well-being. I work all day at the rock quarry, and what's the first thing that happens when I get home? I get attacked by Dino, her stupid pet dinosaur. And she never offers to drive the car—I always have to. Do you realize how hard that is on my feet?" Wilma: "My husband is verbally abusive. He never *talks* to me; he just *yells*. All I ever hear is *Wi-i-i-l-ma-a-a-a!*"
- Thurston Howell III and Lovey (from *Gilligan's Island*)—Thurston: "My wife is mentally unstable. You should have seen all the clothes and money she packed for a 'three-hour' boat tour." Lovey: "I suspected my husband was having an affair when Mary Ann started making coconut cream pies for him when it wasn't even his birthday. Both Mary Ann and Ginger had their eyes on my husband—and his money—from the first day we landed on the island."
- Santa and Mrs. Claus—Santa: "My wife is trying to destroy my career. Two weeks ago I caught her switching some names on my 'naughty' and 'nice' lists." Mrs. Claus: "My husband works only one day a year. The rest of the time he's either gambling with his elf buddies, or he's out on the town with Frosty the Snowman."

Give the teams a few minutes to prepare. Then have each team present its skit. If you feel like participating, you could serve as judge and "preside" over each skit.

Afterward, say: **We're going to be talking about divorce today. Other than in the skits we just performed, have you ever seen the subject of divorce played for laughs? If so, when?** Kids will probably be able to think of several TV shows and movies that feature a humorous take on divorce. **Do you think divorce is a humorous topic? Why or why not?**

The Breakdown on Break-Ups

(Needed: Copies of Repro Resource 5, pencils, chalkboard and chalk or newsprint and marker, prizes [optional])

Distribute copies of "Personal Perspective" (Repro Resource 5) and pencils. Give group members a minute or two to answer the questions on the sheet. When they're finished, give them a chance to mingle about and have other group members fill out the sheet. Group members should get responses from as many others as possible. Afterward, go over their results. Ask several volunteers to share the percentages they came up with for the first part. From these, try to get an average for the group.

Then say: **Statistics say that today one of every two marriages ends in divorce. Of the families that you know, would you say that figure is high, low, or just about right? How does our group percentage compare to that?** Get several responses.

Then ask: **Based on the responses you got on Part 2 of the sheet, how would you summarize our group's feelings about divorce? About divorced people remarrying?** Ask a few volunteers to explain their responses.

Say: **People give all kinds of reasons for divorce in real life, on TV, and in the movies. Let's see how many of these reasons we can name.** Write group members' responses on the board as they are named. If no one mentions them, you might want to suggest reasons like "irreconcilable differences" (a general term that can apply to almost any personality clash between spouses), "incompatability" (not being able to live together), physical or emotional abuse, infidelity, money problems, etc.

O P T I O N S

SMALL GROUP

URBAN

Afterward, ask: **On a scale of 1 to 10—with 10 being the most difficult—how hard would you say it is for a couple to get divorced in our society today?** Probably most group members will agree that it's very easy to get a divorce today.

How hard *should* it be for a couple to get a divorce? Why? Give several group members an opportunity to share their opinions. Some may say that making divorce easy contributes to the skyrocketing divorce rate. Others may say that increasing the difficulty of getting a divorce could jeopardize the well-being of spouses trapped in dangerous marital circumstances.

STEP
3

What Does God Say?

(Needed: Bibles, paper, pencils, chalkboard and chalk or newsprint and marker, copies of Repro Resource 5, copies of Repro Resource 6)

Have group members reassemble into the teams they formed in Step 1. Distribute paper and pencils to each team. Write the following Scripture references on the board: Matthew 5:27-32; Mark 10:2-12; and I Corinthians 7:1-16. Instruct each team to look up the passages on the board and create a new list (similar to the one on Part 3 of Repro Resource 5) of circumstances in which God permits divorce. Unlike the list on Repro Resource 5, however, this list will be based on what the Bible actually says.

Give the teams a few minutes to work; then have each one share its findings. Matthew 5:27-32 indicates that marital unfaithfulness (or "cheating") may be grounds for divorce. Mark 10:2-12 mentions no circumstance under which divorce is OK. I Corinthians 7:1-16 suggests that if a Christian is married to a non-Christian and the non-Christian wants to leave the marriage, the Christian should let him or her go— for the sake of peace in the home. [NOTE: These passages indicate that marrying a divorced person is adultery. How does that compare with the popular opinion of your group members?]

Make a list of the teams' responses on the board, next to the list you created in Step 2. Compare the two lists. Note how many "unbiblical" reasons people offer for divorce. Then have group members compare the second list on the board with the lists they came up with for Part 3 of Repro Resource 5. Are there any circumstances they *thought* were covered in the Bible that actually weren't?

O P T I O N S

EXTRA ACTION

SMALL GROUP

LARGE GROUP

HEARD IT ALL BEFORE

LITTLE BIBLE BACKGROUND

FELLOWSHIP & WORSHIP

SHORT MEETING TIME

To help your group members apply biblical principles to real-life situations, distribute copies of "Divorce-O-Meter" (Repro Resource 6). Give kids a few minutes to complete the sheet. Then go through the situations one at a time, asking volunteers to share their responses.

Point out that the Bible is silent on many specific issues concerning divorce—such as abuse (physical or emotional), drug use, homosexuality, and failing to provide financially for the family. However, most Christians would agree that if a person (or his or her child) is in physical danger from his or her spouse, he or she should seek safety immediately. The person should then try to convince his or her spouse to seek professional help. Divorce should not be the first option for *any* couple—regardless of the circumstances.

Afterward, ask: **Do you think the Bible's view of divorce is too restrictive? Should there be more circumstances under which divorce is OK? Explain.** Allow several group members an opportunity to share their opinions.

Have someone read aloud Malachi 2:16. Then ask: **Why is the Bible so "strict" on divorce? Why does God hate it? Why is there very little difference between the divorce rate among Christians and the divorce rate among the rest of society?** Get several responses.

Divorce's Other Victims

(Needed: Volunteer speaker)

Say: **Not all of us will have an opportunity to talk a couple out of getting divorced. But there are other ways we, as Christians, can deal with this problem issue. First, we can help the other people affected by divorce.**

Before the session, you'll need to recruit a guest speaker. Find someone whose parents divorced when he or she was young. This speaker could be someone from your church, perhaps a young adult most of your group members know. Ask this person to speak to the group for a few minutes about the emotions he or she experienced during his or her parents' divorce. Also ask your speaker to describe how he or she eventually got over the pain of the divorce. Were there any family members or Christian friends who were especially comforting to him or her? If so, what did these people do?

After your speaker finishes talking, open up the floor for questions. You might also give group members who come from divorced families an opportunity to share their stories.

Then ask: **What can we do to help kids we know whose parents have divorced?** (Spend time with them; listen to them when they share their feelings and frustrations; don't treat them—or their parents—differently than we would treat other people; etc.)

Think before You Commit

(Needed: Paper, pencils)

Say: **A second way we can deal with this issue of divorce is to take steps now to prevent ourselves from becoming another divorce statistic. In most cases, the problems in a marriage that led to divorce were probably apparent when the couple was dating. However, the couple chose to overlook the problems, hoping that they would go away.**

What are some potential marital problems that could be spotted during a dating relationship? (One of the partners not being a Christian; a partner with abusive tendencies; an unfaithful partner; radically different views on money, raising kids, etc.; substance abuse; etc.)

What should a person do if he or she recognizes some potential problems in his or her dating relationship? (Check with his or her partner to see if he or she is willing to take steps to correct the problem—perhaps through professional counseling. If the person is not willing to do so, it may be time to end the relationship.)

Point out that the short period of grief following the end of a dating relationship is a worthwhile sacrifice when compared to the potential pain of a miserable marriage and divorce.

Distribute paper and pencils. Say: **At most weddings, the bride and groom recite vows. The purpose of these vows is to guide the couple's actions throughout the marriage. When these vows are broken, trouble begins. In the same way, we can create some dating commitments to guide our actions as we get romantically involved with members of the opposite sex. These commitments could prevent us from getting into relationships that might eventually lead to divorce. Take**

some time now to write down at least four commitments that you will follow as you date.

Give group members a few minutes to work. When everyone is finished, ask volunteers to share their commitments. Use the following suggestions to supplement group members' ideas.

- Do not date non-Christians.
- Do not date people who have a reputation of being sexually promiscuous.
- Do not date people who drink or use drugs at all.
- Do not date people who have violent tendencies or who are verbally abusive to others.

As you wrap up the session, encourage group members to keep their commitment sheets in a place where they will be seen often. As your young people get involved in relationships, they should periodically check the sheets to make sure their relationships are on track.

PERSONAL PERSPECTIVE

1 | Write your name in the space below if at least one of your parents has been divorced. | Write your name in the space below if neither of your parents has ever been divorced.

Total number of people in the group: _____

Approximately _____ 10% _____ 20% _____ 30% _____ 40% _____ 50%
_____ more than 50% of the people in this group come from a family that has experienced divorce.

2 Draw an "X" on each of the lines below to indicate your responses to the questions.

Do you believe divorce is wrong?

_____

Always   Usually   It depends on   It's none of
                                                      the circumstances.   my business.

Do you believe divorced people should remarry?

_____

Always   Usually   It depends on   It's none of
                                                      the circumstances.   my business.

3 List as many circumstances as possible in which God permits divorce.

DIVORCE -O- METER

For each of the following situations, draw an arrow in the appropriate place to indicate what you think should be done. Your answers should be based on the principles in Matthew 5:27-32; Mark 10:2-12; and I Corinthians 7:1-16.

 1. A husband is physically abusing his wife.

 2. A wife is habitually abusing drugs and refuses treatment.

 3. One of the marriage partners has an affair.

 4. One of the marriage partners reveals that he or she is a homosexual.

 5. One of the marriage partners refuses to accept Jesus Christ as Lord and Savior.

 6. One of the marriage partners discovers that his or her spouse is sexually abusing a child.

 7. One of the marriage partners is verbally abusing his or her spouse.

 8. A wife is abandoned by her husband.

 9. A husband is not financially providing for his family.

STEP 1

Have kids form pairs. Give each pair several large graham crackers, a cup of canned cake frosting, a butter knife, and a dozen small candies. Explain that each pair has three minutes to make a "gingerbread" house of its own design. When time is up, ask each pair: **Is this home worth saving?** If both partners say no, crush the house. If one says no, crush the house. If both say yes, offer them an incentive (candy, a quarter, etc.) to let you wreck the house. See what happens. Then give a prize to any pair that won't let you ruin its house. Ask: **How did you decide whether your "home" was worth saving?** Ask those who let you wreck their houses: **How did it feel when I crushed what you'd worked on?** Ask those whose partners unilaterally decided the house wasn't worth saving: **Was it fair to let just one partner wreck your "home"?** Use this as an illustration of how divorce works—one or both partners in a marriage decides the relationship isn't worth saving. Ask: **What kinds of "homewrecker" attitudes and actions are splitting people up today?**

STEP 3

Bring a lock that needs a key to be opened. Also bring several keys that look like they might fit the lock (but don't) and several stick-on labels. Have kids label the keys with reasons people give for divorcing. If adultery is mentioned, make sure that label goes on the key that *does* open the lock. (If it isn't mentioned, put that label on the right key yourself.) Mix the keys together. After kids search the Bible passages for permissible reasons for initiating a divorce, have volunteers try all of the keys to see which could legitimately "unlock" the bonds of marriage.

STEP 2

Have kids form pairs. Ask each pair to list as many movies as it can think of that contain scenes in which a husband or wife does something that might be considered grounds for divorce. (An obvious example is *Fatal Attraction,* in which a husband has an affair.) Give the pairs three minutes to work. Then have each pair read its list and explain what happens in each film that might be considered grounds for divorce. Give the rest of the group an opportunity to question whether a particular action is grounds for divorce or not. Lead in to a discussion on how easy it is to get divorced in our society today.

STEP 3

Rather than handing out Repro Resource 6, have kids form two groups. Instruct one group to look up Matthew 5:27-32 and I Corinthians 7:1-16, and write down the key principles of the passages. (Matt. 5:27-32 indicates that marital unfaithfulness ["cheating"] may be grounds for divorce. I Cor. 7:1-16 suggests that if a non-Christian wants to leave his or her marriage to a Christian, the Christian should let him or her go—for the sake of peace in the home.) Instruct the other group to look up Mark 10:2-12 and Malachi 2:16a, and write down the key principles of the passages. (Neither passage mentions any circumstance under which divorce is OK.) When the groups are finished, read aloud the situations on Repro Resource 6. Have each group decide, based on its assigned passages, whether each situation is grounds for divorce or not. It's likely that the groups will disagree on at least a couple of the situations. Afterward, ask: **Why do some Bible passages seem to indicate that divorce is *always* wrong while others seem to suggest that under certain circumstances it's OK?** Encourage most of your kids to offer their opinions.

STEP 1

Begin the session with a "human knot" activity. Have all of your group members bunch together tightly in a huddle. Instruct them to extend their arms into the middle of the huddle and clasp two other hands in the bunch. After everyone is "joined together," explain that the object of the activity is for kids to get untangled *without letting go of each other's hands.* This means that kids will have to step over or crawl under each other's arms, twist and maneuver in tight spaces, drag each other through the maze of people, etc. If kids aren't able to untangle themselves after several minutes of trying, call a halt to the activity. Then compare the difficulty kids had untying the "human knot" with the difficulty divorcing couples have untying the "marriage knot."

STEP 3

Have kids form nine small groups (or pairs). Assign one of the situations on Repro Resource 6 to each group. Instruct each group to come up with a realistic scenario based on its situation (supplying names to the characters involved, details about their situation, etc.). Then have each group come up with a convincing argument as to why its situation is grounds for divorce. After a few minutes, have each group briefly present its scenario and argument. Then give the rest of your group members an opportunity to argue *against* divorce in that situation, basing their arguments on the Bible passages listed on Repro Resource 6. After all of the groups have shared, lead in to a discussion on whether or not the Bible's view on divorce is too restrictive.

STEP 3

Kids may know that the Bible opposes divorce, but feel deep down—as many adults do these days—that such a position is too old-fashioned. After all, times have changed since the Bible was written. Point out that in Mark 10:2-12, Jesus makes it clear that God opposes divorce because of the way He designed people—male and female, meant to become "one flesh" in an inseparable way. A lot of things have changed since Creation and since Jesus walked the earth, but our basic design hasn't. And if you want to get technical, you could mention that Jesus' statement is a lot more recent than Moses' rules, which allowed divorce in a variety of circumstances.

STEP 5

Kids may tune out repeated warnings not to date non-Christians. "We'd just be going out," they may say, "not getting married." Deal with this by asking kids exactly when and how they would break up with a non-Christian to make sure they didn't get married. Ask a few guy-girl pairs to act out a scene in which a Christian has to tell a non-Christian he or she's been dating for six months that they can't go out anymore. If kids want to know why the breakup is happening, say: **You tell me. At what point would you stop the relationship to keep it from going too far?** Having to get specific, and seeing the awkwardness of such a breakup, may help kids understand why it's better not to start such a relationship in the first place.

STEP 3

Kids with little Bible background may be confused by the seemingly contradictory Bible passages concerning divorce. So in the Bible study, focus your attention primarily on Mark 10:6-9. Ask: **How does God feel about marriage?** (He holds it in esteem and considers it sacred and special.) **What does "the two will become one flesh" mean?** (When a man and woman are united in marriage, they are no longer viewed as two different entities; they become one.) Point out that, therefore, divorce is not simply a matter of two people going their separate ways; it's a matter of tearing apart "one flesh."

STEP 5

Kids who are new to the faith may not understand why Christians shouldn't date non-Christians. So spend a few minutes reviewing 2 Corinthians 6:14-18. Point out that the ideal relationship (marriage or dating) involves two people growing closer together as they grow closer to God. However, if one person in the relationship is not a Christian and has no desire to grow closer to God, he or she will disrupt not only the relationship, but his or her partner's spiritual growth as well.

STEP 3

As you discuss Mark 10:9 ("Therefore what God has joined together, let man not separate"), give each group member two links of a chain or necklace. Encourage kids to keep the links as a reminder of God's desire for us to be "linked together" with one special person for our entire life.

STEP 5

If you have kids from divorced families in your group, meet with them privately sometime before the session to talk about some specific problems and concerns they have as a result of their parents' divorce. Some kids may mention that they have no one to attend father-son or mother-daughter outings with. Other kids may relate the agony of having to decide which parent to live with. Assure all of the kids that their responses will be kept anonymous. As you wrap up the meeting, read (or write on the board) some of the specific concerns and problems the kids named. Then close the session in prayer, asking various group members to choose one of the problems to pray for. Encourage kids to continue praying for these problems throughout the week.

STEP 1

If you don't have any guys available for the opening skits, add the following props to help the girls portraying the men get "in character."

• For the "Homer and Marge Simpson" skit, Homer will need a large box of doughnuts.

• For the "Fred and Wilma Flintstone" skit, Fred will need a baseball bat with padding added to it to make it look like a prehistoric club.

• For the "Thurston Howell III and Lovey" skit, Thurston will need a sport coat.

• For the "Santa and Mrs. Claus" skit, Santa will need a large white beard.

STEP 4

Distribute paper and pencils. Give your girls a choice of the following options:

• Write a letter to a friend whose parents are in the process of getting a divorce.

• Write a letter to your parents, letting them know how you feel about their divorce and how it has affected your life.

• Write a letter to your parents, encouraging them to stay together.

Make sure your girls know they don't have to share their letters with anyone if they don't wish to; but if they're willing, collect the letters and read them anonymously to the group.

STEP 1

Probably all of your guys have said at one time or another, "I can't believe *she's* going out with *him!*" As a group, come up with a list of guys who are married to or dating people who are much better looking than they are. Your list might include celebrities, guys your group members know at school, or perhaps even some of your group members themselves. After you've come up with several names, ask: **What do you think girls see in these guys?** Use your discussion to introduce the topic of compatibility and incompatibility in relationships.

STEP 5

At the beginning of Step 5, distribute paper and pencils. Instruct your guys to write down (in order) the top seven characteristics they look for in a girl. Their lists may include physical characteristics ("blonde hair"), social characteristics ("popular"), spiritual characteristics ("Christian"), etc. After a few minutes, collect the lists. Then read each one aloud, compiling a master list on the board of characteristics that are named by more than one guy. After you've compiled a master list, ask: **How many of these characteristics would contribute to a strong marriage?** Help your guys see that characteristics like blonde hair and a nice smile are appealing, but they're not the kinds of things we should build our relationships—even dating relationships—on.

STEP 1

Set up a mock "Newlywed Game." Pair up three guys and three girls. Have the girls leave the room. Then ask the guys three questions about their "spouse." Each question should have three possible answers. Guys will write down the answer they think their partner will choose. For example, you might say: **You come home from work to find dinner on the table. Knowing your wife, is that dinner most likely (a) a TV dinner, (b) homemade lasagna, or (c) a pizza she had delivered?** After you've asked the questions, bring the girls back. Ask each girl the same questions you asked the guys. If one of her answers matches one of her partner's answers, the couple get a point. For the second round, have the guys leave the room; ask the girls three questions about their "husbands." Then bring the guys back in to try to match the answers. Award prizes to the winning couple. Lead in to a discussion on how important compatibility is in a marriage. Ask: **If a husband and wife aren't compatible, should that be grounds for divorce? Why or why not?**

STEP 5

Have guys and girls pair up to play "Stay Together." "Bind" the members of each pair by tying their ankles together. Then set up an obstacle course in your room (using tables, chairs, trash cans, etc.) for the pairs to navigate. Using a stopwatch, time the members of each pair to see how quickly they complete the course while tied together. If the partners become untied, they must start over at the beginning of the course. Award prizes to the winning pair. Afterward, point out that marriage is sometimes like an obstacle course—with pitfalls, things to avoid, and things to be "conquered" together. The key to marriage, just like the obstacle course, is staying "bound" together.

STEP 1

Show some video scenes (which you've screened beforehand) in which unmarried couples argue. Then ask whether your kids think each couple should get married, and what the chances of a divorce are if such a marriage takes place. Here are some examples of couples and films you might use: John Cusack and Ione Skye in *Say Anything;* Billy Crystal and Meg Ryan in *When Harry Met Sally . . .*; Al Pacino and Michelle Pfeiffer in *Frankie and Johnny;* Kathleen Turner and Michael Douglas in *Romancing the Stone;* Ron Howard and Cindy Williams in *American Graffiti.*

STEP 5

Play and discuss one or more of the following contemporary Christian songs that talk about being wise in romantic relationships. For instance, play "I Love You" by Amy Grant. Then ask: **Do you think the couple described in this song is likely to get a divorce? Why or why not? What kinds of "changes" might take place in a romantic relationship? How can people prepare for them?** Or play "All I Needed to Say" by Michael W. Smith. Then ask: **What situation is this song describing? How can kids avoid painful breakups like this? How might this song help a Christian guy or girl who's just broken up with someone because that person isn't a Christian?** Or play "We've Got a Secret" by Tanya Goodman. Then ask: **What is this couple's secret? What "pressures" and "storms" might they face? How could God's love keep couples together?** Or play "Circle of Two" by Steve and Annie Chapman. Then ask: **What is this song about? How could praying together help a couple? Is this only for married people, or should people who are dating pray together too? Explain.**

STEP 1

Try a shorter opener. Before the session, put a set of the following objects in each of several bags—the number of bags to be determined by the number of teams you decide to have. The objects are as follows: a peeled banana, a marshmallow, a hard-boiled egg in the shell, a tomato, and a piece of cake. Give each team a bag. Announce that each team has one minute to break its objects in half, using only fingers. The team that makes the *cleanest* breaks—with the least ragged, straightest edges—wins. The winners get their pick of the broken foods; the losers have to eat the rest. Discuss the difficulty of breaking these objects without making a mess. Tie this into the myth that divorce can be a clean, painless break with the past; in reality, divorce hurts because it breaks something that wasn't meant to be broken. In Step 2, instead of having kids mingle to gather answers for Repro Resource 5, just have them raise their hands to indicate how many come from families that have experienced divorce; let kids fill out the rest of the sheet individually.

STEP 3

Rather than having everyone study all three passages, have kids form three teams; assign each team one passage. Skip Step 4. In Step 5, omit the commitment-writing exercise. Instead, simply ask group members to seriously consider the four suggested commitments listed near the end of Step 5.

STEP 2

After your group members list as many reasons as they can think of for divorce, show some pictures of Hollywood celebrities—some of whom have been divorced and some of whom haven't. Have your group members guess which celebrities have been divorced. Then ask: **Do you think it's more difficult for celebrities to remain married than it is for other people? Why or why not?** Afterward, point out that *all* married couples face obstacles in their relationship.

STEP 4

If many of your group members live in low-income housing developments, it's likely that at least some of them have single, never-married parents. So while the topic of divorce may not *directly* affect these kids, some of the same principles may apply to their family situation. Invite a few of these single (never married) parents to share with your group some of the hardships and triumphs they've experienced in raising their kids alone. Then give kids an opportunity to ask some questions. (You might want to screen the questions before they're asked to make sure they're appropriate.) Afterward, brainstorm ways your group members can help kids from divorced and single-parent (never married) families.

STEP 1

Turn the opening activity into a competition between your high schoolers and your junior highers. Instruct each group to brainstorm a list of several fictional couples—and a list of reasons each couple might give for divorcing. (You might read some of the examples in the session to give kids an idea of what you're looking for.) After a few minutes, have two members from the high school group—representing one of the fictional couples on their list (without revealing who the couple is)—start reading the list of reasons the couple might give for divorcing. After each reason is read, members of the junior high team will have an opportunity to guess who the couple is. See how many clues (reasons) it takes before the junior highers are able to guess who the couple is. Then have two junior highers read a list of reasons for divorce while your high schoolers attempt to guess who the couple is. The team that correctly guesses its opponent's couple using the fewest clues gets a point. Play as many rounds as you have time for.

STEP 4

To help your kids consider the wide-reaching effects of divorce, get them to look at it from two different points of view. Ask your high schoolers to brainstorm a list of the effects of divorce on the parents who are actually divorcing. Ask your junior highers to brainstorm a list of the effects of divorce on the divorcing couple's kids. Instruct each group to list as many effects as it can think of. After a few minutes, have each group share its list. Afterward, ask: **Who do you think suffers worse in a divorce: the husband and wife or their kids? Why?** Regardless of the answer your kids arrive at, help them see that divorce is a terrible experience for everyone involved.

STEP 4

Ask: **How many of you have attended a wedding in which the bride and groom recited vows that they'd written themselves? If so, how did their vows differ from "traditional" vows?** Get a few responses. Then give kids an opportunity to write vows for their *own* wedding. First, read a traditional wedding vow (". . . in sickness and in health, for richer or for poorer, 'til death do us part"). Then ask: **What would you add to this vow or change for *your* wedding? Write it down.** Give kids a few minutes to work. When they're finished, ask volunteers to read and explain the vows they wrote. Lead in to a discussion on why it's sometimes hard to keep wedding vows.

STEP 5

Randomly assign kids to two equal-sized teams. Have the two teams sit on opposite sides of the room. Then say: **Statistics say that one of every two marriages ends in divorce. So, statistically speaking, if everyone in this room got married, all of you** (point to one of the teams) **would end up divorced. How does that make you feel?** Give kids an opportunity to respond to the statistic and its implications. Then have the members of each team brainstorm a list of things they could do to reverse the skyrocketing divorce-rate trends. (Most of their suggestions will probably focus on their own individual relationship habits. That's OK.) After a few minutes, have each team share its list.

Just an Alternative Lifestyle? (Homosexuality and Gay Rights)

YOUR GOALS FOR THIS SESSION:

Choose one or more

☐ To help group members identify and explain their personal views on homosexuality and gay rights.

☐ To help group members understand what the Bible says about homosexuality.

☐ To help group members choose God-honoring ways to respond to homosexuals and gay agendas in our society.

☐ Other:_____

_____

Your Bible Base:

Genesis 2:20-25;
    18:16—19:29
Leviticus 20:13
Romans 1:24-27; 7:14-25
I Corinthians 6:9-11
Galatians 6:7
Ephesians 5:21-33; 6:10-8
Hebrews 12:4-13
I John 1:9; 3:9

What's My Secret?

(Needed: Poster board, markers, chairs)

Before the session, you'll need to choose five group members to participate in a game. Interview each participant separately and find out something about him or her that no one else in the group knows. (Make sure the information isn't embarrassing.) Write each person's secret on a piece of poster board.

To begin the session, line up five chairs at the front of the room. Ask the five group members you spoke with earlier to sit in the chairs. Then, one at a time, have other group members come to the front of the room and try to guess which secret goes with which person. Each contestant will place the various pieces of poster board in front of the appropriate people to indicate his or her guesses. Then you will announce how many correct answers the person got. Continue until someone guesses all five secrets correctly.

Afterward, ask: **What if we had a person in the group whose secret was that he's gay? How would you react?** Encourage group members to answer honestly. If they would be uncomfortable around such a person, they should say so.

Explain: **Today we're going to be talking about homosexuality and gay rights. We're going to find out not only what the Bible says about these issues, but also what the Bible says about how we should respond to them.**

OPTIONS

EXTRA ACTION

SMALL GROUP

LARGE GROUP

HEARD IT ALL BEFORE

FELLOWSHIP & WORSHIP

MOSTLY GIRLS

EXTRA FUN

MEDIA

SHORT MEETING TIME

URBAN

JR.HIGH HIGH SCHOOL COMBINED

What about Homosexuality and Gay Rights?

(Needed: Copies of Repro Resource 7, pencils, chalkboard and chalk or newsprint and marker)

To get an idea of how your group members feel about homosexuality and gay rights issues, distribute copies of "What Do You Think?" (Repro Resource 7) and pencils. Give group members a few minutes to complete the sheet. When everyone is finished, go through the questions one at a time, asking several group members to share their responses for each one.

Afterward, ask: **How do most of your friends feel about homosexuals? How do most of the kids at your school feel about them?** Get responses from several group members. Do *not,* however, allow anyone to name names in the discussion.

Do you believe homosexuality is a sin? Why or why not? If there are group members with differing opinions on this issue, encourage a brief debate on the topic. Ask each person to explain his or her position; then allow time for rebuttals. Explain that you'll be looking at what the Bible says about homosexuality in a few minutes.

Do you think homosexuals are mistreated in our society? Do you think they're discriminated against? Explain.

What political and legal rights should homosexuals have in our society? List group members' suggestions on the board as they are named.

Do gays and lesbians qualify as a minority in the same way that African-Americans or Hispanics do? Why or why not?

Keep in mind that you're not necessarily looking for the "right" answers to these questions. You're looking for group members' opinions. No one should feel hesitant about responding, fearing that he or she will give a "wrong" answer.

STEP 3

God's Word on Homosexuality

(Needed: Bibles, paper, pencils, index cards with Scripture references written on them, chalkboard and chalk or newsprint and marker, team prizes [optional])

Have group members form four teams. Distribute paper and pencils to each team. Before the session, you'll need to prepare twelve index cards—three for each team. On one side of each card, write one of the following Scripture references. On the other side, write the number of the team to which that passage is assigned.

The assignments are as follows:
- Group #1—Genesis 2:20-25; Genesis 18:16—19:29; Leviticus 20:13
- Group #2—Romans 1:24-27; Romans 7:14-25; 1 Corinthians 6:9-11
- Group #3—Galatians 6:7; Ephesians 5:21-33; Ephesians 6:10-18
- Group #4—Hebrews 12:4-13; 1 John 1:9; 1 John 3:9

After you've prepared the cards, hide them around the room.

At this point in the session, explain that each team must find its three hidden cards, look up the Scripture passages written on them, and answer the following questions (write them on the board):
- How do these passages relate to the issue of homosexuality?
- According to these passages, how does God respond to sin?
- According to these passages, how does God treat sinners?

After all of the teams have finished, ask each one to share its findings. Use the following information to supplement the teams' answers.

Group #1—Genesis 2:20-25 makes it clear that God's original design was for men to be with women and women to be with men. Therefore, homosexual practice goes against God's design. Genesis 18:16—19:29 relates the story of Sodom and Gomorrah, two cities that were destroyed because of the wickedness of their citizens. One of the forms of wickedness in the cities was homosexual activity (19:4-5). Because of God's love for His people, He promised not to destroy the cities if just 10 righteous people were found. However, because 10 righteous people could not be found, God's holiness demanded punishment for sin. [NOTE: For more information on the sins of Sodom and Gomorrah, see Ezek. 16:49-50 and Jude 7.] Leviticus 20:13 demonstrates the severity with which God dealt with homosexual sin under the Old Testament law.

Group #2—Romans 1:24-27 tells us that "God gave them over in the sinful desires of their hearts to sexual impurity" and "shameful lusts." This sexual impurity and shameful lust includes homosexual activity.

Sometimes, rather than punishing sexual misconduct immediately and dramatically (as He did in Sodom and Gomorrah), God allows the sin itself to run its course as an act of judgment. In Romans 7:14-25, Paul describes a conflict that could apply to many people who struggle with homosexuality: "I do not understand what I do. For what I want to do I do not do, but what I hate I do" (vs. 15). Paul also offers a solution to such ambivalence and confusion, a rescue from our sinful nature: Jesus Christ. I Corinthians 6:9-11 lists various people who "will not inherit the kingdom of God" (vs. 9). Included among the list are "homosexual offenders" (vs. 9). Note that all of these passages condemn much more than homosexual practice. Heterosexual promiscuity is just as much a sin as homosexual promiscuity. The root sin is rebellion against God. Homosexual practice is just one of many symptoms of the root sin.

Group #3—Galatians 6:7 warns us that any sin (including homosexual activity) will eventually result in punishment. Ephesians 5:21-33 outlines God's plan for healthy relationships—husbands and wives loving each other. In Ephesians 6:10-18, Paul outlines a strategy for people to fight Satan's attacks—attacks that might include homosexual temptation. God cares so much for us that He wants us to be prepared for such attacks.

Group #4—Hebrews 12:4-13 tells us that the Lord's discipline for sins (which would include homosexual activity) should not be viewed as a rejection by the Lord. God disciplines those whom He loves. I John 1:9 emphasizes that if we confess our sins—no matter what those sins are—God will forgive us for them. I John 3:9 tells us that a person "who is born of God" (a Christian) will not continue to live a life that is characterized by sin—which would include a homosexual lifestyle.

Afterward, ask: **Based on these passages, how would you respond to gay rights activists who claim that people are born homosexual, and are simply following their natural tendencies in pursuing homosexual lifestyles?** (Passages like Gen. 2:20-25 and Matt. 19:4-6 make it clear that God created us for heterosexual relationships. The question isn't one of heredity—it's one of obedience. We're all born with a tendency to sin. Even if homosexuality is hereditary, that doesn't make practicing it right in God's eyes. There is no excuse for sin.)

Is it wrong to be tempted by homosexual activity? After a couple of kids have responded, emphasize that being tempted by something is not wrong. After all, Jesus Himself faced temptation from Satan (Matt. 4:1-11). Purposefully dwelling on the temptation and giving in to it is wrong. We might say that homosexual *orientation* is not sin, but homosexual *lust* and *practice* is. In the same way, being tempted to have heterosexual sex isn't sinful, but deliberately lusting after someone and engaging in sex outside of marriage is a violation of God's design for us.

STEP 4

What Should Our Response Be?

(Needed: Bibles, copies of Repro Resource 8, pencils, poster board, markers)

OPTIONS

LARGE GROUP

FELLOWSHIP & WORSHIP

MOSTLY GIRLS

MOSTLY GUYS

EXTRA FUN

MEDIA

URBAN

EXTRA CHALLENGE

Have someone read aloud John 3:16 and Matthew 7:1-5. Then ask: **How should these two passages influence the way we treat homosexuals and gay rights activists?** (John 3:16 points out that God loves the people of the world so much that He gave His only Son, so that whoever—homosexuals or heterosexuals alike—believes in Him will have everlasting life. If God loves someone that much, who are we to shun him or her because of his or her sexual orientation? Matthew 7:1-5 reminds us not to focus too heavily on the sins of others because, in the process, we may tend to overlook our own sins. We should not try to relate to homosexuals from a position of moral superiority. Christian witness, as an old saying suggests, is simply one beggar [sinner] telling another beggar where to find food [redemption].)

Have group members form pairs. Distribute copies of "What to Do?" (Repro Resource 8) to each pair. Instruct the members of each pair to read each situation and write down some ideas (based on the principles in John 3:16 and Matt. 7:1-5) as to how they would respond.

After a few minutes, go through the situations one at a time and have each pair share its responses. Use the following information to supplement the pairs' answers.

Situation #1—Perhaps the best solution would be to convince the girl that the youth group leader is someone who can be trusted and who can help her with her sexual confusion. Or you might encourage her to seek help from a pastor or a qualified counselor. Then you could accompany her and give her moral support, if necessary. In the meetings that follow, you should make it a point to spend time with her and show her that you're not avoiding her. Also, *under no circumstances* should you repeat what she told to any other group members!

Situation #2—Responding in a God-pleasing manner to someone who is shouting in your face is difficult. One possible solution is not to say anything at all. Someone looking for a verbal fight is probably going to tee off on anything you say.

Situation #3—Rather than confronting these women in haste and driving them away from the church, perhaps it might be best to allow the Holy Spirit to work in their lives. His work might eventually involve the pastor (or some official governing board of the church) meeting with the women, but it also might involve other methods of making them aware of their sin.

Situation #4—As with Situation #2, the first thing you need to do in this situation is say a quick prayer, asking God to give you wisdom and guide your words as you respond to the man. It would also be helpful to remember that if you don't know the answer to a question, it's OK to say so. There's nothing wrong with not having all of the answers.

As you wrap up the session, give group members an opportunity to pray about their own involvement with the issue of homosexuality. Perhaps some of your group members are experimenting with homosexual activity or are questioning their sexual orientation. Perhaps others have brothers, sisters, or close friends who are gay or lesbian. And perhaps others have strong anti-gay biases or have even participated in gay-bashing activities. Whatever their concerns, give group members an opportunity to share them with God. Also invite kids to talk with you privately about their concerns. If you don't feel qualified to help them on your own, be prepared to refer them to your pastor or to a qualified counselor.

What Do You Think?

1. Place a check mark next to the statements you agree with.

Gay people should have the right to . . .
____ Solicit sex in public places.
____ Be openly gay while teaching in a public school.
____ Serve without restriction in the military.
____ Get married and receive all of the benefits that a married heterosexual couple would receive.
____ Have explicitly gay businesses, such as bars and entertainment places that cater to gays.
____ Live a publically gay lifestyle while holding public office.
____ Display sexual affection toward members of the same sex in public.
____ Be ordained pastors and ministers.
____ Be leaders in churches, serving in staff positions and as elders, deacons, teachers, etc.
____ Special legislation that preserves their legal rights as a minority group.

2. Draw an "X" on the following lines to indicate your opinions.

I believe that those who practice homosexuality are

Abnormal ———————————————————————————— Normal

Immoral ———————————————————————————— Moral

Perverted ———————————————————————————— Healthy

Practicing
learned behavior ——————————————————————— Born
                                                     homosexual

Condemned   Loved
by God ————————————————————————————— by God

Unacceptable ————————————————————————— Acceptable

3. Is it possible to be a practicing homosexual and a Christian?
____ Yes   ____ No   ____ Uncertain

4. Draw an "X" on the following line to indicate your opinion.

As Christians, we should reject and hate sin, but love (with God's love) the sinner.

_____
Agree   Not Certain   Disagree

NOTES

WHAT TO DO?

SITUATION #1

At a youth group retreat, you get into a long conversation with a girl who hasn't been in the group very long. She mentions that she doesn't feel like she fits in well with the others in the group, but she's hesitant to say why. After some questioning on your part, she finally confides to you that she doesn't have the same feelings about guys—in a romantic sense—that other girls seem to have. In fact, she's afraid that she sometimes has romantic feelings for other girls. Although she's never acted on those feelings, she's afraid she might be a lesbian. She begs you not to tell anyone else in the group— especially the leaders. What would you do?

SITUATION #2

The legislators of your state are considering a gay rights bill that would recognize homosexuals as a legitimate minority group. You and a few of your friends go to the capital to attend a protest rally. While there, you are confronted by militant gay rights activists. One of them walks up to you and screams in your face, "Why don't you go bomb an abortion clinic, you self-righteous fascist?! We don't need a bunch of brainwashed Christian kids out here protesting something they don't understand! We don't try to interfere with your right to call yourself a Christian, so why are you trying to interfere with our right to call ourselves gay?" How would you respond?

SITUATION #3

A lesbian couple has recently started attending your church. The two of them haven't flaunted their relationship or tried to stir up any controversy, but they make no secret of the fact that they are lesbians. They seem genuinely interested not only in what the pastor says, but also in the general church proceedings. Some of the members of the church are starting to get uncomfortable with the women's presence. They want the pastor to confront the couple about their relationship. What do you think should be done?

SITUATION #4

While you're visiting a member of your church who's been hospitalized, you encounter a man who's dying of AIDS. When he finds out you're a Christian, he starts asking you questions like "If God didn't want me to be a homosexual, why did He make me attracted to men?" "Do you think I'm a sinner because I'm gay?" "Do you think God loves homosexuals as much as He loves straight people?" "Do you think there are any gays in heaven?" "Do you think God gave me AIDS to punish me?" You can't tell whether the man is just trying to challenge your faith or whether he's really interested in your answers. How would you respond?

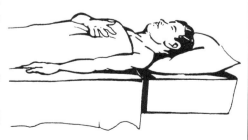

NOTES

STEP 1

Play a short game of touch football, basketball, floor hockey, or charades. Before you start, secretly tell one person on each team to try to score points for the other team. When the "normal" players complain about the result, stop the game. Ask: **What was unusual about the "orientation" of these two players? Why did it bother you? What do people mean when they talk about "sexual orientation"? Why is it such a big issue these days?**

STEP 2

When you make copies of Repro Resource 7, make half of the copies on pink paper. After handing out all of the copies, declare that no self-respecting member of the group would want a pink copy. Those with pink copies have one minute to get rid of theirs. However, they must abide by the following rules: (1) No one may destroy a copy. (2) Everyone who is asked to trade copies must do so. (3) Everyone must be holding a copy when the minute is up. After a minute of frenzied copy-trading, stop the proceedings. Ask: **Why did you go along with this? Did you believe the pink copies really had something wrong with them? Does the color pink have any special meaning to you? Why might some guys avoid wearing pink clothes? Why do so many people avoid doing things that might label them as "gay"?** After kids respond to these questions, have them complete the sheet.

STEP 1

The opening activity may not work well with a small group. Instead, have kids form pairs. Give each pair five minutes to list as many fictional characters as possible who kept at least one secret about themselves. The pairs' lists may include movie and TV characters, comic-book superheroes, characters in books, etc. When time is up, have each pair share its list and explain the secret that each character kept. Award prizes to the pair that comes up with the most characters. Then lead in to the two questions at the end of Step 1.

STEP 3

With a small group, you may have an opportunity to discuss the media sources that influence your kids' opinions on homosexuals and homosexuality. Ask: **What are some movies and TV shows you've seen recently that feature gay or lesbian characters? How were those characters presented? What is the general attitude of Hollywood toward homosexuality? Do you agree with that attitude? Why or why not? How much influence do you think the media has on kids' attitudes toward homosexuals and homosexuality?**

STEP 1

Have kids pair up for a "staring contest." When you say **Go,** each person will stare into his or her partner's eyes for as long as possible. The first of the partners to blink or look away loses the match. (You'll need several volunteers to monitor the matches.) Have the winners pair up for a second round. Continue until only one person remains. Crown him or her "Stare Master" and award him or her a prize. To introduce the topic of the session, point out that staring is often our first reaction when we see something that's radically different from what we're used to seeing. Say: **Let's say you're in a restaurant with your friends. One of the people at the table whispers to the entire group, "I think those guys at the next table are gay." How do you think you and your friends would respond? Why?** Encourage kids to respond honestly.

STEP 4

Rather than using Repro Resource 8 according to the instructions in the session, try a different approach. Have kids form small groups. Instruct the members of each group to come up with the most difficult situation regarding homosexuality that they can think of—the situation that would be hardest for them to respond to. (For instance, one group might come up with a situation in which a person finds out his or her brother is gay.) If necessary, read some of the accounts on Repro Resource 8 to give kids an idea of what you're looking for. After a few minutes, have each group share its situation. Then give the rest of the group members an opportunity to offer biblical solutions or advice (based on the passages you looked at earlier) for the situation.

STEP 1

The Bible's view of homosexuality may not come as a surprise to your kids. That's OK—except for those who feel they might be homosexual. These kids may feel alienated as soon as you announce the topic. So avoid referring to homosexuals as if you assume there are none in your midst. For example, change **"What if we had a person in the group whose secret was that he's gay?"** to **"What if you knew that the secret of a person in our group is that he's gay?"** Instead of talking about "how we should respond to" these issues, talk about "how to deal with" them. The differences are subtle. But to teens struggling with their sexual identity, choosing your words carefully could make the difference between being heard and being tuned out.

STEP 3

Some kids may not be satisfied with the answer to the "natural tendencies" question. God did create the human race as a whole to be heterosexual, but does that mean no one could be born with an abnormal sexual orientation? After all, people are born with genetic abnormalities. Explain: **Even if someone could prove that homosexual tendencies are inborn, it wouldn't make homosexual activity right. Some people may be born with a tendency to become alcoholics or to be violent. That doesn't mean alcoholism and violence are OK, or that people with these tendencies should "do what comes naturally" instead of getting help. Everyone is born with a tendency to sin; it's part of our old natures. Those who belong to Christ don't have to be slaves to their old natures. They may struggle with temptations including homosexuality, but they don't have to give in—whether or not they were born more vulnerable to certain temptations than to others.**

STEP 2

Kids with little Bible background may hold one of two opinions about homosexuals. They may view gays with contempt, not tempering their prejudices with God's command to love; or they may be completely accepting of the gay lifestyle, influenced by the media's portrayal of homosexuality as just an "alternate lifestyle." To introduce the Bible's position on how we should respond to homosexuals, use an illustration. Say: **In the middle of art class, your teacher is called away. As soon as she leaves, the class erupts into chaos. Some kids start throwing paint at each other, splashing it all over the walls and floor in the process. Others start overturning desks. Still others start throwing easels around like Frisbees. When the teacher comes back, she freaks. She grabs one of the desk overturners and drags him into the hall to find out what happened. Do you think the kid should be disciplined for what he did? Explain.** (Yes. He's guilty of doing something wrong and deserves punishment.) **Do you think he deserves any more punishment than the other kids in the class?** (No. All are equally guilty.) Draw the parallel to homosexuality. Point out that God views homosexual practice as sin and deserving of punishment. However, we are *all* guilty of sin. (See Rom. 3:23.) The Bible instructs us to forgive and love each other as God forgives and loves us. (See Col. 3:13 and John 13:34.)

STEP 3

Instead of forming teams for the Bible study, focus as a group on two passages: Genesis 2:20-25 and I John 1:9. Ask kids to summarize the two passages in one sentence. (For instance, someone might suggest "Homosexual practice goes against God's design, but God will forgive people for homosexual sin.")

STEP 1

Begin the session with a game of "Odd Man Out." Allow kids to mingle around the room and talk to each other for a minute or two. Then call out a number. When you do, kids will have to quickly form groups made up of the number of people you called. So if you call, **Three,** kids will form groups of three by joining arms. Those who aren't able to get into a group are eliminated. Once in a group, each person should share a time when he or she felt left out. After a minute or two, have kids mingle again. Then call out another number—perhaps **Five.** Kids must then form appropriate groups again. Those who don't get into groups are eliminated. Once in a group, each person should share about another time when he or she felt left out. Continue the process until only two people remain. Declare them the winners. Then lead in to a discussion on homosexuals, who often feel "left out" of society. If your group is small, skip the group forming and simply discuss times when each group member felt left out.

STEP 4

As a group, work on a poster that illustrates (perhaps humorously) the principle of Matthew 7:1-6. When you're finished, hang the poster somewhere in your room to remind kids of the attitude we should have toward other "sinners." Then lead your group in a time of prayer, thanking God for the truth of John 3:16.

STEP 1

After your girls have completed the "Secret Game," ask: **Have you ever told someone something in confidence, only to find out later that the whole school knows about it? If so, how did it feel to have your confidence betrayed? How did you feel about the person who betrayed your confidence? What did you do as a result of that situation?** Talk for a few minutes about the need people sometimes have for confidentiality. Ask: **Is there ever a time you *should* break a confidence?** Discuss situations in which outside help may be needed. Then ask: **What if we had a person in the group whose secret was that she's struggling with lesbian feelings?** Get several responses.

STEP 4

Add one more situation to your discussion of Repro Resource 8. Say: **You've been captain of the volleyball team for two years. This year you have a new coach who's absolutely wonderful. You've learned a lot from her, and she gets along with the team very well. It looks like it will be a winning season in more ways than one. Soon, though, you begin to hear rumors that her roommate isn't just a roommate; they're lesbians. What would you do?** (First of all, we know what the Bible says about gossip. But if the rumors are true, you can still interact with the coach and learn from her God-given talents and abilities. If you're uncomfortable being around her, you may wish to talk with a youth group leader, pastor, or trusted adult who can keep a confidence. Depending on how open the coach is about her relationship, you may be able to share with her some of your feelings. No matter what you do, though, it's important to remember that the coach is a child of God, and that God loves her just as much as He loves you.)

STEP 2

Bring in a newspaper or magazine article that deals with a recent "gay bashing" incident. (You may need to check some resources at your local library to find such an article.) Read the article to your group, particularly focusing on quotes made by the "gay bashers" to explain their actions. Then ask: **Do you know of anyone who's ever participated in a gay-bashing incident? If so, what's the person like? Why did he or she participate?** The way your guys talk about the people they know who've participated in gay-bashing incidents should give you a clue as to your guys' attitude toward homosexuals. After a couple of guys have shared, ask: **What is "gay bashing"?** Help your guys see that "gay bashing" does not always have to involve physical harm; it might also involve things like perpetuating stereotypes, making derogatory comments, telling dirty jokes about homosexuals, etc. Lead in to the first question in Step 2.

STEP 4

As you wrap up the session, help your guys focus on any prejudices they may have toward homosexuals. Ask them to respond honestly (if not aloud, at least to themselves) to the following questions: **When you hear that someone has "come out of the closet" and declared himself to be a homosexual, what's your first reaction? Do you think girls are more likely to show Christian love to a lesbian than guys are to show Christian love to a gay man? Explain. Why might some guys be hesitant to show Christian love to homosexuals? What might prevent *you* from showing Christian love to a homosexual?**

STEP 1

Have kids arrange their chairs in a circle for a game of "Hot Potato." Hand a raw potato to one person. Explain that when you say **Go,** he or she must pass the potato to the person on his or her right. The potato will continue to be passed until you say **Stop.** (Emphasize that you'll have your back turned to the action, so you won't be able to see who has the potato.) At that point, the person holding the potato is out; he or she must remove his or her chair from the circle. After group members "tighten up the circle," start the game again. Continue until only one person remains. Crown him or her "Mr. (or Mrs.) Potato Head" and award him or her a prize (perhaps a gift certificate for french fries at a local fast-food restaurant). Afterward, explain that the "hot potato" you'll be talking about in this session is homosexuality.

STEP 4

Prepare a quiz on different kinds of phobias (fears of certain things). List the names of various phobias on one side of the sheet and possible definitions (some accurate, some humorous) on the other side. Among the phobias you might use are acrophobia (fear of heights), ailurophobia (fear of cats), hydrophobia (fear of water), claustrophobia (fear of small or closed places—not the fear of Santa), arachnophobia (fear of spiders—not the fear of a Middle Eastern country), and mysophobia (fear of dirt and germs—not the fear of small rodents). The object of the quiz is for kids to match each phobia with its correct definition. After distributing the quiz, give kids a few minutes to work on it. Award prizes to those who get the most correct answers. Then ask: **What is homophobia?** (An aversion to homosexuals.) Lead in to a discussion on how Christians should respond to homosexuals.

STEP 1

Play one or more of the following songs recorded by Elton John: "Your Song," "Nikita," "Blue Eyes," "Goodbye Yellow Brick Road," and "Someone Saved My Life Tonight." Ask: **How do these songs make you feel? Which would you classify as love songs?** Then mention Elton John's self-proclaimed bisexuality. Ask: **If you knew that the singer was directing the song(s) we just heard at a man rather than a woman, how would it change your feelings about the song(s)? Why? Does that tell you anything about your attitude toward homosexuality? If so, what?**

STEP 4

Show scenes from two or more of the following movies-on-video in which homosexual (or apparently homosexual) characters are portrayed. Pre-screen the scenes yourself for appropriateness; rather than showing an objectionable scene to "prove" the character's sexual orientation, you might explain that the orientation is established elsewhere in the film. *Personal Best* (Mariel Hemingway as a lesbian athlete); *Zorro, the Gay Blade* (George Hamilton as Don Diego's effeminate brother); *Longtime Companion* (several gay characters affected by the AIDS epidemic); *An Early Frost* (Aidan Quinn as an AIDS victim). Ask: **Did these characters seem like real people or stereotypes? Do you tend to think of homosexuals as real people? How do you think God sees them? If you were making a movie that included a homosexual character, what might the character be like? How would you want things to turn out for the character? Why?**

STEP 1

Try a shorter opener. Have kids form two teams. Team A must sing the Christmas carol "Deck the Halls" as Team B simultaneously sings the theme from the old *Flintstones* TV show. The first team that names what the two songs have in common wins a prize. (The answer: Both songs contain the word *gay*.) Ask: **What does the word *gay* mean in these songs? What does it usually mean today? How do you react when you hear the word? Why?** In Step 2, cut the first section (the agree-disagree statements) from the rest of Repro Resource 7 so that responses from that section can be tallied by a couple of volunteers while the group discusses the rest of the sheet. Announce the result of the tally at the end of Step 2.

STEP 3

Skip the card-finding activity. Study just the following passages, assigning them to individuals or teams: Genesis 2:20-25; Romans 1:24-27; I Corinthians 6:9-11; I John 1:9; 3:9. In Step 4, use just Situations #1 and #4 if you don't have time to use all of the ones on Repro Resource 8.

STEP 1

To begin the session, have your group members vote on their favorite professional athlete. First, you'll need to get a list of nominees. Have group members suggest athletes from several different sports and explain why those athletes deserve to be nominated. Once you've got a list of at least seven nominees, have kids vote on their favorite. After declaring a winner, ask: **What if I told you that _____ (your kids' favorite athlete) was gay? Would that change your opinion of him (or her)? Why or why not?** Use this discussion to introduce the session topic.

STEP 4

Add the following situation to your discussion of Repro Resource 8:

• **Ramon is a gay hustler who works the street on your block. He's always making lewd comments and propositions to the guys in the area. One day you overhear a couple of older guys in the neighborhood planning an attack on Ramon. What would you do?**

STEP 1

Have your junior highers and high schoolers compete in a game of "One of These Things Is Not Like the Other." Instruct each group to brainstorm several sets of items. Each set should include three things that go together and one that doesn't. The other group will then try to guess which object doesn't belong in the set. Encourage kids to give their sets some thought. While they need to make sure that one item is distinct from the others, they shouldn't make it so obvious that the other group is able to guess it right away. For instance, one group might list "Calvin & Hobbes," "The Far Side," "The Lockhorns," and "Family Circus." The distinct item in this set is "Calvin & Hobbes" because it's a comic *strip*; the others are comic *panels* (one frame). Award a point each time a group stumps the other. Then give prizes to the group with the most points at the end of the game. Use the activity to lead in to a discussion on whether homosexuals are "like" other people in society.

STEP 2

It's likely that much of your junior highers' (and perhaps your high schoolers') knowledge of and opinions on homosexuals are based on information from their peers— a dubious source at best. So you may want to spend a few minutes trying to find out what they know (or think they know) and think of homosexuals. Ask: **What are some slang terms you or your friends use when you talk about homosexuals? Where did these words come from? Why are they associated with homosexuals? Do you ever use those words when you're talking about people you know *aren't* homosexuals? If so, why? Do you think you could recognize a homosexual on the street? If so, how?** Encourage several kids to respond.

STEP 3

Give your kids an opportunity to apply, in a debate setting, biblical principles concerning homosexuality. Have kids form two groups. Instruct the members of one group to brainstorm as many arguments as possible that gay-rights activists might give to support their position. Instruct the members of the other group to brainstorm as many biblical principles as possible to refute the gay-rights arguments. After a few minutes, start the debate and give each team an opportunity to refute the other's arguments.

STEP 4

As a group, create a question-and-answer brochure outlining some of the biblical principles you've discovered concerning homosexuality in this session. Among the questions you might address are "Is homosexuality a sin?" "How should we answer homosexuals who argue that their sexual preference is hereditary and beyond their control?" and "What should be our response to the gay-rights movement?" After creating the brochure, send it to your pastor (or board of elders) for approval. If the pastor (or board) makes changes or additions to the brochure, incorporate them in a second draft of the work. Once the brochure is completed, consider making it available to interested people in the church.

DATE USED:

Approx. Time

STEP 1: *What's My Secret?* _____
- ❏ Extra Action
- ❏ Small Group
- ❏ Large Group
- ❏ Heard It All Before
- ❏ Fellowship & Worship
- ❏ Mostly Girls
- ❏ Extra Fun
- ❏ Media
- ❏ Short Meeting Time
- ❏ Urban
- ❏ Combined Jr. High/High School

Things needed:

STEP 2: *What about Homosexuality and Gay Rights?* _____
- ❏ Extra Action
- ❏ Little Bible Background
- ❏ Mostly Guys
- ❏ Combined Jr. High/High School

Things needed:

STEP 3: *God's Word on Homosexuality* _____
- ❏ Small Group
- ❏ Heard It All Before
- ❏ Little Bible Background
- ❏ Short Meeting Time
- ❏ Extra Challenge

Things needed:

STEP 4: *What Should Our Response Be?* _____
- ❏ Large Group
- ❏ Fellowship & Worship
- ❏ Mostly Girls
- ❏ Mostly Guys
- ❏ Extra Fun
- ❏ Media
- ❏ Urban
- ❏ Extra Challenge

Things needed:

Hawks and Doves
(War and Peace)

Choose one or more

☐ To help group members identify and explain their personal views on war and peace.

☐ To help group members understand what the Bible says about pacifism and just wars.

☐ To help group members make biblically informed, God-honoring decisions concerning their involvement in and support of any wars the nation might face.

☐ Other:_____
_____

Your Bible Base:

Exodus 14:13-14
I Samuel 15:1-3; 17:47
Matthew 5:43-48
Acts 4:18-20
Romans 12:14-19; 13:1-5

This Is War?

(Needed: A deck of playing cards, table, team prizes [optional])

To begin the session, have group members form two teams. Then announce that war has been declared between the two teams. Quickly add, however, that you're not talking about a *fighting* war; instead, you're talking about the card game "War."

Have the two teams line up single-file facing each other, with a table between them. Place a deck of cards face down on the table. The first person in line for each team will draw a card. The person with the higher card wins the "battle" and goes to the end of his or her team's line. [NOTE: Aces are high for this game.] The person with the lower card is out, and must sit down. If the two contestants tie, the next two people in line draw cards. If the player from Team A draws a higher card, then both contestants from Team B must sit down. The game continues like this until one team's players are all eliminated.

If you have a small group, you might want to have the teams play a couple of rounds. You might also want to award prizes to the winning team.

Afterward, ask: **When I say the word "war," what images come to mind?** This rather generic question could provide some insight into your group members' thoughts on the subject. Some kids might mention the negative aspects of war like killing, bombing, destruction, invasion, etc. Others might mention things like protecting freedom, liberating countries, serving your country, etc.

A History of War

(Needed: Chalkboard and chalk or newsprint and marker, cut-apart copy of Repro Resource 9)

Ask: **How many wars has our country fought?** List the various wars on the board as kids name them. For Americans, these wars might include the Revolutionary War, the War of 1812, the Spanish-American War, the Civil War, World War I, World War II, the Korean War, the Vietnam War, and the Persian Gulf War. [NOTE: If you're using this material outside the U.S., supply your own information here.]

Have kids form teams. Cut apart a copy of "Wars of America" (Repro Resource 9). Distribute one or more (depending on the size of your group) of the cards from the sheet to each team. Instruct each team to read the information on its card—the war being described, the stated purpose of the war, and the number of people killed during the war. Then, based on this information, the team should decide whether the war was justifiable or not. Give the teams a few minutes to discuss. Then have each team share and explain its conclusion.

Afterward, ask: **How did you decide whether or not a war was justifiable?** (Perhaps by weighing the purpose of the war against the cost, including loss of life.)

For those of you who decided a war was *not* justifiable, would you have changed your mind if fewer people had been killed? If only 1,000 people had died, would the war have been justifiable? What about 100? What would you consider to be an acceptable loss in terms of the number of people killed? Why?

Besides loss of life, what other factors can we use in determining whether a war is justifiable or not? (The destruction and loss of property caused by the war; changes in the quality of living for the people affected by the war; the political circumstances surrounding the war; etc.)

Explain that people who favor the use of war to solve problems between nations are sometimes known as "hawks." People who oppose the use of war are sometimes known as "doves." Then ask: **Would you say our country has been more of a "hawk" or a "dove" throughout its history? Explain.**

Are you proud of our nation's history concerning war? Why or why not? Encourage several kids to respond.

STEP
3

War in the Bible

(Needed: Bibles, index cards with Scripture passages written on them, pencils)

If no one mentioned it earlier, point out that the ultimate factor in determining whether a war is justifiable or not is what God thinks of it. Ask: **Do you think God is more of a "hawk" or a "dove"?** Chances are your group members will be divided on this issue. Some of them may think God is more of a "hawk" because of all the bloody battles fought by the Israelites—God's chosen people— in the Old Testament. Others may think He is more of a "dove" because of His loving nature.

Before the session, you'll need to prepare several index cards. Write each of the following passages on one of the cards: Exodus 14:13-14; 1 Samuel 15:1-3; 1 Samuel 17:47; Matthew 5:43-48; Romans 12:14-19; Romans 13:1-5.

Have group members reassemble into the teams they formed in Step 2. Distribute one or more of the cards (depending on the size of your group) to each team. Instruct each team to look up its assigned passage and determine whether the passage supports pacifism (not fighting in a war) or fighting a war for a just cause. If team members think the passage supports pacifism, they should write "Peace" on the back of the card. If they think the passage supports fighting a war for a just cause, they should write "War" on the back of the card. If they're unsure about what the passage is saying, they should write "Undecided" on the back of the card.

After a few minutes, have the members of each team read aloud their assigned passage and explain how they interpreted it and why. Allow group members who disagree with the teams' conclusions to share their opinions.

Use the following information to supplement your discussion of the passages.

- *Exodus 14:13-14*—In this passage, Moses assures the Israelites that they will have to do nothing to defend themselves against the Egyptians. He promises that the Lord will do their fighting for them. This would seem to support the Christian pacifist view that we should leave all of our fighting and wars to God.
- *1 Samuel 15:1-3*—In this passage, the Lord commands Saul and the Israelites to attack and completely destroy their enemies, the

Amalekites. This would seem to support the notion that some
wars are just and are in line with God's will.

- *I Samuel 17:47*—This passage suggests that the Lord does not
use "sword or spear" to accomplish His purposes.
- *Matthew 5:43-48*—Those who support the Christian pacifist
view use this passage as one of the central supports of their
philosophy. They say that as Christians, our responsibility is to
love our enemies—not only our personal enemies, but our
national enemies as well. They argue that war is certainly not
an expression of love.
- *Romans 12:14-19*—This passage is also used by Christian pacifists
to support their beliefs. Instructions like "Bless those who
persecute you"; "Do not repay anyone evil for evil"; and especially
"If it is possible, as far as it depends on you, live at peace with
everyone" seem to support the pacifist view.

Have group members focus on verse 19: "Do not take revenge, my
friends, but leave room for God's wrath, for it is written, 'It is mine to
avenge; I will repay,' says the Lord."

Ask: **Do you think it's possible that the Lord might use
one nation to avenge the actions of another nation? In other
words, do you think it's possible that war between two
countries is God's way of avenging?** Refer group members back
to I Samuel 15:1-3.

- *Romans 13:1-5*—Supporters of the just-war philosophy use this
passage to back their views. They say that submitting to the
authority of national leaders means fighting in wars deemed
necessary and justified by those leaders. To not fight in a war,
then, is to disobey our leaders.

Ask: **Does this passage mean we have to do everything
our leaders tell us to do? What about the people in Nazi
Germany—were they required to obey Hitler?**

Have someone read Acts 4:18-20. Explain that Peter and John were
ordered by the Sanhedrin not to speak or teach in the name of Jesus.
The two men disobeyed the order, knowing that it was contrary to
God's will. They obeyed God's law rather than the law of the Sanhedrin.

Ask: **Do you think it's possible that not fighting in a war
might also be an example of obeying God's law rather than
human law? Explain.** Get responses from several group members.

After all of the passages have been read and discussed, ask: **Do you
think the Bible, as a whole, supports pacifism or fighting a
war for a just cause?** Instruct those who think the Bible supports
pacifism to move to the left side of the room. Those who think the Bible
supports fighting a war for a just cause should move to the right side of
the room. Ask several people from both sides of the room to explain
their reasoning.

STEP 4

The Personal Aspect of War

(Needed: Copies of Repro Resource 10, pencils)

O P T I O N S

With group members still sitting on both sides of the room, distribute copies of "A Matter of Conscience?" (Repro Resource 10) and pencils. If possible, have group members pair up with someone sitting on the opposite side of the room. The partners should go through the situations on the sheet, sharing with each other their responses to each situation. Encourage debate and questioning between the partners.

After a few minutes, have the members of each pair share their responses and some of the "highlights" of their discussion/debate regarding each situation.

Then ask the following questions to the entire group:

Under what circumstances, if any, would you be willing to go to war for our country?

Do you think it's right that some citizens should be allowed not to fight in wars even though they enjoy the freedom bought with the price of so many deaths in past wars?

If you were drafted and ordered to fight in a war that you believed was unjust, what would you do?

Get responses from as many group members as possible. You might also ask them to share any biblical principles they can think of to support their decisions.

Wrap up the session with a time of group prayer. Have group members form a circle. Ask several of them to pray aloud for the following things:

- men and women in the armed forces
- young men and women who are considering entering the military
- soldiers faced with the prospect of using force and perhaps even killing someone
- the nation's leaders who make decisions concerning military actions
- Christians who are trying to sort out their beliefs concerning war
- areas of the world in which people are engaged in war
- all efforts to promote peace (1 Tim. 2:2) so that the Gospel may be spread freely.

NOTES

WARS OF AMERICA

REVOLUTIONARY WAR

Purpose: To establish American independence from Great Britain

Number dead: Approximately 35,700

WAR OF 1812

Purpose: To prevent Great Britain from interfering with American shipping trade

Number dead: Approximately 5,000

SPANISH-AMERICAN WAR

Purpose: To establish Cuban independence from Spain

Number dead: Approximately 5,000

CIVIL WAR

Purpose: To abolish slavery and settle other disputes between the North and the South

Number dead: Approximately 620,000

WORLD WAR I

Purpose: To make the world safe for democracy and to prevent the spread of power of the Central Powers (most notably Germany)

Number dead: Approximately 8,500,000 military deaths, in addition to millions of civilian deaths

WORLD WAR II

Purpose: To make the world safe for democracy and to prevent the spread of power of the Axis (most notably Germany, Italy, and Japan)

Number dead: Approximately 17,000,000 military deaths, in addition to tens of millions of civilian deaths

KOREAN WAR

Purpose: To liberate South Korea from the invading forces of Communist North Korea

Number dead: Approximately 3,000,000

VIETNAM WAR

Purpose: To liberate South Vietnam from the invading forces of Communist North Vietnam

Number dead: Approximately 2,000,000

PERSIAN GULF WAR

Purpose: To liberate Kuwait from the invading forces of Saddam Hussein and his Iraqi army

Number dead: Approximately 100,000

A MATTER OF CONSCIENCE?

Situation #1

Your nation declares war on a Communist country in Asia. Critics are saying the situation "could become another Vietnam." Your older brother is drafted for the war. What would you want him to do? Why?

Situation #2

A Middle East nation ruled by a dictator invades a neighboring country, wipes out that country's armed forces, terrorizes its citizens, and claims that country's land and resources for itself. Your country is asked to declare war on the invading nation and send troops to liberate the invaded country. What do you think should be done? Why?

Situation #3

A soldier on a peace-keeping mission in an African nation is ordered to use force to break up a mob demonstration. The soldier doesn't believe force is necessary. What should he do?

Situation #4

You're invited to participate in a demonstration to protest your country's involvement in a war between two Eastern European countries. Several of your friends are going to participate in the demonstration. What would you do? Why?

Situation #5

The Cold War has ended. As a result, there are very few threats to world peace. Most countries are slashing their defense budgets and using that money to fund other government programs. Your country, however, has done very little defense-budget cutting. Defense supporters say that your country must be equipped to fight two different wars at the same time, in case the need arises. Therefore, they say, defense production must continue as before. Opponents say that since no military threats exist, the money from the defense budget should be used in other, more important, areas—such as reviving the economy, funding a national health-care program, creating jobs for the unemployed, etc. What do you think should be done? Why?

STEP 1

Begin the session with "Military Tag." Assign a rank to each person: General, Colonel, Major, Lieutenant, Sergeant, Corporal, or Private. Instruct kids to keep their rank a secret. Give each person 10 "medals" (Post-it™ Notes). Have each person write his or her initials on his or her medals. Then give kids one minute to stick all of their medals on each other. Kids may stick as many medals on any one person as they want to. But anyone who happens to stick a medal on a superior officer loses the game. (The above ranks are listed in order of superiority.) After one minute, see who won and who lost. Ask: **Who stood the best chance of winning this game?** (Generals, who had no superior officers.) **Who stood the best chance of losing?** (Privates, who had the most superiors.) **If you were in the military, what rank would you want? Why? How do you think it would feel to be in the military?**

STEP 2

Help kids visualize the casualty numbers on Repro Resource 9. Bring several bags of dried beans. Announce that each bean represents one death. Have kids form teams. Assign each team one of the wars on the sheet. Distribute the bags of dried beans among the teams. Instruct each team to start counting out the number of beans needed to represent the deaths in its assigned war. After one minute, stop the proceedings. Then estimate how long it would take each team to finish counting at its current rate. For example, if the "Vietnam War" team counted 200 beans in one minute, it would take 10,000 minutes (over 166 hours—nearly a week) to represent its deaths.

STEP 1

The "War" game probably wouldn't work well with a small group. Instead, try a game of "Who Would Win?" Have kids form two teams. Explain that you will name two people or groups of people, and ask: **If these people got into a fight, who would win?** Each team will choose (or be assigned) one of the combatants and, in 30 seconds, come up with a convincing argument as to why he or she (or they) would win the fight. The team that comes up with the most convincing argument (according to your judgment) gets a point. The team with the most points at the end of the game is the winner. Among the potential combatants you might suggest are the Chicago Bears (or any professional football team) vs. the New York Rangers (or any professional hockey team); the Atlanta Braves (or any professional baseball team) vs. the Seattle Supersonics (or any professional basketball team); Tonya Harding vs. Nancy Kerrigan; David Letterman vs. Jay Leno; Guns 'N' Roses vs. Pearl Jam; etc.

STEP 4

Go through Repro Resource 10 as a group. Skip the three questions that follow in the session. Instead, distribute paper and pencils. Ask each group member to summarize (in one paragraph) his or her feelings toward war. The summary should explain whether he or she believes there's such a thing as a "just" war. It should also explain whether he or she would be willing to fight in a war—and if so, under what conditions. After a few minutes, collect the sheets. Read each response aloud without revealing who wrote it. Afterward, emphasize the need for tolerance of each other's beliefs. Then wrap up the session with the group prayer activity described in the session.

STEP 1

Begin the session with "Human Stratego." Using tape, divide the floor of your room into small squares—like a chess board. Have kids for two teams. Give each player a card that has one of the following things on it: a number between 1 and 9, a picture of a bomb, or a picture of a flag. [NOTE: Only one person on each team should have a flag on his or her card. The other items should be evenly distributed among players.] Explain that the object of the game is to capture the other team's flag. To do this, teams must "attack" each other. Each player will start the game standing in a square, facing the other team. The teams will take turns moving people (one square per move). When a player from one team gets to a square occupied by an opponent, each will reveal what's on his or her card. The person with the lower number wins the "battle"; the other person is out of the game. If a person moves to a square occupied by a "bomb," he or she is out—unless he or she is an "8." In that case, the "bomb" is removed from the game. If a person moves to a square occupied by a "flag," his or her team wins. "Bombs" and "flags" may not move. Everyone else may move one square in any direction per turn. So not only should teams use strategy in moving their players, they should also use strategy in positioning their flag and bombs. After giving teams a few minutes to set up, begin the game. Afterward, introduce the topic of war.

STEP 3

Have kids form groups. Ask half of the groups to come up with a situation that illustrates the principle of Romans 12:14-19. Ask the other half to come up with a situation that illustrates Romans 13:1-5. After a few minutes, have each group share its situation. Then discuss how the principles apply to war.

STEP 2

Kids who've studied the wars at school may find the stated purposes on Repro Resource 9 to be simplistic. For example, "To make the world safe for democracy" made an inspiring wartime slogan, but historians might say the reasons for American involvement in the world wars were more complex. Opinions differ over why the U.S. was involved in Vietnam. And some believe the U.S. acted as it did in the Persian Gulf to protect oil supplies as well as to liberate Kuwait. Give kids a chance to add their viewpoints rather than expecting them to simply accept the information on the sheet.

STEP 3

Kids who are familiar with passages like these may come to the discussion with a troubling question: Why does God seem so warlike in the Old Testament and so loving in the New Testament? Note that scholars disagree over the answer to this question. But you may want to point out the following: (1) The God of both testaments is the same God, and perfect (though not easy to understand) at all times; (2) God wanted to protect His people (Israel) in the Old Testament from other nations, and sometimes gave specific instructions to Israel's leaders that included war; (3) with the coming of Christ in the New Testament, anyone who received Him could belong to God, which meant that protecting God's kingdom was no longer a matter of national boundaries; (4) God has a final battle planned (see the Book of Revelation), which indicates that He still reserves the right to be involved in war; (5) despite His limited, specific instructions for ancient Israel to conduct war, God's standards for individual behavior—living at peace with each other rather than killing each other—have remained constant.

STEP 3

Kids with little Bible background may have a hard time reconciling their image of a loving, gracious God with the Lord's Old Testament commands to the Israelites to attack and completely wipe out their enemies. (You may want to set aside a session or two in the future to explore the history of God's chosen people.) So skip the question at the beginning of Step 3 concerning whether God is a "hawk" or a "dove." Also skip the Exodus passage and the two passages from I Samuel. Instead, focus on Matthew 5:43-48; Romans 12:14-19; 13:1-5; and Acts 4:18-20. Ask: **Do you believe that loving our enemies extends to wartime situations? Why or why not? Romans 12:18 says, "As far as it depends on you, live at peace with everyone." How *far* should we go to keep peace? Explain. What is our responsibility to our country? Should we volunteer to serve in a war? Must we serve if we're drafted? Explain.** Lead in to the final question in Step 3.

STEP 4

If your kids are uncomfortable with group prayer, close the session by discussing I Timothy 2:1-2. Ask: How often do you pray for the leaders of our country? How often do you thank God for the freedom and peace in our country? Why is it so easy to take things like freedom and peace for granted? Encourage your kids to begin regularly praying for our country's leaders, that they may make wise decisions so that we may live peaceful and quiet lives.

STEP 3

After discussing the various Bible passages supporting both points of view in the "just war" issue, introduce one more passage. Have someone read aloud Ephesians 6:12 ("For our struggle is not against flesh and blood, but against the rulers, against the authorities, against the powers of this dark world and against the spiritual forces of evil in the heavenly realms."). Emphasize that regardless of where we stand on the issue of human war, all Christians are joined together in the fight against the forces listed in this verse. Then lead your group in singing "Onward Christian Soldiers."

STEP 4

It's likely that sometime during the session, some of your kids disagreed and argued with each other concerning the issue of war. So rather than end the meeting on a note of dissonance, give your kids an opportunity to agree on something. Ask someone to read aloud Exodus 14:13-14. Then, as a group, work on a poster that communicates the truth that "God will fight for you." Close the session in prayer, thanking God that He *does* fight for us.

MOSTLY GIRLS

STEP 1

Your girls may mention that they think of war as something that primarily affects men. Take a few minutes to talk about the many ways women are affected by war, which includes women serving in combat. After some discussion, ask: **What do you think of women being more directly involved in fighting, as some were during the Persian Gulf War?** Allow for discussion on both sides of the issue. Then move on to Step 2.

STEP 3

Ask your girls if they can think of any biblical examples of women who were involved in war. After a minute or two of discussion, instruct group members to read Joshua 2 and Judges 4. These passages contain the stories of three different women—Rahab, Deborah, and Jael—and the three very different roles they played in times of war. As your girls are reading, have them make note of the women and the roles they played. After everyone is finished reading, ask volunteers to share their findings. Ask: **Was anyone surprised by what you read in these passages?** Some of your group members may be quite surprised to discover some of the ways God worked through women (especially in such male-oriented times) during times of war.

MOSTLY GUYS

STEP 1

Perhaps one of the best ways to introduce the topic of war is to get your guys to discuss their all-time favorite war movies. (To "break the ice," you might want to share your favorite one first.) Have your guys explain why they think the movie is so great, describe some of the best scenes in the movie, and summarize how the movie deals with the issue of war. (For instance, old World War II movies like *The Sands of Iwo Jima* view war as an extension of one's patriotic duty; movies like *Platoon* and *Full Metal Jacket* vividly depict the horrors of war.) From this opening discussion, you should be able to get a sense of where most of your guys stand on the issue.

STEP 3

Have your guys form two teams. Give each team a large sheet of paper and several colored markers. Instruct the members of one team to draw a picture of the type of person that comes to mind when they think of a "hawk" (someone who favors war). Instruct the members of the other team to draw a picture of the type of person that comes to mind when they think of a "dove" (someone who opposes war). After a few minutes, have each team display and explain its picture. See what kind of stereotypical notions your guys have about people on both sides of the issue.

EXTRA FUN

STEP 1

Begin the session with "Battle of the Sumo Warriors." Using tape, make a circle about 10 feet in diameter in the middle of the floor. Call for two volunteers to come to the circle. Tie four large, fluffy pillows around each volunteer's torso. Then have the contestants stand facing each other, close enough that their pillows are touching. Explain that at your signal, the two will try to push each other out of the circle—without using their hands. If a player touches an opponent with his or her hands, he or she is disqualified. Award a prize to the winner of each round. Play as many rounds as you have time for (pairing up contestants of roughly equal size and strength). Afterward, use the "battling warriors" idea to introduce the topic of war.

STEP 3

Set up a "dodgeball war." You'll need several rubber playground balls. Tape a line across the middle of the floor. Have kids form two teams. Put the teams on opposite sides of the line. Designate one team to be the "Hawks" and the other to be the "Doves." Explain that the Hawks will be the aggressors. Their goal is to eliminate the Doves from the game by hitting them with the dodgeballs. The Doves, on the other hand, will remain "passive." Their goal is to dodge or catch the balls thrown at them. If a ball is caught in midair, the person who threw it is out. Doves may not throw balls at the Hawks. Neither team may cross the line at any time during the game. (Players who do are out.) Because the Doves won't be throwing the balls back at the Hawks, you may need to stop the game occasionally to kick the balls back to the Hawks. Continue until one team is eliminated. Afterward, lead in to a discussion on what "hawks" and "doves" believe about war.

MEDIA

STEP 1

Show scenes (which you've screened beforehand) from one or more of the following videos.

• *Glory*. This film tells the Civil War story of a Union regiment composed of African-American soldiers. Play the climactic scene in which the soldiers make a suicidal but symbolic march on a Confederate stronghold. Ask: **How did this scene make you feel? What impression does it give of war? Do you think these soldiers died in vain? Why or why not?**

• *Top Gun*. This movie features high-tech weaponry and steel-nerved pilots. After showing a fast-paced, in-the-air segment, ask: **How did this scene make you feel? What impression does it give of being in the military? Do you think the word *hero* applies to fighter pilots like these? Why or why not?**

• *Dear America: Letters Home from Vietnam*. This documentary consists mainly of soldiers' letters from the Vietnam War. Try to include a confident letter from early in the film and a poignant one from later in the film. Ask: **How do these letters make you feel? What impression do they give you of war? If you were in a war, what kinds of letters would you write home? Why?**

STEP 4

Play one of the following songs: "The Battle Is the Lord's" by Harvest, "End of the Book" by Michael W. Smith, "Destined to Win" by DeGarmo and Key, "Mighty Fortress" by Steve Green, or "We Are His Hands" by White Heart. Ask: **What does this song say about fighting evil or doing good? Should that message be applied to the question of whether to fight in a war? If so, how? If not, why not? If you took the message of this song seriously, would you be likely to serve as a soldier in a war? Why or why not?**

SHORT MEETING TIME

STEP 1

For a shorter opener, try a "21-Bag Salute." Have group members stand in a circle. Put a large supply of paper bags in the middle of the circle. At your signal, the first person will grab a bag, return to his or her "post," inflate the bag, and pop it—all within 10 seconds. Repeat with the next person, working your way around the circle. Anyone who takes more than 10 seconds, or whose bag doesn't make a suitable pop (you be the judge), is out. Continue until you run out of bags or players. Use this to lead into a discussion of kids' feelings about guns, the military, and war. In Step 2, give an entire copy of Repro Resource 9 to each group member. After giving kids two minutes to study the sheet, vote as a group to choose the "most justifiable" and "least justifiable" wars. Give a few volunteers a chance to explain their votes.

STEP 3

Instead of distributing index cards, forming teams, and reporting results, read the passages aloud to the whole group, one passage at a time. Have kids move from one side of the room (the "hawk" side) to the other (the "dove" side) after each passage. In Step 4, use just the first three situations. Skip the prayer circle at the end if necessary.

URBAN

STEP 1

Before the session, find some pictures that show the aftermath of war on a city—bombed-out buildings, streets littered with debris, "shell-shocked" citizens, etc. (Before-and-after pictures of Sarajevo, Yugoslavia would work well.) Compare the areas shown in these pictures with some of the worst parts of your city. Do you see any similarities? (Abandoned buildings, streets littered with garbage and junk, "shell-shocked" citizens, etc.) Point out the references to "war" that many people use when talking about the inner city—the *war* on drugs, gang *wars*, etc. Ask: **Do you ever feel like you're living in a war zone? Explain.** Use this discussion to introduce the topic of war.

STEP 4

Say: **The philosopher William James once said that to end war, we must be ready to wage "the moral equivalent of war." In short, those who believe in peace must begin to fight against war with the tools of active, nonviolent behavior.** Point out that there are two types of nonviolent people. There are *passive* people, who see a fight taking place and keep their distance, preferring not to get involved; and there are *active* people, who jump in the middle of a fight to try to break it up. Suggest that in the inner city, active nonviolence is "the moral equivalent of war." Come up with three scenarios that involve violent confrontation—two that your kids are likely to face on the street or at school, and one that involves an international conflict. Have group members decide what they, as individuals or as part of a larger group, could do to "disarm" each situation through active nonviolence.

STEP 2

Have your junior highers compete against your high schoolers in a game of "Higher or Lower" to guess the approximate number of fatalities in each war. Bring a player from each team to the front of the room. Have the two players face each other (a la *Family Feud*). Ask: **Approximately how many people died in the Revolutionary War?** Have the high schooler guess first. If the guess is wrong, announce whether the actual number is higher or lower. Then have the junior high schooler guess. Continue until one of the players guesses correctly. Award a point to his or her team. Go through the rest of the wars listed on the sheet in the same manner (using different players from each team). At the end of the game, give prizes to the winning team.

STEP 4

Your junior highers (and most of your high schoolers) would probably relate well to personal anecdotes and opinions about war from people who've experienced it firsthand. Ask a couple of veterans from your church or community to talk briefly with your group about their experiences and feelings concerning war. Leave some time at the end of the presentation for your kids to ask questions. (You may want to be prepared with a couple of questions yourself to "break the ice.")

STEP 3

Say: **A non-Christian friend of yours is confused. He knows the Bible well enough to know that one of the Ten Commandments is "You shall not commit murder." But he just heard someone talking about I Samuel 15, in which God commands the Israelites to kill all of the Amalekites. "It sounds like God can't make up His mind," your friend comments. How would you respond?** Have kids form pairs. Instruct each pair to come up with a response to the non-Christian's comments. After a few minutes, have each pair share its response.

STEP 4

As you wrap up the session, focus on Romans 12:18: "If it is possible, as far as it depends on you, live at peace with everyone." As a group, brainstorm a list of ideas as to how a *country* or *nation* might "live at peace with everyone." Might it require disarming all nuclear weapons? Might it involve reassigning all military personnel to strictly humanitarian efforts? After you've come up with a list of ideas, discuss the potential results of such actions. Would other countries be influenced by the example and follow suit? Would the peacekeeping country suddenly become vulnerable to hostile nations?

DATE USED:

Approx. Time

STEP 1: *This Is War?* _____
- ❏ Extra Action
- ❏ Small Group
- ❏ Large Group
- ❏ Mostly Girls
- ❏ Mostly Guys
- ❏ Extra Fun
- ❏ Media
- ❏ Short Meeting Time
- ❏ Urban
Things needed:

STEP 2: *A History of War* _____
- ❏ Extra Action
- ❏ Heard It All Before
- ❏ Combined Jr. High/High School
Things needed:

STEP 3: *War in the Bible* _____
- ❏ Large Group
- ❏ Heard It All Before
- ❏ Little Bible Background
- ❏ Fellowship & Worship
- ❏ Mostly Girls
- ❏ Mostly Guys
- ❏ Extra Fun
- ❏ Short Meeting Time
- ❏ Extra Challenge
Things needed:

STEP 4: *The Personal Aspect of War* _____
- ❏ Small Group
- ❏ Little Bible Background
- ❏ Fellowship & Worship
- ❏ Media
- ❏ Urban
- ❏ Combined Jr. High/High School
- ❏ Extra Challenge
Things needed: